In Conversation with God

Meditations for each day of the year

Volume One
Advent – Christmas – Epiphany

Francis Fernandez

In Conversation with God
Meditations for each day of the year

Volume One
Advent – Christmas – Epiphany

SCEPTER
London – New York

This edition of *In Conversation with God – Volume 1* is published:
in England by Scepter (U.K.) Ltd., 21 Hinton Avenue, Hounslow
TW4 6AP; e-mail: scepter@pobox.com;
in the United States by Scepter Publishers Inc., P. O. Box 211, New
York, NY 10018; e-mail: info@scepterpublishers.org

This is a translation of *Hablar con Dios – Vol I*, first published in
1986 by Ediciones Palabra, Madrid, and in 1988 by Scepter.

With ecclesiastical approval

British Library Cataloguing in Publication Data

Fernandez-Carvajal, Francis
In Conversation with God — Volume 1
Advent, Christmas, Epiphany.
1. Christian life — Daily Readings
I Title   II Hablar con Dios   *English*
242'.2

ISBN Volume 7   978-0-906138-36-6
ISBN Volume 6   978-0-906138-25-0
ISBN Volume 5   978-0-906138-24-3
ISBN Volume 4   978-0-906138-23-6
ISBN Volume 3   978-0-906138-22-9
ISBN Volume 2   978-0-906138-21-2
ISBN Volume 1   978-0-906138-20-5
ISBN Complete set 978-0-906138-19-9

Cover design & typeset in England by KIP Intermedia, and printed
in Singapore.

Contents

Contents

40.1 Approaching Our Lord in friendship and trust.
40.2 The name of Jesus. Invocations.
40.3 Our relations with the Blessed Virgin and St
   Joseph.

THE CHRISTMAS SEASON – 3 JANUARY
41. The prophecy of Simeon   277
41.1 The Holy Family in the temple. The meeting with
   Simeon. Our meetings with Jesus.
41.2 Mary, Co-redemptrix with Christ. The meaning of
   pain.
41.3 Our Lady teaches us to co-redeem. Offering up
   pain and contradictions. Atonement. Apostolate
   with those around us.

THE CHRISTMAS SEASON – 4 JANUARY
42. Naturalness and simplicity   283
42.1 Simplicity and naturalness of the Holy Family.
   Simplicity as an outward sign of humility.
42.2 Simplicity and an upright intention. Consequences
   of spiritual childhood. Being simple in our dealings
   with God, with others and in spiritual guidance.
42.3 Things which are opposed to simplicity. Fruits of
   this virtue. The means to attain it.

THE CHRISTMAS SEASON – 5 JANUARY
43. The faith of the Kings   289
43.1 Firmness in faith. Overcoming human respect, comfort, attachment to worldly goods, to seek Our Lord.
43.2 Faith and docility in moments of darkness and
   disorientation. Letting ourselves be helped.
43.3 The only important thing in our life is to reach
   Our Lord.

Contents

Contents

* * * * * *

Table of Moveable Feasts

Year	Ash Wednesday	Easter	Ascension	Pentecost	First Sunday of Advent
2012	22 Feb	8 Apr	17 May	27 May	2 Dec
2013	13 Feb	31 Mar	9 May	19 May	1 Dec
2014	5 Mar	20 Apr	29 May	8 Jun	30 Nov
2015	18 Feb	5 Apr	14 May	24 May	29 Nov
2016	10 Feb	27 Mar	5 May	15 May	27 Nov
2017	1 Mar	16 Apr	25 May	4 Jun	3 Dec
2018	14 Feb	1 Apr	10 May	20 May	2 Dec
2019	6 Mar	21 Apr	30 May	9 Jun	1 Dec
2020	26 Feb	12 Apr	21 May	31 May	29 Nov
2021	17 Feb	4 Apr	13 May	23 May	28 Nov
2022	2 Mar	17 Apr	26 May	5 Jun	27 Nov
2023	22 Feb	9 Apr	18 May	28 May	3 Dec
2024	14 Feb	31 Mar	9 May	19 May	1 Dec
2025	5 Mar	20 Apr	29 May	8 Jun	30 Nov

FIRST SUNDAY OF ADVENT

1. ADVENT:
IN EXPECTATION OF OUR LORD

1.1 Keeping watch in the period before the coming of the Messiah.

Grant your faithful, we pray, almighty God, the resolve to run forth to meet your Christ with righteous deeds at his coming, so that, gathered at his right hand, they may be worthy to possess the heavenly Kingdom.[1]

Everybody knows, even those of us who have lived most unadventurously, says Ronald Knox in a sermon on Advent, *what it is to plod on for miles, it seems, eagerly straining your eyes towards the lights that, somehow, mean home. How difficult it is, when you are doing that to judge distances! In pitch darkness, it might be a couple of miles to your destination, it might be a few hundred yards. So it was, I think, with the Hebrew prophets, as they looked forward to the redemption of their people. They could not have told you, within a hundred years, within five hundred years, when it was the deliverance would come. They only knew that, some time, the stock of David would burgeon anew; some time, a key would be found to fit the door of their prison house; some time, the light that only showed, now, like a will-o'-the-wisp on the horizon would broaden out, at last, into the perfect day.*

This attitude of expectation is one which the Church wants to encourage in us, her children, permanently. She sees it as an essential part of our Christian drill that we

---

[1] *Collect of the Mass*

should still be looking forward; getting on for two thousand years, now, since the first Christmas Day came and went, and we must still be looking forward. So she encourages us, during Advent, to take the shepherd-folk for our guides, and imagine ourselves travelling with them, at dead of night, straining our eyes towards that chink of light which streams out, we know, from the cave at Bethlehem.[2]

When the Messiah came, few really were expecting him. *He came unto his own and his own received him not.*[3] Most men of that time had been blind to what was most essential in their lives and in the life of the world.

Watch, therefore, Our Lord tells us in today's gospel. *Wake from sleep,*[4] St Paul echoes. For we too can forget what is most fundamental in our existence, what our life here on earth is about.

Summon the nations, say to the peoples: See, our God and Saviour is coming! Tell it, proclaim it; cry aloud.[5]

The Church reminds us of this with a four-week period of preparation, so that we can get ourselves ready to celebrate Christmas once more. And at the same time so that, with the first coming to the world of God made Man, we may be heedful of those other 'advents' of God – first when we die, and then again at the end of time. The holy season is thus a time of preparation and of hope.

Come, O Lord, and do not delay. Let us make straight His path...The Lord is soon to arrive. If we are aware that our sight is clouded and that we don't see

---

[2] R. A. Knox, *Sermon on Advent*, 21 December 1947
[3] John 1:11
[4] cf Rom 13:11
[5] *Divine Office, Responsorial Psalm, Monday of the 1st Week of Advent*

clearly the radiance emanating from Bethlehem, from the infant Jesus, it is time to rid ourselves of whatever impairs our vision. Now is the time for a specially good examination of conscience and for a thorough interior purification which will befit us to receive and to welcome that expected guest who is God. It is the moment to take note of the things that separate us from Him, to loosen their hold and cast them from us. Our examination, then, must penetrate to the very roots of our actions and scrutinize deep down in our hearts the motives which inspire our actions.

1.2 The principal enemies of our sanctity: the three concupiscences. Confession, a way of preparing for Christmas.

As we really do want, not vaguely but seriously, to draw and be drawn closer to God at this time, let us look down into our souls in depth. There we will find the real enemies that sustain their unremitting warfare to keep us away from Him. There, in one form or another, are the main obstacles that obstruct and hinder the growth of our Christian life: *the lust of the flesh and the lust of the eyes and the pride of life.*[6]

The lust of the flesh is not confined only to the disordered tendencies of the senses in general or to the disorder of sensuality in particular. It also refers to that love of comfort, to that reluctance to stir ourselves or even to be alert, which drives us to seek that which is least uncomfortable, what is most pleasurable, the path offered us that seems the shorter and less arduous, even at the cost of our failing in faithfulness to God.

The other enemy is the lust of the eyes, a deep-seated greed that sees nothing of value in what cannot be laid

---

[6] 1 John 2:16

hands on.

*The eyes of the soul are dulled; reason thinks itself
to be self-sufficient, dispensing with God as unnecessary.
It is a subtle temptation supported by the dignity of the
very intelligence our Father God has given us that we
may know and love him freely. Seduced by this
temptation, the human intelligence regards itself as the
centre of the universe, reverting with delight to the words
of the serpent in Genesis, 'you shall be like Gods' (Gen
3:5) and, being filled with love of self, turns its back on
God's love.*

*Our existence can, in this way, surrender itself
unconditionally into the hands of the third enemy, 'pride of
life'. This is not merely a matter of ephemeral fantasies,
the fanciful products of vanity or self-love: it is an all-
embracing presumption. Let us not fool ourselves; this is
the worst of all evils, the root of every conceivable
deviation.*[7]

Since God is coming to us, we have to get ready for
Him, to prepare ourselves. When Christmas arrives, Our
Lord should find us with everything in order and our soul
fit to receive Him, just as He ought to find us in our final
encounter with Him. We have to make what adjustment
is required to correct the course of our lives and turn ourselves to God who also comes to us. Man's whole
existence is a constant preparing to see God, who draws
ever closer. We have an appointment. But in Advent the
Church helps us with this solemn consideration in mind
to ask in a special way: *Lord, make me know your ways.
Lord, teach me your paths. Make me walk in your truth,
and teach me: for you are God my Saviour.*[8]

Let us ready ourselves for this encounter in the

---

[7] St. J. Escrivá, *Christ is passing by*, 5-6
[8] *Responsorial Psalm, Cycle C*, Ps 24

Sacrament of Penance. Just before Christmas in 1980, Blessed John Paul II was with over two thousand children in a Roman parish. And he began his catechesis with this dialogue: *How are you preparing for Christmas? By praying*, shout back the children. *Very good, by praying*, the Pope says, *but also by going to Confession. You must go to Confession so that you can go to Communion later. Will you do that?* In an even louder voice, those thousands of children replied: *We will!* And John Paul II tells them, *Yes, you ought to go.* Lowering his voice he whispers: *The Pope will also go to Confession so as to receive the Child Jesus worthily.*

We too will do the same in the weeks between now and Christmas, with an ever greater love and deeper contrition. For we can always receive this sacrament of the divine mercy with better dispositions as the result of a deeper examination of our souls.

1.3 Remaining watchful through prayer, mortification and examination of conscience.

At that time, Jesus said to His disciples: Take heed, watch and pray; for you do not know when the time will come...Watch, therefore – for you do not know when the master of the house will come, in the evening or at midnight, or at cockcrow, or in the morning – lest he come suddenly and find you asleep. And what I say to you I say to all: Watch![9]

To maintain this state of alertness we need to struggle, for we all have a tendency to live with our eyes fixed on the things of the earth. Especially during this time of Advent let us not forget that *our hearts are darkened by gluttony and drunkenness and the cares of this life*, and so lose sight of the supernatural dimension

---

[9] Mark 3:33-37

which every action of ours should have as its milieu. St
Paul compares this guard over ourselves to that of *the
well-armed soldier who does not allow himself to be
taken by surprise.*[10] *This adversary tries to wreak havoc
in whatever way he can; and since he does not devise his
tactics without attention to detail, neither should we.*[11]

We will remain at the ready if we are attentive to our
personal prayer, which enables us to avoid lukewarmness
and the dwindling and cooling of our desire for sanctity.
We will be constantly on the alert if we do not become
slipshod about those little mortifications which keep us
awake to the things of God. We will remain attentive
through a refined examination of conscience, which
makes us look to those points at which, almost without
noticing it, we are departing from our path.

Brothers, St Bernard says to us, *God reveals to you,
as he did to the children, what is hidden from the learned
and wise: the true ways of salvation. Meditate on them
with the greatest attention. Steep yourselves in the
meaning of these Advent days. And above all, pay heed to
him who is approaching; think whence he comes and
whither it is he advances; consider his purpose in
coming, the ripeness of the times, the route he may
choose for his approach. Such speculation cannot but be
good. Our curiosity is far from being an idle one. The
Universal Church would not celebrate this Advent time
with such solemnity of devotion did it not contain within
it some great mystery.*[12]

*Let us go forth with a clean heart to receive the
supreme King, for he is to come, and he will not delay,*
we read among the Advent Antiphons of the Liturgy.

---

[10] cf 1 Thess 5,4-11
[11] St Teresa of Avila, *The Way of Perfection*, 19,13
[12] St Bernard, Sermon on the six aspects of Advent, 1

Holy Mary, our Hope, will help us to improve in this season of Advent. She awaits with hushed recollection the birth of her Son, who is the Messiah. All her thoughts are directed towards Jesus, who will be born in Bethlehem. At her side it will be easy for us to dispose our souls in such a way that the arrival of Jesus will not find us distracted by other things which have little or no importance in the light of the coming of God.

FIRST WEEK OF ADVENT – MONDAY

2. PREPARING TO RECEIVE JESUS

2.1 The joy of Advent. The joy of receiving Our Lord in Holy Communion.

Psalm 121, which we read in today's Mass, was a hymn sung by pilgrims as they approached Jerusalem: *I was glad* – chanted these pilgrims as they drew near the city – *when they said to me: 'Let us go to the house of the Lord.' Our feet have been standing within your gates, O Jerusalem!*[1]

This same joy is appropriate to the season of Advent, in that each passing day marks another step towards the celebration of our Redeemer's birth. It is, moreover, a figure of the happiness we feel when we go, rightly disposed, to receive Holy Communion.

It is inevitable that along with this joy we should feel progressively more unworthy as the moment for receiving Our Lord comes closer. If we decide to receive, it is because He wishes to remain in the species of bread and wine precisely to serve as food; and so He gives strength to the undernourished and the infirm. He is not there as a reward for the strong, but as a remedy for the weak. And we are all weak and in some degree ailing.

However thorough our preparation, it will appear to us insufficient and in no way adequate for the reception of Jesus in the Blessed Sacrament. St John Chrysostom preached in such terms so that those who heard him

---

[1] Ps 121:1-2

might dispose themselves worthily to receive Holy Communion. *Is it not ridiculous*, he asks, *to be so meticulous about bodily things when the feast draws near, as to get out and prepare your best clothes days ahead..., and to deck yourself in your very finest, all the while paying not the slightest attention to your soul, which is abandoned, besmirched, squalid and utterly consumed by desire...?*[2]

If we sometimes feel 'cold' emotionally, or otherwise find ourselves lacking in fervour, we ought not for that reason to refrain from going to Communion. We will get out of the state of numb insensibility we are in by making acts of faith, hope and love and by praying for an increase in these supernatural virtues. If it is a matter of lukewarmness or of falling into a dullness of routine, we have it in our hands to extricate ourselves from this situation, since we can count on the help of grace for our rehabilitation. But let us not confuse mere nervous or physical exhaustion or ordinary and inevitable tiredness with a deplorably genuine spiritual mediocrity or a pernicious routine that increases its grip on the soul day by day. Whoever makes no proper preparation, whoever makes no effort to avoid or dispel distractions when Jesus comes into his heart, will inevitably fall into luke-warmness. To go to Communion with our imagination deployed on distractions and our mind preoccupied with other thoughts is a recipe for dropping one's spiritual temperature. To be lukewarm is to give no importance to the sacrament we are receiving.

The worthy reception of Our Lord's Body will always be an opportunity to set ourselves aflame with love. *There will be those who say: 'that is exactly why I don't go to Communion more often, because I realize my*

---

[2] St John Chrysostom, *Homily* 6; PG 48, 276

love is cold...' If you are cold, do you think it sensible to move away from the fire? Precisely because you feel your heart frozen you should go 'more frequently' to Holy Communion, provided you feel a sincere desire to love Jesus Christ. 'Go to Holy Communion', says St Bonaventure, 'even when you feel lukewarm, leaving everything in God's hands. The more my sickness debilitates me, the more urgently do I need a doctor.[3]

When we think of the God who awaits us we can joyfully sing in the inmost depths of our soul: *I was glad when they said to me: Let us go to the house of the Lord...*

Our Lord is also glad when he sees our efforts to dispose ourselves well to receive him. Let us meditate on the means and on the thoughtful interest we take in our preparation for Holy Mass, by avoiding distractions and banishing any feeling of routine, so that our thanksgiving afterwards may be intense and loving, uniting us to Christ throughout the rest of the day.

2.2 *Lord, I am not worthy...* Humility in receiving the Blessed Sacrament. Getting ready to receive Our Lord, imitating the centurion of Capharnaum.

The Gospel of the Mass[4] recall the words of a gentile, a centurion in the Roman army. These words: *Domine non sum dignus* – Lord, I am not worthy... have been included in the Liturgy of the Mass since the early centuries of Christianity and Christians have always used them as the immediate preparation for Communion.

The leading Jews of the town had asked Jesus to relieve the suffering of this non-Jew, this foreigner, by curing a very dear servant of his, who was, it seems, at the

---

[3] St Alphonsus Liguori, *The practice of love for Jesus*, 2
[4] Matt 8:5-13

point of death.[5] The reason they wanted help for him was that this well-disposed stranger had built a synagogue for them, or had munificently donated the wherewithal to have it built.

When Jesus drew near to the house, the centurion uttered the words that are repeated in every Mass (using the word 'soul' in place of 'servant'): *Lord, I am not worthy that thou shouldst enter under my roof; say but the word and my soul shall be healed.* One word from Christ cures, purifies, comforts and fills with hope.

The centurion is a man of deep humility, generous, compassionate and with a high regard for Jesus. Since he is a gentile, he does not presume to go himself to Our Lord, but sends others whom he considers more worthy, that they may intercede for him. *Humility,* comments St Augustine, was *the door by which Our Lord entered to take possession of what was already his own.*[6]

Faith, humility and refinement are united in this man's soul. That is why the Church commends his example to us and uses his words as preparation for receiving Jesus when He comes to us in Holy Communion: *Lord, I am not worthy...*

The Church not only invites us to repeat his words, but also to imitate his dispositions of faith, humility and refinement. *We want to tell Jesus that we accept his un-merited and unique visit, repeated all over the world, which is made even to us, to each one of us. We want to tell him also that we feel amazed and unworthy at such a response to our asking. But we feel happy too – happy at what He has granted to us and to the world. And we want also very much to tell him that such a great marvel does not leave us indifferent and unmoved; it does not leave us*

---

[5] cf Luke 7:1-10
[6] St Augustine, *Sermon 6*

with a tenuous and wavering faith, but arouses in our hearts such a warmth of enthusiasm that it will never cease to burn in the hearts of those who truly believe.[7]

It is wonderful to see how the Roman officer of Capharnaum was doubly united to the sacrament of the Eucharist. First, obviously, through his words, which priest and faithful say every day before Communion in the Mass. And, secondly, because it was in the synagogue of Capharnaum, which the centurion had built, that Jesus first said that we must eat of his Body if we are to have life within us: *This is the bread which has come down from heaven* – Jesus said – *not such as our fathers ate and are dead; he who eats this bread will live for ever.* And St John adds: *This he said in the synagogue as he taught in Capharnaum.*[8]

2.3 Further preparation of soul and body to receive the Sacrament fruitfully. Frequent Confession.

To prepare ourselves to receive Our Lord in Communion means first of all to make sure we shall receive him in a state of grace. To receive Communion in a state of mortal sin would be to commit a most grievous offence, a sacrilege. We should never go to receive Our Lord if there is a well-founded doubt as to whether we have committed a serious sin in thought, word or action. *Whoever, therefore, eats the bread or drinks the cup of the Lord in an unworthy manner will be guilty of profaning the body and blood of the Lord.* Therefore, St Paul continues: *Let a man examine himself, and so eat of the bread and drink of the cup. For anyone who eats and drinks without discerning the body of the Lord eats and*

---

[7] Paul VI, *Homily*, 25 May 1967
[8] John 6:58-59

drinks judgement upon himself.[9]

 The person who freely receives communion has to be reminded of the command: 'May each one examine himself' (1 Cor 2:28). And the practice of the Church declares that this examination is necessary so that no one conscious of mortal sin, however contrite he believes himself to be, may approach the Holy Eucharist without having previously been to sacramental confession.[10]

 The Sacraments of the new Law, though they produce their effects 'ex opere operato', nevertheless produce a greater effect proportionately if the dispositions of the recipients are better...[11]

Hence the importance of a thorough preparation of soul and body, of the desire for purification, of treating this holy sacrament with appropriate loving awe, of receiving it with the greatest possible piety. The struggle to live constantly in the presence of God throughout the day is an excellent preparation, as is the fight to fulfil our daily duties as well as possible. So too is feeling the need to make amends to Our Lord whenever we commit some error. And we should also try to fill the day with short acts of thanksgiving and spiritual communions. In this way, little by little, we will form a habit, so that in work or play, in family life, in whatever we do, our hearts will be centred on God.

Together with these interior dispositions, and as a necessary manifestation of them, are the dispositions of the body: the fast prescribed by the Church, posture, dress, etc., which are signs of respect and reverence.

As we finish our prayer let us consider how Mary received Jesus after the message of the angel. Let us ask

---

[9] 1 Cor 11:27-28
[10] Paul VI, *Eucharisticum Mysterium*, 37
[11] St Pius X, Decree, *Sacra Tridentina Synodus*, 20 December 1905

her to teach us to communicate *with the purity, humility and devotion* with which she received Him in her most holy womb, *with the spirit and fervour of the saints*, even though we feel ourselves to be unworthy and insignificant.

3. THE MESSIAH: *PRINCE OF PEACE*

3.1 Peace, a gift of God. It is lost through sin, pride and insincerity.

Peace is one of the great goods constantly implored from God in the Old Testament. It is this gift that is promised to the people of Israel as a reward for their fidelity,[1] and it is seen as a work of God[2] from which flow uncountable benefits. But real peace came to the world only with the coming of the Messiah. That is why at the Nativity of our Lord the angels proclaim it, singing: *Glory to God in the highest and peace on earth to men of good will.*[3] Advent and Christmas are especially opportune times for the growth of peace in our hearts; they are also times to pray for peace in this world, torn as it is by conflict and widespread dissension.

Behold: the Lord is coming in power – to bring peace to his people and give them eternal life.[4] Isaiah reminds us in the first reading of the Mass that in the Messianic era *the wolf shall live peacefully with the lamb, and the leopard lie down with the kid, and the calf and the lion and the beast of the field dwell together.*[5] With the Messiah's coming, the peace and harmony the world knew at the beginning of creation are restored and a new order is inaugurated.

---

[1] Lev 26:6
[2] Is 26:12
[3] Luke 2:14
[4] *Divine Office, Antiphon*
[5] cf Is 11:1-10

The Lord is the *Prince of peace*,[6] and from the very moment of his birth he brings us a message of peace and joy – the only true peace and the only real joy – which later he will sow wherever he goes: *Peace be with you; it is I, do not be afraid.*[7] The presence of Christ in our lives is always the source of a calm and indestructible peace: *It is I, do not be afraid*, he tells us.

The teaching of Our Lord constitutes *the good news of peace.*[8] And this same peace is also the treasure he has passed on to his disciples in every age: *Peace I leave you; my peace I give you; not as the world gives it do I give it you.*[9] *Earthly peace, which comes from love of our fellow-man, is a type and a result of the peace of Christ issuing from God the Father. The incarnate Son himself, the Prince of peace, reconciled all men to God through his cross. In his own flesh he killed hatred, and after he had risen he poured out the Spirit of charity into the hearts of men.*[10] The peace of God completely transcends an earthly peace, which can so easily be superficial and unreal, stemming often from selfishness, and not at all incompatible with injustice.

Christ is *our peace*[11] and our joy. Sin, on the other hand, sows nothing but loneliness, anxiety and sadness in the soul. Christian peace, so necessary for apostolate and good fellowship, is the product of interior order, of a consciousness of our own failings and virtues, of unfailing respect for others and a complete confidence in God, who, we know, will never abandon us. It is the

---

[6] Is 9:6
[7] Luke 24:36
[8] Acts 10:36
[9] John 14:27
[10] Second Vatican Council, *Gaudium et spes*, 78
[11] Eph 2:14

consequence of humility, of awareness of our divine filiation and of the struggle against our own passions, which tend always towards disorder and disruption.

We lose our peace through sin, through pride and by not being sincere with ourselves and with God. Peace can also be lost through impatience; when we are unable to see the providential hand of God in times of difficulty and contradiction.

The sincere confession of our sins is one of the main ways God has given us to recover the peace that has been lost through sin or by the failure to correspond with his grace. *Peace with God, the result of justification and the rejection of sin; peace with our fellow-men, the fruit of love dispersed by the Holy Spirit; peace with ourselves, the peace of conscience proceeding from victory over our passions and over evil.*[12] The recovery of peace, if it has been lost, is one of the best signs of love for those around us, and its acquisition also the first task in preparing our hearts for the coming of the infant Christ.

3.2 True peace gives joy and serenity to those who lack them.

In the beatitude in which he proclaims the gift of peace, *Our Lord is not merely seeking to do away with all kinds of controversy and enmity between men; he is asking more of us: that we try to bring peace, no less, to those who hate us.*[13]

The Christian is a man open to peace, and his presence should spread tranquillity and happiness around him. But we are talking about real peace, not about those false states that are substitutes for it. Blessed are we when we know how to bring peace to the afflicted, when

---

[12] John Paul II, *Address to UNIV-86*, Rome, 24 March 1986
[13] St John Chrysostom, *Homily on St Matthew* 15:4

we serve as instruments of unity in our families, among our workmates and in all those we meet in the course of our daily lives. To put this vitally important commitment into practice, we have to be very humble and conciliatory, for *pride does nothing but cause dissension.*[14] The man who carries peace in his heart knows how to communicate it almost unthinkingly, and others look to him for support and for peace of mind. It is an enormous help in the apostolate. We Christians have to spread the interior peace we have in our hearts, wherever we find ourselves.

Our Lord blesses in a special way those who pray for peace among nations and work, with a right intention, to obtain it. Above all, He blesses those who offer prayer and sacrifice in order to reconcile men with God. This is the first task in any kind of apostolic activity. The apostolate of Confession, which moves us to bring our friends to this Sacrament, must deserve a special reward in heaven, for it is surely the best source of peace and joy there is in the world. *Those confessionals scattered about the world where men declare their sins don't speak of the severity of God. Rather do they speak of his mercy. And all those who approach the confessional, sometimes after many years weighed down with mortal sins, in the moment of getting rid of this intolerable burden, find at last a longed-for relief. They find joy and tranquillity of conscience which, outside Confession, they will never be able to find anywhere.*[15]

Those who have the peace of God and pass it to those around them *will be called the children of God.*[16] St John Chrysostom explains why: *Truly it has been the*

---

[14] Prov 13:10
[15] John Paul II, *Homily*, 16 March 1980
[16] cf Matt 5:9

work of the only-begotten One: to unite those who were apart and to reconcile those who were at war with one another.[17] Within our own family, at our place of work, and among our friends, cannot we too, in this time of Advent, impart a deeper sense of union with God among those around us and a still more loving and joyful fellowship?

3.3 Divine filiation, the foundation of our peace and of our joy.

When a man forgets his eternal destiny, and when the horizons of his life are limited by his earthly existence, he is content with a fictitious peace, with a mere outward appearance of tranquillity. All he asks is the illusory security of attaining the greatest possible material well-being with the least effort. In this way he builds an imperfect and unstable peace, since it is not rooted in the dignity of the human person, a person made in the image and likeness of God and called to his divine sonship. You must never be content with these substitutes for peace, for their fruit produces the most bitter disillusionment. Jesus Christ emphasized this when he said to his disciples shortly before his ascension into heaven: Peace I leave with you; my peace I give you; not as the world gives do I give it to you. (John 14:27)

There are thus two kinds of peace: that which men can make for themselves alone, and that which is the gift of God; ... that which is imposed by force of arms and that which is born in the heart. The former is fragile and insecure; it can be called a mere appearance of peace, for it is founded on fear and mistrust. The latter, on the contrary, is a strong and durable peace, and being founded on justice and love, it permeates the heart. It is a

---

[17] St John Chrysostom, *Homily on St Matthew* 15:4

gift God gives to those who love his Law (cf Ps 119:165).[18]

If we are men and women with true peace in our hearts we will be the better able to live like children of God and will the better be able to live brotherhood with our fellow-men. Also, insofar as we realize that we are children of God, we will be men and women with lasting peace.

Divine filiation is the foundation of the Christian's peace and joy. In it we find the security we need, a fatherly warmth and trust for the future. We live in the assurance that behind all the disappointments of life there is a good reason: *in everything God works for good with those who love him,*[19] says St Paul to the first Christians in Rome.

Considering our divine filiation will help us to be strong in the face of difficulties. *Don't be frightened; don't fear any harm even though the circumstances in which you work are terrible ... God's hand is as powerful as ever and, if necessary, he will work miracles.*[20] We are well protected.

Let us try then, in these days of Advent, to foster peace and joy, overcoming every obstacle. Let us learn to find God in everything, even in the most difficult situations. *Seek his face Who ever dwells in real and bodily presence in his Church. Do at least as much as the disciples did. They had but little faith; they feared; they had no great confidence or peace, but at least they did not keep away from Christ ... Do not keep from him, but, when you are in trouble, come to him day by day, asking him earnestly and perseveringly for those favours which*

---

[18] John Paul II, *Address to UNIV-86*, Rome, 24 March 1986
[19] Rom 8:28
[20] St. J. Escrivá, *Friends of God*, 105

he alone can give ... So, though he discerns much infirmity in you which ought not to be there, yet he will deign to rebuke the winds and the sea, and say: Peace, be still. And there will be a great calm.[21]

Mary, who is Queen of peace, will help us to have peace in our hearts, to recover it if we have lost it and pass it on to those around us. Since the feast of the Immaculate Conception is fast approaching, we will do all we can to turn to her all day long, keeping her closer to us in our work and offering her some special token of our affection.

---

[21] Blessed J. H. Newman, *Sermon for the Fourth Sunday after the Epiphany*, 1848

4. A MERCIFUL MESSIAH

4.1 The need to turn always to the mercy of Our Lord. Meditating on his life so as to learn to be merciful to others.

Large crowds came to him, we read in the Gospel of today's Mass, *bringing the lame, the crippled, the blind, the dumb and many others; these they put down at his feet, and he cured them. The crowds were astonished to hear the dumb speaking, to see the cripples whole again, the lame walking and the blind with their sight restored...*

Jesus called his disciples to him and said: I feel sorry for all these people![1] This is why the heart of Our Lord is so often moved. And in his mercy he was to follow up this episode with the wonderful miracle of the multiplication of the loaves.

The Liturgy has us consider this passage of the Gospel during Advent because an abundance of good things and limitless mercy will be the signs of the coming of the Messiah.

I feel sorry for all these people. This is an overriding reason for giving oneself to others: to be compassionate and to have mercy.

And to learn how to be merciful we must fix our eyes on Jesus, who comes *to save that which was lost.* He does not come to crush the broken reed or to wholly extinguish *the wick that still smoulders,*[2] but to take upon himself our wretchedness and save us from it, and to share in their misfortune with those who suffer and are in

---

[1] Matt 5:7
[2] Luke 19:10

need. Each page of the Gospel is an example of the divine mercy.

We should meditate on the life of Jesus because *Jesus is a summary and compendium of the story of the divine mercy ... Many other scenes of the Gospel also make a deep impact on us, such as his forgiveness of the woman taken in adultery, the parables – the prodigal son, the lost sheep, the pardoned debtor – and the raising to life of the son of the widow at Naim. How many reasons based on justice could Christ have found to work as great a wonder as this last one! The only son of that poor widow had died – he who gave meaning to her life, he who would help her in her old age. Jesus did not perform His miracle out of justice, but out of compassion, because his heart was moved by the spectacle of human suffering.*[3] Yes, Jesus is moved to the heart by human suffering!

The mercy of God is the essence of the whole history of salvation, the reason for all his saving acts.

God is mercy. And this divine attribute is like the engine supplying the power that energizes the life-story of every human being. When the apostles wanted to sum up God's revelation, his mercy always appeared to them to be the essence of an eternal and gratuitous plan springing from God's generosity. With good reason could the Psalmist affirm: *the earth is full of the steadfast love of the Lord.*[4] Mercy is constant in God's attitude to mankind. And recourse to it is the universal remedy for all our ills, including those for which we thought there was no answer.

Meditating on the mercy of God should fill us with great confidence *now and at the hour of our death*, as we

---

[3] St. J. Escrivá, *Christ is passing by*, 7
[4] Ps 33:5

pray in the Hail Mary. What a joy to be able to say to
God, with St Augustine: *All my hope lies solely in your
great mercy!*[5] Solely in that, Lord. On your mercy rests
all my hope. Not on my merits, but on your mercy.

**4.2 Our Lord's special compassion and merciful
welcome for repentant sinners. Going to the sacrament of mercy. Our behaviour towards others.**

In a special way, God shows his mercy towards
sinners: he pardons them their sins. The Pharisees often
criticize him for this. He rebuts their criticisms saying: *It
is not those who are well who have need of a physician,
but those who are sick.*[6]

We who are sinners are sick of soul and need to have
recourse many times to divine mercy: *Show us, O Lord,
your mercy; and grant us your salvation,*[7] the Church
repeats continually in this liturgical season.

On so many occasions, every day even, we will need
to have recourse to the merciful Heart of Jesus and say:
Lord if you will, you can make me clean.[8] Especially in
these circumstances, *the knowledge of God, the God of
mercy and benign love, is a constant and inexhaustible
source of conversion, not only as a momentary interior
act, but also as a stable disposition, like a state of mind.
Those who come to know God in this way, those who so
regard him, cannot live without being incessantly
transformed by him.*[9] Truly, we too can exclaim: *How
great is the mercy of the Lord, and his forgiveness for*

---

[5] St Augustine, *Confessions*, 10
[6] Matt 9:12
[7] Ps 84:8
[8] Matt 8:2
[9] John Paul II, Encyclical, *Dives in misericordia*, 13

those who turn to him![10] How great is the divine mercy towards each one of us!

This leads us to turn frequently to God, in repentance for our faults and sins, especially in that sacrament of divine mercy we call Confession.

But God has placed a condition on our obtaining his compassion and mercy for our offences and weaknesses. The condition is that we too should have a heart of compassion for those around us. In the parable of the good Samaritan[11] Our Lord teaches us the attitude we should adopt towards a neighbour in distress. We are not permitted to 'pass by on the other side' in detached indifference. Rather, we must 'go' to him. *A good Samaritan is he who stops to relieve the suffering of another, no matter who or what he is. This stopping will not be merely from curiosity, but rather from the desire of making ourselves available. It is a specific interior disposition of the heart which also has its emotional side. Good Samaritans are those who are affected by the suffering they see around them; they are genuinely moved by their neighbour's misfortune.*

If Christ, who knows the interior of man, emphasizes this compassion, this means that it is important for our whole attitude towards the suffering of others. Therefore one must cultivate this sensitivity of heart, which bears witness to 'compassion' towards a suffering person. Sometimes this compassion remains the only or the principal expression of our love for and of our solidarity with the sufferer.[12]

In our own home, in our office or workshop, is there not some person who is handicapped either physically or

---

[10] Sir 17:29
[11] Luke 10:30-35
[12] John Paul II, Apostolic Letter, *Salvifici doloris*, 28

morally, who needs, perhaps urgently, our time, our affection and our attention?

4.3 The works of mercy.

Throughout Sacred Scripture there is an urgency on God's part to see that men also have stirrings of sympathy and deep-seated feelings of mercy, that they too have this *compassion for another's misery which moves us to remedy it if at all possible.*[13] Our Lord promises us happiness if we have a merciful heart towards others, and gives assurance that *we will obtain mercy* from God in the same measure as we ourselves show it to our fellow men.

The scope for mercy is as great as the extent of the human suffering that needs to be remedied. And, since mankind is subject to misery and calamity in the physical, intellectual and moral order ... the possible works of mercy are innumerable – as many as men have needs – though traditionally, by way of example, fourteen 'works of mercy' have been cited, since in them this virtue is capable of being exercised in a special way.

Our attitude of compassion and mercy must, in the first place, be shown towards those who are near us – our family, our friends, our close associates – to those whom God has placed at our side, and then to those beyond who are most in need.

Mercy will frequently consist in our attention to the health, the recreation and the nourishment of those whom God has commended to our care. The sick merit a special attention in terms of our company and our real interest in their illness, as we show them how and help them to offer their sufferings to God ... In a society dehumanized by frequent attacks on the family, more and more old people

---

[13] St Augustine, *The City of God*, 9,5

and those who are ill are left without consolation and affection. Visiting them in their loneliness is a work of mercy that has never been more necessary. The time spent in keeping them company is rewarded by God in a special way: *As you did it to one of the least of these my brethren, you did it to me,*[14] says Our Lord.

Alongside the so-called material works of mercy, we should also carry out those that are spiritual. In the first place it is our privilege and duty *to correct those in error*, with our advice when the opportunity arises, and charitably, without ever causing offence. Secondly, it is *to teach those who don't know*, especially with regard to ignorance of religion, an ignorance which is the great enemy of God; it increases daily in alarming proportions so that catechesis has become a work of mercy of prime importance and urgency. Next comes giving *counsel to the doubting*, honestly and with the right intention, so as to help them on their way to God. Then follows the *consolation of the afflicted*, by sharing their sorrow and encouraging them to recover their happiness in their supernatural understanding of the pain they suffer. *Pardon those who have offended us*, promptly and as often as necessary, without giving excessive importance to the offence. We are advised too, *to give help to the needy*, carrying out this service generously and joyfully: and, finally, we have to *pray for the living and the dead*, feeling ourselves linked in a special way through the Communion of Saints to those we owe most because of family relationships, friendship etc.

Our attitude of merciful benevolence towards others must extend to many different aspects of life, because, says St John Chrysostom, *nothing can make you such an imitator of Christ as your concern for others. Although*

---

[14] Matt 25:40

*you fast, although you sleep on the floor, even though, I
dare to say, you kill yourself, if you are not attentive to
your neighbour, you have done very little; you are very
far from being an image of Christ.*[15]

Thus we will ourselves obtain God's mercy and
perhaps also merit it for others in that immense depth of
mercy that *extends from generation to generation,*[16] as
our Lady prophesied to her cousin St Elizabeth.

Let us call down the divine mercy on ourselves who
are so much in need of it. Let us also ask for it to be
extended to our generation through Mary, Mother of
mercy, our life, our sweetness and our hope. Now that
the feast of the Immaculate Conception is so near, our
confident reliance on the Virgin Mary will, if we have
recourse to her, be more continuous and more loving.

---

[15] St John Chrysostom, *Commentary on the 1st Epistle to the
Corinthians*
[16] Luke 1:50

FIRST WEEK OF ADVENT – THURSDAY

5. *I COME TO CARRY OUT THE WILL OF THE FATHER*

5.1 Identifying our will with that of God. How God shows us his Will. The Will of God and holiness.

A person's life can be built on many different kinds of foundations: on rock, on clay, on smoke, on air ... Only the Christian has a firm foundation which securely supports him: *the Lord is the everlasting rock.*[1]

In the Gospel of the Mass He tells us about two houses.[2] In one of them, perhaps the builder wanted to economize on material for the foundations; or perhaps he was in a hurry to finish it. He did not take as much care as he should have. Our Lord calls such a builder *a fool.* The two houses were completed and looked identical but they had very different foundations. One of them was firmly bedded on rock, but not the other. Time passed and there arose problems that would put the solidity of their construction to the test. One day a storm arose. The rain poured down, floodwater began to rise and hurricane winds hurled themselves against those buildings men had erected.

The time had come for proving their stability. One house remained firm and unshaken, the other collapsed with a roar in total ruin.

Our life can be built safely only on Christ himself, our sole hope, our sure foundation. And this means, first of all, that we strive to identify our will with his. Ours is

---

[1] *First reading of the Mass* Is 26:5
[2] Matt 7:21;24-27

not a more or less superficial adherence to a faint and barely distinguishable historical figure called Jesus Christ, but an adherence to his manifest will and to his clearly discernible and knowable person. *It is not those who say to me, Lord, Lord, who will enter the kingdom, but he who does the will of my Father in heaven.* We read this also in the Gospel of today's Mass.

God's Will is the compass-needle which at every moment accurately points the way that takes us to him. At the same time, this course is the path to our own happiness. The fulfilment of the Divine Will also gives us tremendous fortitude to overcome obstacles.

What a joy to be able to say at the end of our days: I have always tried to seek and to follow God's Will in everything! The successes we have had will not gladden us half so much, nor will the failures and the sufferings we have undergone matter in the slightest. What will matter to us, and matter a lot, is whether we have loved God's Will in preference to our own and made its implementation active in our lives, whether the Divine Will showed itself, as it does at times, in a more general way, or, on other occasions, in a more immediate and very specific form. Always perceptible, it will be seen clearly enough if we do not become blind to that light of the soul we call conscience.

The loving fulfilment of God's Will is, at the same time, the summit of all holiness. *All Christ's faithful then will grow daily more holy in the conditions their life imposes, its duties and its circumstances. These things will be the means of their advance in holiness, if they combine their faith with an acceptance of everything that comes from the hand of their heavenly Father, and if they are co-operative with the divine will...*[3] It is here that we

---

[3] Second Vatican Council, *Lumen gentium*, 41

demonstrate our love for God as well as the closeness of our union with him. And God will make clear what his Will is by means of the Commandments, the indications, the counsels and precepts of our holy Mother the Church, and the duties that are involved in one's own vocation and state in life.

The recognition and love of the Divine Will in these duties will give us the strength to carry them out as perfectly as possible. And in them we will find the opportunity to practise the human and supernatural virtues. God's Will is intimately bound up with meeting each day with a loving smile, with the fulfilment of our duties no matter how difficult they are and, with the help, both supernatural and human, that we give to those at our side.

5.2 Other ways in which God's Will is manifested in our lives: obedience. Imitating Jesus in his ardent desire to carry out his Father's Will. Humility.

God's Will is made clear to us in a specific way through those persons to whom we owe obedience and allegiance, and through the advice we receive in spiritual direction.

Obedience is not based on the qualities (such as personality, intelligence, experience or age) of the person who commands. Jesus, being God, was infinitely superior to Mary and Joseph, yet *he was subject to them*.[4] But there is more. *Christ has introduced the kingdom of heaven on earth. He has revealed its mystery to us and brought about our redemption 'by his obedience'*.[5]

Those who think that obedience is a servile subjection unworthy of man, proper only to the very

---

[4] Luke 2:51
[5] Second Vatican Council, *Lumen gentium*, 3

young or to those in some way lacking in maturity, have to take into account that *Christ Jesus ... became obedient unto death, even death on a cross.*[6] Christ obeyed out of love by carrying out the Will of his Father. This is the meaning of Christian obedience: that which is owed to God and to his commandments; that which is owed to the Church and to our parents, and that which in one way or another rules our conduct in our professional and social activities, each one in its proper place.

To obey as Jesus obeyed it is necessary to have an ardent desire to fulfil the Will of God in our lives and to be humble – that is, to recognize our relationship and where we stand in it. A soul dominated by pride leaves no space for the spirit of obedience. Only one possessed of the virtue of humility can joyfully accept criteria other than his own, especially those coming from God, to which we must conform our actions and our attitudes.

The person who is not humble will openly refuse to obey some commands, while appearing to accept others, though without really in the latter instance making room for them in his heart. For he will submit them to critical debate and impose restrictions accordingly. He will thus lose sight, altogether, of the supernatural meaning of obedience. *Let us be forewarned, then, for we will always tend to be self-centred and this temptation can occur in many ways. God wants us to show our faith when we obey, for he doesn't express his Will with drums and trumpets. Sometimes he suggests his wishes in a whisper, deep in our conscience; and we must listen carefully to recognize his voice and be faithful.*

He often speaks to us through other people. But when we see their defects or doubt whether they are well-informed – whether they have grasped all the aspects of

---

[6] Phil 2:8

the problem – we feel inclined to disobey.[7] Nevertheless, our desire to fulfil the Will of God will overcome this and other obstacles that oppose themselves to our obedience.

Humility gives us peace and joy in carrying out a command in all its details. Humility leaves us free to obey happily. *So long as we yield humbly to the voice of another we overcome ourselves in our hearts,*[8] we overcome our own selfishness and break its enslaving bonds.

In apostolate, obedience is indispensable. All the effort, the human means, the mortifications we put into it is otherwise worthless. In God's eyes it will all be useless without obedience. A whole life energetically dedicated to a human task would be fruitless, if we did not count on God's help. Even our most resounding successes will be ultimately valueless if we lack in their execution the desire to accomplish God's will. *God does not need our deeds but our obedience.*[9]

5.3 Carrying out God's Will when it hurts, or becomes apparently thankless or difficult.

God's Will is also shown in those things He allows to happen that do not turn out as we had hoped. They are often even directly opposed to our wishes or apparently at variance with what we have perhaps prayed for fervently and perseveringly. Then it is time to redouble our prayers and fix our eyes more steadily on Jesus Christ. Especially is this true when events make life unusually hard and misfortunes come: personal illness, material setback or disaster, the death of a loved one, the

---

[7] St. J. Escrivá, *Christ is passing by*, 17
[8] St Gregory the Great, *Morals*, 35,14
[9] St John Chrysostom, *Homilies on St Matthew*, 56,5

sufferings of those who are dear to us ...

Our Lord will unite us with his prayer: *not what I will, Father, but as thou wilt.*[10] *Not my will but thine be done.*[11] He even wants to share with us at times all the sorrow that comes from injustice and lack of understanding. But he also taught us to obey *unto death, even death on a cross.*[12] If we are sometimes made to suffer greatly, God will not be offended by our tears. But we must say at once: *Father, thy will be done.* There can be moments in life when heavy blows fall on us, accompanied perhaps by darkness and deeply-felt anguish and grief, times when God's Will is so difficult to accept that we are tempted to discouragement. The sight of Our Lord in the garden of Gethsemane will show us how to react; we must embrace God's Will unconditionally and without limits of any kind, while we persevere in prayer.

Throughout life there will often be times when we will necessarily have to act in complete conformity with the Will of God our Father. It is precisely then that in our personal prayer we will say within ourselves: *Is it what you want, Lord? ... Then it's what I want too!*[13] And there will come peace and tranquillity to our soul and to our surroundings.

Faith will make us see a higher wisdom behind the screen of each occurrence: *'God knows better.' We men have little understanding of how his fatherly and gentle care leads us towards him.*[14] Jesus Christ will relieve us of all our burdens, and they will be made holy.

---

[10] Mark 14:36
[11] Luke 22:42
[12] Phil 2:8
[13] St. J. Escrivá, *The Way*, 762
[14] A. del Portillo, Preface, *Friends of God*

There is a providence behind every happening. Whether we see it or not, everything is arranged and disposed to serve for the salvation of everyone in the best way possible. Yes, absolutely everything, whether it occurs in the general course of the world's events or in the little everyday universe of our job or occupation or family. Everything that happens can and ought to help us to encounter God, and thus to find peace and serenity of soul: *in everything God works for good with those who love him.*[15]

The accomplishment of God's Will is the true source of tranquillity and peace. The saints have left us an example of an unconditional fulfilment of the divine Will. St John Chrysostom expresses it thus: *On each occasion I say: 'Lord, thy will be done! It's not what this or that one wants, but what You want me to do.' This is my fortress, this is my firm rock, this is my sure support.*[16]

Let us finish our prayer by asking in unison with the Church: *O God, eternal majesty, whose ineffable Word the immaculate Virgin received through the message of an Angel and so became the dwelling place of divinity, filled with the light of the Holy Spirit, grant we pray, that by her example we may in humility hold fast to your will.*[17]

---

[15] Rom 8:28
[16] St John Chrysostom, *Homily before his exile*, 1-3
[17] *Collect, Mass for 20 December*

FIRST WEEK OF ADVENT – FRIDAY

6. INCREASING OUR FAITH

6.1 The need for faith. Asking for it.

The deaf, that day, will hear the words of a book and, after shadow and darkness, the eyes of the blind will see. But the lowly will rejoice in the Lord even more, and the poorest exult in the Holy One of Israel![1]

The new era of the Messiah is proclaimed by the prophets to be full of joy and of marvels. The Redeemer will ask only one thing of us: faith. Without this virtue the kingdom of God will not come among us.

The Gospel of today's Mass tells of two blind men who follow after Christ shouting for him to cure them. *Son of David, take pity on us*, they say. Our Lord asks them: *Do you believe I can do this?*[2] When they reply 'Yes, Lord', he sends them away cured with the words: *According to your faith, be it done to you.*[3] In the same way he restores the sight of another man in Jericho: *Go your way; your faith has made you whole. And immediately he received his sight and followed him on the way.*[4] He assures the father whose daughter has died: *Do not fear; only believe and she shall be well.*[5] A few moments earlier he has cured a woman who has suffered for twelve years from an internal haemorrhage. Coming up behind him, she has touched the fringe of his cloak.

---

[1] *First reading of the Mass* Is 29:17-24
[2] Matt 9:27-31
[3] Matt 9:28-29
[4] Mark 10:52
[5] Luke 8:50

Daughter, your faith has made you well. Go in peace.[6]
To the Canaanite he will say: *Woman, great is thy faith.*
And later: *be it done to you as you desire.*[7] For those who
believe there are no obstacles. *All things are possible to
him who believes,*[8] he says to the father of the boy
possessed by a dumb spirit.

The apostles open their hearts and minds to Our
Lord in all simplicity. They know their faith is often not
great enough to take in the things they see and hear. So
one day they ask Jesus: *Increase our faith!* And Our Lord
replies: *If you had faith as small as a grain of mustard
seed, you could say to this sycamore tree, be rooted up,
and be planted in the sea, and it would obey you.*[9]

We too are in the same situation as those first
followers of Christ. Our faith falters when we see how
few are our resources, when we are faced with
difficulties in our apostolate and with events that we have
to learn to understand from a supernatural point of view.

If we live with our eyes fixed on God we need fear
nothing: *Faith, if it is strong, protects the whole house.*[10]
It protects our whole life. With faith we can achieve
results far in excess of our own scanty powers; literally
nothing will be impossible. *Christ lays down one
condition: we must live by faith; then we will be able to
move mountains. And so many things need moving ... in
the world, but, first of all in our own hearts.*[11] Let us
imitate the apostles and humbly but manfully ask Our
Lord to have pity on us, for we know how weak and

---

[6] Luke 8:48
[7] Matt 15:28
[8] Mark 9:23
[9] Luke 17:9-10
[10] St Ambrose, *Commentary on the Psalms*, 18,12,13
[11] St. J. Escrivá, *Friends of God*, 203

cowardly we are. *Lord, increase our faith*, we say to him in our prayer. Holy Mary, ask your Son to increase our faith, so often weak and feeble!

With this confidence we await the birth of Our Lord, and for this reason we pray with the Church: *O God, who sees how your people faithfully await the feast of the Lord's Nativity, enable us, we pray, to attain the joys of so great a salvation and to celebrate them always with solemn worship and glad rejoicing.*[12]

6.2 Faith, our greatest treasure. Guarding it. Communicating it.

Faith is the greatest treasure we have, so we must use all the means at our disposal to conserve it and increase it. It is only logical, therefore, that we should defend our faith against anything that could endanger it; being careful about what we read (especially in these times when error is rampant), by avoiding shows that can soil the heart, by being on our guard against the temptations of the consumer society and alert to the danger of television programmes that can endanger the treasure we have received. Let us put into practice the means for acquiring an adequate religious formation, necessarily all the more solid the more difficult the environment that surrounds us and the situations in which we are compelled to lead our lives. Let us try to recite attentively the Creed at Mass on Sundays and feast-days, making a true profession of the faith that is in us.

In these times of doctrinal confusion we must take particular precautions not to give way in the content of our faith, not even in the slightest degree, for *if one yields ground on any single point of Catholic doctrine, one will later have to yield in another, and again in another, and so*

---

[12] *Collect, Mass for 3rd Sunday of Advent*

on until such surrenders come to be something normal and acceptable. And, when one gets used to rejecting dogma bit by bit, the final result will be the repudiation of it altogether.[13]

If we keep watch over our faith and reflect on it in our daily lives, we will know how to communicate it to those around us. We will bear the same witness to the world as the early Christians did: they were firm as a rock in the face of incredible difficulties. Many of our friends, observing how consistent is our behaviour with the faith we profess, will be moved by this calm and firm witness and will themselves come closer to Our Lord.

So everyone who acknowledges me before men, I also will acknowledge before My Father who is in heaven.[14] What a wonderful promise to inspire us to an apostolic life!

To acknowledge God before men is to be a living witness to his life and to his words. We want to fulfil our daily tasks, to carry out everything we do, according to the doctrine of Jesus Christ, and we should be disposed to make our faith transparent in every one of our family and professional obligations. Let us stop and think for a moment of our work, of our colleagues, of our friendships: are we seen as people whose lives are totally consistent with our faith? Do we lack the courage to speak to our friends about God? Are we restrained by human respect, by what other people will think of us? Do we concern ourselves with the faith of those who, in one way or another, God has placed in our charge?

One consequence of a strong faith is optimism, and the certainty that things will go well. God's power goes with us and drives away all possibility of fear. He who

---

[13] St Vincent of Lerins, *Narrations*, 23
[14] Matt 10:32

has given us a vocation to holiness and a divine mission
will also give us the grace to fulfil it.

6.3 Mary's faith.

At all times we ought to follow the example of Our
Lady, she whose whole existence was grounded on faith,
but especially in this season of Advent, which is a time of
waiting, a time of sure hope, before the Messiah is born
of her virginal womb. *Blessed art thou who hast
believed,*[15] said her cousin Elizabeth.

See with wonder the confidence and serenity of the
Virgin Mary at the discovery of her vocation. She is the
Mother of God! She is that creature of whom, from the
beginning of Genesis, the Sacred Books have been
speaking, the one who would crush the head of the
enemy of God and of men,[16] the one so often proclaimed
by the prophets.[17] Yahweh *has regarded the low estate*,
the simplicity, *of his handmaiden.*[18]

Take the trusting serenity of the Virgin Mary in the
secret she kept from Saint Joseph. Mary loved Joseph and
she saw him suffer.[19] She trusted in God. It is possible
that in following our own vocation or in carrying out
God's will, we may be afraid of making our loved ones
suffer. He knows how best to arrange things. *God knows
best.*[20] She was to understand later. The accomplishment
of God's will, which always involves faith, is the greatest
good for ourselves and for those with whom we normally
come in contact, or have dealings with.

---

[15] Luke 1:45
[16] Gen 3:15
[17] cf Is 7:14; Mic 5:2
[18] cf Luke 1:48
[19] cf Matt 1:18-19
[20] A. del Portillo, Preface, *Friends of God*

Think of the faith of Our Lady in the difficult moments that preceded the birth of Jesus. St Joseph knocked on many doors that Christmas eve and Our Lady heard many refusals. Think of her faith in the face of that rapid flight into Egypt, of God fleeing to a foreign land!

Consider too Mary's trust every single day of those thirty years when Jesus led his hidden life in Nazareth, when there were no miraculous signs of her son's divinity, nothing but simple and ordinary work ... .

Ponder the faith of Mary on Calvary. *This was how the Blessed Virgin made progress on the pilgrimage of faith. She maintained her union with her son right up to the cross. There, by the divine plan, she took her stand, endured bitter grief with her only child, shared with a mother's heart in his sacrifice by giving a loving consent to the offering of the victim who had taken birth from her.*[21]

Mary lives with her eyes fixed on God. She has placed all her trust in the Almighty and surrendered herself entirely to him. She asks this for us, too: that we may live with unbreakable trust in Jesus, untroubled amidst all the storms of life and eager to pass on the same attitude to those around us. This is what she wants for us, her children. And, above all, she wants some day to see us in heaven, beside her Son.

Joining in the Liturgy of the Church we pray: *O God, through the child born of the Blessed Virgin you revealed to the world the splendour of your glory. Help us to preserve undiminished our faith in the great mystery of the Incarnation, that it may remain forever the centre of our lives.*[22]

---

[21] Second Vatican Council, *Lumen gentium*, 58
[22] *Prayer, Mass for 19 December*

7. THE GOOD SHEPHERD PROCLAIMED BY THE PROPHETS

7.1 Jesus Christ the Good Shepherd promised by the prophets. His knowing us each one by name.

When you turn to the right or when you turn to the left, your ears shall hear a word spoken behind you: 'This is the way, walk in it.'[1] One of the greatest gifts God can give us in this life is a clear view of the road that leads to him and the opportunity to rely on someone who will help us to recover from our errors and wrong turnings so that we can get back once more onto the right track.

Many times in the course of their history the chosen people lost their bearings and strayed from the right path, falling into the greatest confusion and dismay because they had no true guides. This is how God finds his people: *like sheep without a shepherd,* as today's Gospel relates.[2] *And when he saw the crowds he felt sorry for them because they were harassed and dejected, like sheep without a shepherd.* Their guides had behaved more like wolves than like true shepherds of their flock.

Throughout the long waiting of the Old Testament the prophets had proclaimed, with centuries still to go, the imminent arrival of the Good Shepherd, the Messiah, who would lead his flock with loving care. He would be the *one shepherd*[3] who would seek the lost lamb that had

---

[1] *First reading of the Mass*, Is 30:21
[2] Matt 9:35-38; 1:6-8
[3] Ezek 34:23

gone astray, who would bind up its wounds and cure it of its sickness.[4] With him the sheep would be safe, and in his name they would have other good shepherds whose mission likewise would be to care for and lead them: *I will set shepherds over them who will look after them, and they shall fear no more, nor be dismayed; neither shall they be missing, says the Lord.*[5]

I am the good shepherd,[6] says Jesus. He has come into the world to gather together God's flock.[7] For as St Peter says: *You were straying like sheep, but have now returned to the Shepherd and Guardian of your souls.*[8] The Good Shepherd comes to return the lost sheep to its flock,[9] to guide it,[10] to defend it,[11] to feed it,[12] to judge it,[13] and to lead it finally to the eternal pastures *irrigated by springs of living water.*[14]

Jesus is the Good Shepherd proclaimed by the prophets. In him, to the letter, are all the prophecies accomplished. He knows each one of his sheep and calls it *by its name.*[15] Yes. Jesus knows us personally. He calls us, seeks us and heals us. There is no need for us to feel lost, submerged in a huge mass of nameless humanity. To him each one of us is unique. We can say with perfect

---

[4] cf Ezek 34:16
[5] Jer 23:4
[6] John 10:11
[7] Matt 15:24
[8] 1 Pet 2:25
[9] Luke 15:3-7
[10] John 10:4
[11] Luke 12:32
[12] John 10:12
[13] Matt 25:32
[14] Apoc 7:17
[15] John 10:3

accuracy: *He loved me and gave himself up for me.*[16] He
distinguishes my voice among many others. No Christian
has the right to say he is alone. Jesus Christ is with him.
If he is lost in the by-ways of wrongdoing, the Good
Shepherd is already out searching for him. Only the
perverse will of the sheep can bring to naught the
vigilance of the shepherd – a plain refusal to return to the
sheepfold. That and that alone.

7.2 Our Lord's leaving good shepherds in his Church.

As well as applying to himself the title of Good
Shepherd, Christ also compares himself to the *door*
through which the sheep enter the fold, which is the
Church. The Church *is a sheepfold whose one and only
door is Christ. It is also a flock of which God himself is
said in prophecy to be the Shepherd, and whose sheep,
though undoubtedly led by human shepherds, are nevertheless guided and fed continually by Christ himself, the
Good Shepherd and Prince of shepherds, who gave his
life for his sheep.*[17]

Jesus has ordained that there be in his Church good
shepherds so that in his name they may watch over and
lead his sheep.[18] At the head of all these, as his Vicar on
earth, he established Peter and his successors,[19] to whom
we owe a special veneration, love and obedience. Together
with the Pope, and in communion with him, are the
bishops to whom we pay similar homage as successors to
the apostles.

Priests are good shepherds, especially in the
administration of the Sacrament of Penance in which all

---

[16] Gal 2:20
[17] Second Vatican Council, *Lumen gentium*, 6
[18] Eph 4:11
[19] John 21:15-17

our wounds and illnesses are healed. *They remind us,* said John Paul II, *that their priestly ministry ... is ordered, in a special way, to the great solicitude of the Good Shepherd, a solicitude for the salvation of all men ..., that men may have life, and have it more abundantly, so that none may perish, but that they may have eternal life.*[20]

Every Christian also should be a good shepherd to his fellow men, especially by means of fraternal correction, example and prayer. Let us consider often that, in one way or another, we are to be the good shepherds of those whom God has placed at our side. We have a duty to help them, through example and prayer, to walk in the way of holiness and to persevere in their correspondence to the gifts and indications of the Good Shepherd, who leads us to the pastures of eternal life.

The role of good shepherd is a most demanding one. It involves much love and a great deal of patience.[21] It requires courage,[22] ability[23] and meekness, as well as quickness of mind[24] and a great sense of responsibility[25]. The neglect of this mission can bring about serious harm to the people of God:[26] *the bad shepherd leads even his strongest sheep to their death.*[27]

The good shepherd must fulfil four conditions. First of all he must have 'love': charity was the very first virtue Our Lord demanded of Peter before entrusting to him the care of his flock. Secondly, he needs to be 'watchful', so that he may be attentive to the needs of his

---

[20] John Paul II, *Letter to all priests*, 8 April 1979, 7
[21] Is 40:11
[22] 1 Sam 25:7; Is 31:4; Amos 3:12
[23] Prov 27:23
[24] 1 Pet 5:2
[25] Matt 18:12
[26] Is 13:14-15; Jer 50:6-8
[27] St Augustine, *Sermon 46, On the shepherds*

flock. Essential in the third place is 'doctrine', the aim of which is to provide men with the food that will enable them to reach salvation. And, finally, the good shepherd requires 'holiness and integrity of life', which is the foundation of all these qualities.[28]

It is the duty of us all to plead persistently that there will never be a lack of good shepherds in the Church. And we ought to pray particularly for those whom God has made the shepherds of our own souls.

7.3 How we encounter the Good Shepherd in spiritual direction.

Each one of us needs a good shepherd to direct his soul, since no one can map out his own course without a special help from God. Lack of objectivity, the exaggerated love we have for ourselves, and laziness, all conspire to obscure our path to God, leading us to spiritual stagnation, lukewarmness and discouragement. On the other hand, *in the same way that a ship with a good pilot arrives safely in port, so also, will the soul that has a good shepherd safely reach its destination even though it may many times have gone astray.*[29]

Everyone knows that a guide is needed in order to climb a mountain without difficulty. The same thing happens when it is a matter of a spiritual climb ...; and even more so in that here one must avoid the pitfalls set by the devil, who dearly wants to bring us down.[30]

We need spiritual direction so that at the end of our lives we will not have to say what the Israelites said after wandering about the desert without direction or

---

[28] St Thomas of Villanueva, *Sermon on the Gospel of the Good Shepherd*
[29] St John Climacus, *Stairs of Paradise*
[30] R. Garrigou-Lagrange, *The Three Ages of the Interior Life*

meaningful purpose: *for forty years we went round and round the mountain.*[31] We have lived, they said, without rhyme or reason, without knowing where we were going, without our work or study bringing us any closer to God, without letting friendship or family, health or sickness, success or failure take us one step forward towards what is really important: holiness and salvation. So that we won't be in the position of having to say that we too have lived in this way, pointlessly whiling away the time, absorbed in passing fancies simply because we have no supernatural goal to aim at, we need a clear path to travel and a guide to lead us along it.

It may be necessary to entrust the direction of our soul to someone else, for we all need a kindly push if we get discouraged at our setbacks on our road to God. It will be good for us to have a friendly voice which says: *Come on! Don't give in! God's grace is available to help you overcome every difficulty.* Listen to these words inspired by the Holy Spirit: *For if they fall, one will lift up his fellow; but woe to him who is alone when he falls and has not another to lift him up.*[32] With the help of our director we regain our interior composure, and drawing upon forces which we had thought were not there any more, we continue on our way.

It is a special grace from God to be able to rely on such a person who is both friend and confidant and who can help us so effectively in a matter of such great importance. We can open our hearts to him confidently, with human and supernatural intent. What a joy it is to be able to lay bare our most intimate thoughts and feelings, to direct them to God with the help of someone who understands us! He holds us in esteem, opens up to us

---

[31] Eccles 4:10
[32] Deut 2:1

new horizons, supports us and prays for us. He also has special grace from God to enable him to help us. But it is important to find and go to that person who will be truly a good shepherd for us, the one God wants us to go to.

St Luke tells us how the prodigal son felt the need to be rid of the burden that weighed so heavily on his soul. Judas also felt weighed down by the load of his betrayal. The first went where he ought to have gone and found a peace he could never have imagined: he regained his life. Judas should have gone back to Jesus who would have sheltered and comforted him, in spite of his sin, as he did the repentant Peter. But instead, Judas went where he should not have gone: he went to those who were incapable of understanding, and, above all, who were unable to give that unfortunate man what he most needed. *What is that to us? they said to him. See to it yourself.*

In spiritual direction we encounter the Good Shepherd, who gives us the help we need to avoid getting lost and to get back on the right path if we have deviated from it in our progress towards Christ.

Our Holy Mother Mary will always show us the safe path that leads to her Son.

SECOND SUNDAY OF ADVENT

8. THE PRECURSOR.
PREPARE THE WAY OF THE LORD.

8.1 The vocation of John the Baptist. An Advent figure.

O people of Sion, behold, the Lord will come to save the nations and the Lord will make the glory of his voice heard in the joy of your heart.[1]

Behold, the Lord will come ... The Saviour is about to arrive and nobody notices anything. The world goes on as usual, completely oblivious. Only Mary knows – and Joseph who has been told by the angel. The world is in darkness. Christ is still in Mary's womb. And there are the Jews, still arguing about the Messiah, without any idea that he is so near ... Few people are expecting *the Consolation of Israel*: Simeon, Anna ... We are in Advent, a time of waiting.

During this liturgical period the Church proposes the figure of John the Baptist for our meditation. *For this is he who was spoken of by the prophet Isaiah when he spoke of: The voice of one crying in the wilderness: Prepare the way of the Lord, make his paths straight.*[2]

The Messiah's coming was preceded by prophets who announced his arrival from afar, like heralds who announce the arrival of a great king. *John appears as the dividing line between the two Testaments, the Old and the New. Our Lord himself teaches something about John when He talks about 'the law and the prophets down to*

---

[1] *Entrance Antiphon of the Mass*, cf Is 30:19,30
[2] Matt 3:3

*John the Baptist'. He is the personification of antiquity
and the announcement of new times. As representing
antiquity, he is born to elderly parents. As one who is a
harbinger of new times, he shows that he has been a
prophet from his mother's womb. He has not yet been
born when, at Our Lady's arrival, he leaps for joy inside
his mother.*[3] *John is called 'the prophet of the Most
High', because his mission is 'to go before the Lord to
prepare his ways, teaching the knowledge of salvation to
his people'.*[4]

The whole of John's life is determined by this
mission, even from his mother's womb. This is to be his
vocation. His whole purpose will be to prepare, for Jesus,
a people capable of receiving the Kingdom of God. At
the same time he is to give public testimony of Him. John
will not seek personal fulfilment through his work but
has come to *prepare a perfect people for the Lord.* He
will not do it because it appeals to him, but because it
was for this very purpose he was conceived. This is what
all apostolate is about: forgetting oneself and fostering a
true concern for others.

John was to carry out his task to the full, even to the
extent of giving up his life in the fulfilment of his
vocation. Many came to know Jesus through John the
Baptist's apostolic work. It was through an express
indication of his that the first disciples followed Jesus.
And many others were inwardly prepared thanks to his
preaching.

One's vocation embraces one's whole life, and our
whole being works towards fulfilment of the divine
mission. God makes the conversion of many children of
Israel depend on John's future response.

---

[3] cf Luke 1:76-77
[4] St Augustine, *Sermon 293*, 2

In his own place and circumstances, each man has a God-given vocation. The divine will desires many other things that depend on the fulfilment of that vocation. *Many great things depend – don't forget it – on whether you and I live our lives as God wants.*[5] Do we bring the people around us closer to God? Do we give good example in the way we carry out our work, in our family circle, in our social relations? Do we speak about God to our colleagues or fellow-students?

8.2 John's humility. This virtue necessary for apostolate.

Whilst being fully conscious of the mission which has been entrusted to him, John knows that before Christ he is not even *worthy to carry his sandals,*[6] which was what the least of the servants used to do for their master; anybody could do that task. The Baptist does not hesitate to proclaim that he is of no importance compared with Jesus. He does not even identify himself according to his priestly parentage. He does not say, 'I am John, son of Zachary of the priestly tribe of ...' On the contrary, when they ask him, *Who are you?*, John says, *I am the voice of one crying in the wilderness; prepare the way of the Lord, make his paths straight.* He is no more than that – *the voice.* He is only the voice that announces Jesus. That is his mission, his life, his personality. His whole being is defined by Jesus, as should be the case in our own lives, in the life of any Christian. What is important in our lives is Jesus.

As Christ gradually manifests Himself, John seeks to take second place, to disappear. His best disciples will be those who take up his indication to follow the Master at

---

[5] St. J. Escrivá, *The Way*, 755
[6] cf Matt 3:11

the beginning of his public life. *This is the Lamb of God* he says to John and Andrew, pointing to Jesus who is passing by. With great refinement he detached himself from his followers, so that they should go after Christ. John *persevered in sanctity, because he remained humble of heart.*[7] That is why he also merited that wonderful praise of Our Lord's, *Truly I say to you, among those born of women there has risen no one greater than John the Baptist.*[8]

Today, the Precursor still points to the path we have to follow. In our personal apostolate – when we prepare others to meet Christ – we must try not to make ourselves the centre of attraction. What is important is that Christ should be announced, known and loved. Only He has the words of eternal life. Only in Him do we find salvation. John's attitude is an energetic warning against disordered self-love, which is always urging us to put ourselves unduly in the foreground. A desire to draw attention to oneself would leave no room for Jesus.

God also asks us to live without ostentation, without wanting to be heroes. He wants us to lead simple, ordinary lives, trying to do good to everyone and carrying out our duties honestly. Without humility we could not bring our friends closer to God. Our life would then become empty.

8.3 Our role as witnesses and precursors. Apostolate with the people around us.

We are not only precursors, however; we are also witnesses to Christ. Together with the grace of Baptism and Confirmation, we have received the honourable duty of making our faith in Christ known through our words

---

[7] St Gregory the Great, *Treatise on St Luke's Gospel*, 20, 5
[8] Matt 11:11

and our deeds. In order to enable us to carry out this mission, we receive frequently, even daily, the divine food of the Body of Christ. His priests lavish sacramental grace on us and instruct us with the teaching of the divine Word.

All that has been given to us is so much greater than John himself had, that Jesus could say: *The least in the kingdom of God is greater than John.* However, what a difference! Jesus is just about to arrive, and John's whole reason for living is to be the Precursor. We are witnesses of what He came to do; but what sort of witnesses are we? What is our Christian testimony like amongst our colleagues and our families? Is it forceful enough to convince those who do not yet believe in Jesus? Those who do not love Him? Those who have mistaken ideas about Him? Is our life a proof, or does it at least point to the *likelihood* of the truth of Christianity? These questions could help us to live this Advent, so that it is not devoid of apostolic meaning.

Behold the Lord will come ... John knows that God is preparing something very great, something for which he is to be the instrument; and he himself points in the direction that the Holy Spirit shows him. We know much more now about what it was that God had in mind for humanity. We know Christ and His Church, we have the sacraments. The doctrine of salvation has been perfectly marked out for us ... We know that the world needs Christ to reign, we know that the happiness and salvation of all mankind depend on Him. We have Christ Himself; the same Christ whom John the Baptist knew and announced.

We are witnesses and precursors. We have to bear witness and at the same time we have to show others the way. *Our responsibility is great, because to be Christ's witnesses implies first and foremost that we should try to live our lives according to his doctrine, that we should struggle to make our actions remind others of Jesus and his most lovable personality. We have to act in such a way that others will be able to say, when they meet us: This man is a Christian, because he does not hate, because he is willing to understand, because he is not a fanatic, because he is willing to make sacrifices, because he shows that he is a man of peace, because he knows how to love.*[9]

Perhaps, in many cases, today's world does not await anything at all. Or it waits facing in a direction from which nobody will come. Many people have thrown themselves heart and soul into possessing material things as if these were their last end. But their hearts will never be satisfied with these things. We have to show the way to such people and to everyone.

You know, says St Augustine, *what each one of you must do in his own home, with his friend, his neighbour, his servant, his superior, his subordinate. You also know the way in which God provides the opportunity, and the way He opens the door with his word. Do not be content, then, to live at peace with yourselves until you have won them all for Christ, for you have been won for Christ.*[10]

Our family, friends, workmates, those people we come in contact with frequently, should be the first to benefit from our love for God. With our example and our prayer we should reach even people we do not have the chance to talk to.

Our great joy will be that of having brought to Jesus, as John the Baptist did, many who were far away or indifferent. We should never forget that it is God's grace, and not our human strength, that can move souls towards

---

[9] St. J. Escrivá, *Christ is passing by*, 122
[10] St Augustine, *Treatise on St John's Gospel*, 10,9

Jesus. As nobody can give what he does not have, the effort to grow in our interior life becomes more urgent, so that all those we meet and pass on the road can be infected by our superabundant love for God.

The Queen of Apostles will increase our longing and our effort to bring souls to her Son in the certainty that no effort is in vain in the sight of God.

9. APOSTOLATE OF CONFESSION

9.1 The greatest good that we can do our friends – taking them to the Sacrament of Penance.

Stir up your power, O Lord, and come to our help with mighty strength, that what our sins impede, the grace of your mercy may hasten.[1] This liturgical prayer, with which we begin our conversation with God, speaks of proclaiming the coming of Jesus by asking pardon for sins.

Strengthen all weary hands, steady all trembling knees, and say to all faint hearts, 'Courage, do not be afraid' ... God himself is coming to save you. Then the eyes of the blind shall be opened, the ears of the deaf unsealed; then shall the lame leap like the deer, and the tongues of the dumb sing for joy; for water gushes in the desert; streams flow in the wasteland, the scorched earth becomes a lake, the parched land revives with springs of water.[2] Our Lord has brought with him everything good.

The Messiah is very close to us, and during these days of Advent we should get ready to receive him in a new way when Christmas comes. During these days Jesus says in a special manner, *Strengthen all weary hands, steady all trembling knees, and say to all faint hearts, 'Courage, do not be afraid'* ... Every day we meet friends, colleagues, relatives who have lost their sense of what is most essential to their very existence. They feel unable to go towards Our Lord, and they walk along the paths of life as though paralysed, because they have lost

---

[1] *Collect, Mass for Thursday in the First Week of Advent*
[2] *First reading of the Mass, cf Is 35:1-10*

hope. We have to show them the way to the humble cave in Bethlehem. There they will find the meaning of their lives. To do this we have to know the way ourselves. We must have interior life. We have to talk to Jesus and strive, ourselves, to improve in those very things in which our friends have to improve. We must have an unshakeable hope in the supernatural means.

Prayer, mortification and good example will always form the basis of the Christian apostolate. The more petition for others is backed by the sanctity of the suppliant, the more certain it is to be answered. Apostolate springs from a great love for Christ.

In many cases, bringing our friends closer to Christ means taking them to receive the sacrament of Penance, one of the greatest treasures Our Lord has left to his Church. Perhaps no way of helping friends is as great as making it easy for them to go to Confession. Sometimes we will have to help them, with tact and kindness, make a good examination of conscience. Sometimes we will accompany them to the place where confessions are being heard. At other times again, a word of encouragement and affection will suffice, accompanied by a brief and properly-prepared instruction about the nature and value of the sacrament. What joy each time we get a relative, a colleague, a friend, to receive the sacrament of divine mercy! This same joy is shared in Heaven[3] by our Father God and by all the blessed.

9.2 Faith and confidence in God – the paralytic of Capharnaum.

In the Gospel of today's Mass St Mark tells us that Jesus came to Capharnaum and that immediately they knew he was in the house, *many were gathered together,*

---

[3] cf Luke 15:7

*so that there was no longer room for them, not even
about the door.*[4]

Four friends also went to the house carrying a
paralytic; but they could not get near Jesus *because of the
crowd.* Then, perhaps, they managed to find some steps
at the back. In some way they got onto the roof with the
paralysed man. They then removed part of the roof,
making a hole in the tiles. Through it they manoeuvred
the stretcher on which the palsied man lay. They lowered
the stretcher down and left it *in the midst before Jesus.*[5]

Apostolate, particularly the apostolate of Confession,
is somehow similar; it is to get people to Jesus. Now, as
then, Our Lord does the rest. It is He who does what is
really important.

The four friends already knew the Master, and their
hope was so great that the miracle was worked because
of their trust in Him. It is their faith that somehow makes
up for, or completes, that of the paralytic. The gospel
says, *when Jesus saw their faith,* (that is, the friends'
faith), he performed the miracle. There is no specific
mention of the sick man's faith, but that of the friends is
emphasized and dwelt upon. They overcame obstacles
which seemed insurmountable: and they had to convince
the sick man. Their trust in Jesus must have been very
great, because only someone who is himself convinced
can convince others. When they reached the house there
were such crowds that it seemed there was nothing they
could do on that occasion at least. But they were
undaunted. They were able to overcome that obstacle
with their decisiveness, their skill and their concern.
What mattered was the meeting between Jesus and their
friend. They used all the means within their reach so that

[4] cf Mark 2:1-13
[5] cf Luke 5:19

this meeting could take place.

What a great lesson this is for the apostolate that we as Christians have to do. We too will doubtless meet with resistance, sometimes more, sometimes less. Our mission consists fundamentally in bringing our friends face to face with Christ, leaving them at Jesus' side ... and disappearing. No one can transform a soul but God, and only He. Apostolate is in the order of grace, a supernatural order.

Sometimes it may be our fault that others do not come closer to God, because they feel unable of their own effort to reach out to Him. *This paralysed man*, explains St Thomas, *symbolizes the sinner lying in his sin. Just as the paralytic is unable to move, so too is the sinner helpless by himself. Those who carry the man immobilized by his paralysis represent those who, with their advice, lead the sinner towards God.*[6]

If we trust Christ and often seek his company, if we use human initiative as well, we will be able to overcome the obstacles that always present themselves in one way or another in every apostolic undertaking.

Our Lord was impressed by the audacity, which was the fruit of great apostolic hope, of those four friends who did not give up at the first sign of difficulty, or defer things till a more opportune occasion might arise. Indeed, they did not know when Our Lord would pass that way again, or be so close.

We can ask ourselves today in our personal meditation whether we behave like this towards our friends, relatives and acquaintances. Have we given up at the first signs of difficulty when we have decided to help them go to Confession? That is where Our Lord is waiting for them.

---

[6] St Thomas, *Commentary on St Matthew*, 9,2

9.3 Confession – the power to forgive sins – respect, gratitude and veneration as we approach this sacrament.

Jesus looked at the sick man with immense pity. *Have faith, my son,* he says. Then he spoke some words which astounded everyone: *Your sins are forgiven.*

After David had sinned and he went to throw himself at Nathan's feet, Nathan said to him, *Yahweh has forgiven you.*[7] It was God who had forgiven him. Nathan did no more than transmit the message which made David recover his joy and see again the meaning of his life. Jesus, however, forgives in his own name. This was a cause of scandal for the Scribes who were present. *Why does this man speak thus? It is blasphemy! Who can forgive sins but God alone?*

It is quite possible that the paralytic saw his life, all his unworthiness, with special lucidity. Perhaps at that moment he understood, as never before, the need to be clean under that most pure gaze of Jesus, which penetrated with deep compassion to the very depths of his soul. Then he received the grace of forgiveness; it was the reward for having allowed himself to be helped; straightaway he experienced a joy such as he had never before imagined. It is the joy of every contrite and sincere Confession. Now his paralysis no longer mattered to him. His soul was clean and he had found Jesus.

Our Lord reads the thoughts of all men, and he wanted to make it very clear to those of us also, who, centuries later, would meditate on this scene, that he has all power in Heaven and on earth – even the power of forgiving sins, because he is God. He demonstrates it by performing the miracle of restoring this man to perfect health.

---

[7] 2 Sam 12:13

This power of forgiving sins was transmitted by Our Lord to his Church in the person of the Apostles, so that through her priests she could exercise it till the end of time. *Receive the Holy Spirit. If you forgive the sins of any, they are forgiven; if you retain the sins of any, they are retained.*[8]

Priests exercise the power of forgiving sins not through any virtue of their own, but in the name of Christ – *in persona Christi* – as instruments in God's hands. Only God can forgive sins, and he has willed to do so by means of the Sacrament of Penance, through his ministers who are priests. People around us need urgent instruction on this subject, which will enable them to receive this sacrament with greater love.

Let us make good use of today's prayer by thanking Our Lord for leaving such immense power to his Church, our Mother. Thank you, Lord, for putting such a great gift so easily within our reach.

This time of prayer beside Our Lord can also help us to examine what our own Confessions are like. Do we prepare them with a careful examination of conscience? Do we stir ourselves to contrition each time we go? Do we go to Confession as frequently as we have made up our minds to do? Are we completely sincere with our confessor? Do we strive to put into practice the advice we have received? This very day could be a good time to see in the presence of God which of our relatives, friends or colleagues we can help prepare a good examination of conscience. Who are the people who most need a word of encouragement in order to prepare to receive this sacrament in readiness for Christmas? In the depths of their souls they are hoping for it, and God too is waiting for them to turn towards this source of his mercy. We

---

[8] John 20:22-23

must not let them down. It is the greatest present we can give them.

Our Mother Mary, *Refugium peccatorum*, will have compassion on them, and on us.

SECOND WEEK OF ADVENT – TUESDAY

10. OUR SINS AND CONFESSION

10.1 Confession of our sins and purpose of amendment. It must be complete, individual and to a priest.

A voice cries: Prepare the way of the Lord in the wilderness, make straight in the desert a highway for our God. Every valley shall be lifted up and every mountain and hill be made low; the uneven ground shall become level and the rough places a plain.[1]

The best way of getting our souls ready to receive Our Lord at his coming is to make a really well-prepared Confession. This Sacrament is a source of grace and mercy throughout our entire life, but its necessity is especially obvious in this season, when through her liturgy the Church urges and encourages us to prepare to commemorate the birth of Our Lord at Christmas.

She puts on our lips the prayerful petition: *O God, who sent your Only Begotten Son into this world to free the human race from its ancient enslavement, bestow on those who devoutly await him the grace of your compassion on high, that we may attain the price of true freedom.*[2]

Confession is also the sacrament which, together with the Holy Eucharist, prepares us for that all-important meeting with Christ at the end of our earthly life. Our whole life is, in this sense, a continual Advent, a preparation for that final moment for which we are unceasingly, day by day, getting ourselves ready. How comforting it is to realize that it is this same Lord who

---

[1] Is 40:3-4
[2] *Collect, Mass for Saturday of the First Week in Advent*

ardently desires to have us with Him in *the new heaven and the new earth*[3] which He has prepared for us.

Every well-made Confession is an impulse which Our Lord gives us to go ahead, freed from our miseries, with new courage and joy. Christ says to us once more: *Take heart, your sins are forgiven*[4] my child, begin again ... It is He Himself who forgives us when we have humbly told Him our faults. We confess our sins *to God Himself, although in the confessional it is a man – the priest – who listens to us. That man is the humble and faithful servant of this great mystery which has been enacted between the son who returns and the Father.*[5]

The causes of evil are not to be found outside man, but, above all, in the depth of his heart. Its cure also comes from the heart. Consequently Christians must rebel against the debasing of man, through a sincere determination to be truly converted themselves, and must show forth in their own lives the joy of being truly freed from sin ... by means of their sincere repentance, their firm resolution of amendment and the courageous confession of their faults.[6]

For those who have fallen into mortal sin after they have been baptized, this Sacrament of Penance is as necessary for their salvation as is Baptism for those who have not yet been re-born into supernatural life: *It is the means to satisfy man with the righteousness that comes from the Redeemer Himself.*[7] And the Church holds its importance to be so great that *lack of time may oblige*

---

[3] Rev 21:1

[4] Matt 9:2

[5] John Paul II, *Homily at the Parish of St Ignatius*, Rome, 16 March 1980

[6] John Paul II, *Homily*, 5 April 1979

[7] John Paul II, Encyclical, *Redemptor Hominis*, 20

priests to postpone or even to omit other activities, but never that of hearing Confessions.[8]

All mortal sins committed after Baptism, together with any circumstances which may affect their nature, must be brought to the tribunal of Penance in an individual confession made privately to a priest, followed by individual absolution.

The Holy Father asks us all to do everything that we can *to help the ecclesial community to appreciate fully 'the value of individual Confession' as a personal encounter with the merciful and loving Saviour, and to be faithful to the directives of the Church in a matter of such importance.*[9]

We cannot forget that conversion is a particularly profound inward act in which the individual cannot be replaced by others and cannot make the community be a substitute for him.[10]

10.2 Confession is to Our Lord Himself; frequent Confession.

As well as being *complete* in regard to serious sins, Confession must be *supernatural*: we have to remember that we are coming to implore forgiveness from the same Lord whom we have offended, because all sins, including those committed against our fellow man, are direct offences against God.

A confession made with consciousness of its supernatural nature is a real act of love for God. In the depth of our soul we hear Christ say, as he said to Peter: *Simon, son of John, do you love me?* And we too can answer, in

---

[8] *idem*, Rome, 17 November 1978
[9] John Paul II, *Address to the Bishops of Japan*, Tokyo, 23 February 1981
[10] John Paul II, Encyclical, *Redemptor Hominis*, 20

the very words of the Apostle, *Domine, tu omnia nosti, tu scis quia amo te.*[11] Lord, you know everything, you know that I love you ... in spite of everything.

Next to mortal sin, venial sin is the soul's greatest misery, because it prevents us from receiving many actual graces. Each small unfaithfulness is the loss of a great treasure: it decreases the warmth of our love; it increases our difficulty in practising the virtues, which seems harder and harder all the time. And it makes it easier for us to end up committing mortal sin, unless we react promptly.

Our greatest help in the struggle to avoid venial sins comes from Holy Communion and frequent Confession. What is more, in Confession we are given special graces to avoid precisely those defects and sins which we have confessed and repented. To value frequent Confession is a sign of spiritual refinement and love of God. To despise it or to be indifferent to it suggests inward coarseness and frequently a real blindness to supernatural realities.

How often we should go to Confession depends on the needs of each individual soul. Anyone who is seriously determined to fulfil the Will of God in everything and to belong entirely to God will feel a real need to come to this sacrament more often and more regularly: *Confession periodically renewed – the Confession of 'devotion' – has always accompanied the ascent to holiness in the Church.*[12]

10.3 Each Confession benefits the whole Church. The Communion of Saints and the Sacrament of Penance.

In the Sacrament of Penance man is reconciled with

---

[11] John 21:17
[12] John Paul II, *Address to members of the Sacred Apostolic Penitentiary*, 30 January 1981

God and with the Church. It is one of the most intimate and personal of human acts, and brings about many fundamental changes in the sanctuary of each man's conscience. Yet at the same time this Sacrament also possesses a deep and inseparable social dimension and also brings about many changes in the family circle, the studies, the work, the friendly relationships etc., of the person who goes to Confession.

The greatest tragedy in any man's life is sin, because the result of sin is a far-reaching disorder which starts in the very centre of his being and spreads outward to affect all those around him. In the Sacrament of Penance Our Lord sorts out all those misplaced elements; in addition to pardoning the sins, he restores to the soul its lost order and harmony.

A well-made confession brings much good to all those who live and work with us. What is more, it is of benefit to very many other people with whom we come into contact in the course of the day. The grace that we receive in this sacrament means that we say and do everything in a very different way.

Not only that, but when a Christian goes to Confession, the whole Church receives an incalculable benefit. Every time a priest pronounces the words of absolution, She rejoices and is mysteriously enriched, because every Confession, through the Communion of Saints, sends blessings which resound through the whole Mystical Body of Christ.

In the intimate life of the Church – whose cornerstone is Christ – every member supports all the others with his good works and merits, and is at the same time supported by them. We all need to be, and in fact we all are, continually receiving a share of the spiritual benefits which are common to us all. Our own merits are helping our fellow men in every part of the world. In the same way sin, lukewarmness, venial sins and self-satisfied mediocrity weigh down every member of the pilgrim Church: *If one member suffers, all suffer together; if one member is honoured, all rejoice together.*[13]

This is the other aspect of that solidarity which, on the religious level, is developed in the profound and magnificent mystery of the 'Communion of Saints', thanks to which it has been possible to say that 'every soul that rises above itself raises up the world'. To this 'law of ascent' there unfortunately corresponds the 'law of descent'. Consequently one can speak of a 'communion of sin', whereby a soul that lowers itself through sin drags down with itself the Church and, in some way, the whole world. In other words there is no sin, not even the most intimate and secret one, that exclusively concerns the person committing it. With greater or lesser violence, with greater or lesser harm, every sin has repercussions on the entire ecclesial body and on the whole human family.[14]

Whenever anybody makes a sincere and repentant Confession it is a moment of rejoicing not only for the penitent but for everybody. *When she has found the lost coin, she calls together her friends and neighbours, saying: Rejoice with me.*[15] The saints in Heaven, the holy souls in Purgatory, and the Church which is still on pilgrimage through this world rejoice together every time an absolution is given.

'To loosen' the chains of sin is at the same time to tighten the bonds of brotherhood. Ought we not to go to

---

[13] 1 Cor 12:26
[14] John Paul II, Apostolic Exhortation, *Reconciliatio et Paenitentia*, 2 December 1984, 16
[15] Luke 15:9

this Sacrament more joyfully and more regularly when we know that by the very fact of making a good Confession we are helping so many other Christians, and especially those who are closest to us?

Let us ask God, in the words of the Church: *Look with favour, Lord God, on our petitions, and in our trials grant us your compassionate help, that, consoled by the presence of your Son, whose coming we now await, we may be tainted no longer by the corruption of former ways.*[16]

---

[16] *Collect, Mass for Tuesday of the First Week in Advent*

SECOND WEEK OF ADVENT – WEDNESDAY

11. THE WAY OF MEEKNESS

11.1 Jesus, the model of meekness for us to imitate.

The first reading from the prophet Isaiah in today's Mass,[1] together with the responsorial Psalm,[2] invite us to contemplate the greatness of God as opposed to that weakness of our own which we know through the experience of our repeated falls into sin. And they tell us that *the Lord is merciful and gracious, slow to anger and abounding in steadfast love,*[3] and that those who hope in Him *shall renew their strength; they shall mount up with wings like eagles, they shall run and not be weary, they shall walk and not faint.*[4]

The Messiah brought a yoke and a burden to humankind. But this yoke is easy to bear because it liberates us, and the burden does not weigh us down because He Himself carries the heaviest part. Our Lord never oppresses us with his instructions and commands. On the contrary, they make us freer and simplify our life. In the Gospel of today's Mass Jesus says to us: *Come to me, all who labour and are heavy laden, and I will give you rest. Take my yoke upon you and learn from me: for I am gentle and lowly in heart and you will find rest for your souls. For my yoke is easy and my burden is light.*[5] Our Lord proposes Himself as a model of meekness and

---

[1] Is 40:25-31
[2] Ps 102:1-2,8,10
[3] Ps 102:8
[4] Is 40:31
[5] Matt 11:28-30

humility, virtues and dispositions of the heart which always go together.

As Jesus talks to the people who follow Him, *harassed and helpless like sheep without a shepherd,*[6] He wins their trust through the meekness of His heart, always so welcoming and understanding.

The Advent liturgy shows us Christ as *gentle and lowly* so that we can go to Him in all simplicity, and also so that we can prepare for Christmas by trying to imitate Him. Only in this way will we be able to understand what is happening at Bethlehem. Only in this way will be able to get those around us to come with us towards the Baby who is God.

Souls open wide to a heart that is gentle and lowly, like Christ's. There, in His most lovable Heart, the crowds used to find shelter and rest; and even now they still feel strongly attracted by Him and find peace in Him. Our Lord has told us to learn from Him. The fruitfulness of all apostolate will always be very closely bound up with this virtue of meekness.

If we look closely at Jesus we will see how patient He is with the defects of His disciples, and how unweariedly He repeats the same teaching over and over again, explaining it in detail, so that His slow-minded and easily-distracted friends can master His saving doctrine. He never loses patience with their obtuseness and failure to grasp His meaning. Truly, Jesus *who is our master and Lord and at the same time is meek and humble of heart, acted patiently in attracting and inviting his disciples.*[7]

The way to cure our bad temper, impatience and failure to be warm and understanding, is to imitate Jesus

---

[6] Matt 9:36
[7] Second Vatican Council, *Dignitatis Humanae*, 11

in His meekness. This calm and welcoming spirit will be born and develop in us in exact proportion to our efforts to remember the constant presence of God and to think more often about Our Lord's life. *How I wish your bearing and conversation were such that, on seeing or hearing you, people would say: This man reads the life of Jesus Christ.*[8] To contemplate Jesus will especially help us not to be arrogant, and not to lose our tempers when things go wrong.

We must not make the mistake of thinking that this 'bad temper' of ours, which bursts out in very definite circumstances and times, depends on the character of the people around us. *The peace of our spirit does not depend on the good nature and kindness of other people. Our neighbours' good nature and kindness are in no way subject to our control or opinion. That would be absurd. The tranquillity of our heart depends on ourselves. The ability to avoid anger, with all its ridiculous effects, has to come from within ourselves and not be dependent on the nature of other people. The power to overcome the evil in our character must not depend on some perfection outside us, but on our own virtue.*[9]

Meekness is particularly necessary in circumstances where living with other people is very difficult.

11.2 Meekness rooted in great spiritual strength.

Meekness does not go with being feeble or characterless. On the contrary, it is founded on great spiritual strength. The very practice of this virtue calls for continuous acts of such strength. Just as, according to the Gospel, the poor are those who are truly rich, so the meek are those who are truly strong. *Blessed are the*

---

[8] St. J. Escrivá, *The Way*, 2
[9] Cassian, *Constitutions*, 8

meek because they, in this world's warfare, are protected against the devil and against earthly persecutors. They are like glassware so well packed into straw or hay that it is not broken when it is struck. Meekness is like a strong shield which blunts and shatters the sharp arrows of anger. The meek are like people dressed in garments of thick quilted cotton which protect them without harming anyone else.[10] Anger in all its many forms is the material on which this virtue has to work. Meekness controls and directs it, so that it is aroused only when necessary and to the extent to which it is necessary.

Learn from me, for I am gentle and lowly in heart. Comparing it to the majesty of God, who has made Himself a Baby in Bethlehem, we see our own life in its real proportions. And what could have seemed an enormous trial shrinks to its true insignificant size. As we contemplate the birth of Jesus we find that our prayer comes alive, our love becomes wider and deeper and our peace more unshakeable. Close to Him, we learn to consider the various happenings of our everyday life in His presence and so give them their true value, to be silent sometimes when we would have liked to speak, to smile, to be nice to everybody, to wait for the right moment in which to correct a fault. At the same time, we are ready to leap to the defence of truth and the interests of God and of other people with as much force as may be necessary. For there is no opposition between meekness, closely connected as it is with humility, and a righteous anger against injustice. Meekness is not a shelter for cowardice.

An anger which protects the rights of other people is righteous and holy; and most especially the sovereignty and holiness of God. We see the righteous anger of Jesus

---

[10] F. Osuna, *Third Spiritual Alphabet*, III, 4

against the Pharisees and traders in the Temple.[11] Our
Lord found the Temple turned *into a den of robbers*, a
place where there was no reverence, given over to
business which had nothing to do with the true worship
of God. Our Lord was terribly angry, and showed it by
word and deed. The Evangelists have shown us few
scenes as forceful as this one.

And yet, together with His righteous anger with
those who prostitute that holy place, Jesus shows us
simultaneously his great compassion for the needy. *And
the blind and the lame came to him in the Temple and he
healed them.*[12]

11.3 The fruits of meekness. Its necessity for social life and apostolate.

Meekness sets its face against those pointless
displays of violence which at bottom are signs of
weakness, such as impatience, irritation, bad temper and
hatred. It is opposed to all useless waste of energy in
unnecessary anger, which so often originates in little
things that might have been passed over in silence or
with a smile, and which never has any useful results.

Those explosions of bad temper between husband
and wife, which can gradually corrode true love, stem
from a lack of this virtue. So does irritability, with its
serious consequences for the bringing up of children. The
same lack of meekness destroys our peace in prayer,
because instead of talking to God we brood over our
injuries. It is the absence of meekness which leads to that
bad temper in conversation which makes even the most
solid arguments powerless to convince. Mastery of
oneself – which is part of true meekness – is the weapon

[11] John 2:13-17
[12] Matt 21:14

of those who are really strong; it prevents us from answering back too quickly and from speaking wounding words which afterwards we wish we had never said. Meekness knows how to wait for the right moment, and to express its judgements in a way that carries conviction.

The habitual lack of meekness is the result of pride, and produces nothing but loneliness and sterility. *Your ill-temper, your roughness, your unfriendliness, your rigidity (not very Christian!) are the reasons why you find yourself alone, in the loneliness of someone who is selfish, embittered, eternally discontented or resentful; and they are also the reason why you are surrounded not by love but by indifference, coldness, resentment and lack of trust.*

With your good humour, your understanding and your friendliness, with the meekness of Christ as part and parcel of your life, not only should you be happy, but you should bring happiness to everyone around you, to the people you meet on the road of your life.[13]

The meek shall inherit the earth. First they will possess themselves, because they will not be the slaves of their impatience and bad temper; they will possess God, because their souls will always be inclined to prayer, in a continual consciousness of the presence of God; they will possess those around them, because they have the kind of hearts which win friendship and affection, indispensable for everyday social life and for all apostolate. As we pass through the world we must spread around us the *fragrance of Christ,*[14] with our habitual smile, good humour and happiness, love and understanding.

Let us examine ourselves on our readiness to make the sacrifices necessary to make life pleasant for other

---

[13] S. Canals, *Jesus as Friend*
[14] 2 Cor 2:15

people. Let us see if we are able to give way to other people's opinions, instead of claiming to be always right about everything, and if we know how to control our temper and disregard the frictions which are inevitable in daily life. Advent is a good time for strengthening this attitude of mind. We will achieve it if we talk more often to Jesus, Mary and Joseph; if we make a real effort every day to be more understanding with the people around us; if we never stop trying to smooth out the rough edges of our characters; if we know how to go to the Tabernacle to talk over with Our Lord the subjects which are uppermost in our thoughts.

12. BEGINNING AGAIN

12.1 A lifelong struggle against our own defects and passions. The Christian life incompatible with self-satisfied mediocrity.

The liturgy of Advent sets before us the figure of John the Baptist, both as an example of many virtues for us to imitate, and as the one chosen by God to prepare for the coming of the Messiah. With him the Old Testament closes and we are on the threshold of the New.

In the Gospel of today's Mass Our Lord tells us that *from the days of John the Baptist until now, the kingdom of heaven has suffered violence and men of violence take it by force.*[1] The Church suffers violence from the forces of evil and every human soul, with its inclination towards evil as a result of original sin, also suffers that violence. A lifelong struggle will be necessary if we are to follow Our Lord in this life and gaze on Him forever in Heaven. The Christian life is simply not compatible with self-satisfied mediocrity, love of comfort and lukewarmness. *Some people, for His sake, would not even rise from a place which is to their ease and liking, unless by their doing so the sweetness of God came to their mouths and hearts without their moving a step and mortifying themselves by losing any of their useless desires, consolations and pleasures. But until they leave these in order to seek Him, they will not find Him however much they cry to Him.*[2]

Now is an especially good moment to ask ourselves

---

[1] Matt 11:12
[2] St John of the Cross, *Spiritual Canticle*, 3,2

how much we struggle against our own passions, defects, sins and bad inclinations. This struggle *is a violence used to fight your own weaknesses and miseries, a fortitude which prevents you from camouflaging your own infidelities, a boldness to own up to the faith even when the environment is hostile.*

Today, as yesterday, heroism is expected of the Christian, a heroism in great struggles, if the need arises. Normally, however, the heroism will be in the little skirmishes of each day.[3]

Our Lord asks us to keep up this struggle through the whole of our life and, most particularly, during those liturgical seasons when He seems, as it were, to draw especially close to us in His Sacred Humanity. This struggle will often take the specific form of a determination to carry out, with the utmost care, all the duties of piety which we owe Him, not neglecting them for anything else that may turn up, or allowing ourselves to be deflected by our state of mind on a particular day or at a particular moment. Our struggle will concern itself with the way we live charity, trying to improve our characters by making a real effort to be friendly, good tempered and considerate to the people around us; with offering our work to God and then doing it as well as we can; in seeing our surroundings as a field for apostolate; in taking all the appropriate steps to make sure that our own spiritual formation does not stagnate ... As a rule it will be a struggle carried on in small ways. *Let's listen to Our Lord: 'He who is faithful in little is faithful also in much; and he who is dishonest in little is dishonest also in much.' It is as if He were saying to us: 'Fight continuously in the apparently unimportant things which are to My mind important; fulfil your duty punctually; smile at*

---

[3] St. J. Escrivá, *Christ is passing by*, 82

whoever needs cheering up, even though there is sorrow in your soul; devote the necessary time to prayer, without haggling; go to the help of anyone who looks for you; practise justice and go beyond it with the grace of charity.[4]

Our love for Our Lord will express itself in constantly beginning again, as we renew our daily efforts not to be overcome by the love of comfort and laziness, which are always lying in wait for us. *The devil sleepeth not, neither is the flesh as yet dead; therefore cease not to prepare thyself for the battle; for on thy right hand and on thy left are enemies who never rest.*[5] We too must never rest in this joyful struggle towards definite goals. The Lord is at our side and has also given each of us a Guardian Angel who will give us invaluable help if only we ask him.

12.2 Allowing for failures. Beginning over and over again.

As we make our way towards Our Lord we cannot expect to be victorious all the time. Many of our defeats will be of only limited importance, but even when they are really important, reparation and contrition will bring us closer to God more than ever. And with Our Lord's help we will begin again. We will not give way to discouragement or pessimism, which always spring from pride. With patience and humility, we can start all over again once more, even though we see no results.

Very, very often we will hear the Holy Spirit say: Make a new start ..., be constant; that last failure doesn't matter; all the bad things in your life put together don't matter ..., make a new start with deeper humility, asking your Lord for still more help.

---

[4] *ibid*, 77
[5] T. á Kempis, *The Imitation of Christ*, II, 9, 8

In the natural sphere, kindliness is usually the result of prolonged patience, of an effort repeated over and over again and constantly improved, *The scientist goes back over his calculations and renews his experiments by modifying them until he has found the object of his research. The writer shapes and reshapes his sentence twenty times. The sculptor breaks one rough model after another, as long as he cannot express his interior vision ... All human 'creations' are the result of unwearied new beginnings.*[6] In the supernatural sphere, our love for Our Lord will show itself less in those successes which we think we have achieved than in our ability to begin again, to renew the interior struggle. On the other hand, if we neglect or abandon our resolutions and aims in the interior life, we sink into spiritual mediocrity and lukewarmness. On the way that leads to God *to sleep is to die.*[7] Discouragement always has its roots in pride and excessive self-confidence; and it induces us to abandon those resolutions and goals which were once suggested to us by the Holy Spirit speaking in our inmost hearts.

Our failures, perhaps quite unforeseen, can very often lead to progress in our interior life, if we react to them with humility and a firmer determination to follow Our Lord. It has rightly been said that perseverance does not consist in never falling down, but in always getting up again when we do. *When a soldier in a battle is wounded or has to give ground a little, no one is so demanding or so ignorant of military matters as to think that this is a crime. Only those who do not fight are never wounded; those who charge the enemy with the greatest spirit are the ones who receive the most blows.*[8]

---

[6] G. Chevrot, *Simon Peter*
[7] St Gregory the Great, *Homily 12 on the Gospels*
[8] St John Chrysostom, *Second Exhortation to Theodore*, 5

Let us ask Our Lady for the grace never to abandon our interior struggle, however depressing or even catastrophic our previous experience may have been, and for the grace and the humility always to begin again.

Let us also ask Our Lady today that we may always persevere in our apostolate, even if it does not seem to produce any fruit. One day, perhaps when we have already arrived in Heaven, Our Lord will show us the fruits of that apostolate and how, although it sometimes seemed to us to be useless, it was in fact always effective. The seed which is sown always brings forth grain: *some a hundredfold, some sixty, some thirty*[9] ... much grain from a single seed.

12.3 Our Lord wants us to begin again after every failure: our hope is based on this.

Look up and raise your heads, because your redemption is drawing near.[10] The Acts of the Apostles tell us that one day Peter and John were going up to the temple to pray. They met a man who had been lame ever since he was born and he asked them for alms. Then Peter said to him: *I have no silver or gold, but I give you what I have; in the name of Jesus Christ of Nazareth, walk.*[11]

In the name of Jesus Christ ... this is where we have to begin again in the apostolate, and in our struggle against everything that might separate us from God. This is our strength. We don't begin again through our own determination, as if we were claiming to be able to advance under our own steam. By ourselves we can do nothing, but, *I will all the more gladly boast of my*

---

[9] Matt 13:8
[10] Luke 21:28
[11] Acts 3:6

weaknesses, that the power of Christ may rest upon me.[12]
And how great that power is!

Let us imitate St Peter. After a wasted night during which he had caught no fish, he let down the nets into the sea once more, simply because Our Lord told him to. *Master,* he said, *we toiled all night and took nothing! But at your word I will let down the nets.*[13] In spite of their weariness, in spite of its not being the proper time for fishing, those men began once more to let down the nets, which they were already washing in readiness for the next day. They brushed aside all the human considerations which would have made it unreasonable to go on fishing. Peter's confidence in his Lord made him return to the work. Peter obeyed without any further argument.

Our own hope is firmly based on the knowledge that Our Lord wants us to begin again every time we feel that we have failed in our interior life or in our apostolate. 'At your word, Lord, I will begin again.' If we live like this, our interior life will never be haunted by that spectre of discouragement which has plunged so many souls into spiritual mediocrity and unhappiness.

Begin again ... Jesus asks it of us with special affection in these days leading up to Christmas. *Lift up your heart gently, then, after a fall, humbling yourself before God in the knowledge of your wretchedness, without being in the least surprised that you have fallen. Weakness must expect to be weak, feebleness to be feeble and misery to be miserable. Nevertheless, detest the offence against God with all your heart; then, with great courage and confidence in his mercy, go forward on the path of virtue which you had forsaken.*[14]

---

[12] 2 Cor 12:9

[13] Luke 5:5

[14] St Francis de Sales, *Introduction to the Devout Life*, 3, 9

SECOND WEEK OF ADVENT – FRIDAY

13. TEPIDITY AND THE LOVE OF GOD

13.1 Love for God and the danger of tepidity.

Anyone who follows you, Lord, will have the light of life. He is like a tree that is planted beside the flowing waters, that yields its fruit in due season, and whose leaves shall never fade.[1]

Our life does not make sense if we are not following Our Lord closely. *Lord, to whom shall we go? Only you have the words of eternal life.*[2] All our successes, any human happiness that goes to make up our earthly treasure is *chaff driven away by the wind.*[3] Truly we can say to Our Lord in our own personal prayer: *Stay with us, because our souls are full of darkness and you are the one true light; you alone can satisfy the longings that consume us. For we know that above everything that is beautiful and good, the greatest is this: to possess you forever, O Lord.*[4]

He comes to bring us the fire of his love, which fills our pointless lives and makes sense of them. Our Lord's is a demanding love, which always asks for more, and which makes our souls grow in responsiveness to God so that they yield much fruit. Every Christian soul full of the love of God is that tree of which the responsorial psalm speaks, *the tree whose leaves never fade.* It is Christ himself who gives it life. But if the Christian allows his

---

[1] *Responsorial Psalm*, Ps 1:1-4
[2] cf John 6:68
[3] *Responsorial Psalm*
[4] St Gregory Nazianzen, *Epistles*, 212

love to grow cold, if he allows self-satisfied mediocrity to creep into his soul, then he will develop that serious spiritual illness which will make him *like winnowed chaff driven away by the wind*: it is tepidity, which drains all love and meaning from his life, though outwardly it may seem that nothing has changed. His mind and heart become, as it were, blind and deaf: as a result of his own negligence he can no longer see or hear Christ. His soul feels emptied of God and he tries to fill that emptiness with other things, which, not being God, cannot satisfy him. And an especially characteristic discouragement saps his life of piety. He loses all joy and readiness for self-giving, and his faith grows weak because his love has grown cold.

If at any moment we find that our innermost life is becoming estranged from God, we must realize that there is a cure for every disease of the soul, including that of lack of love. We have only to employ the right means in order to re-discover Christ, the hidden treasure who once gave meaning to our lives. It is easier when the sickness is in its initial stages, but it is also possible later on, in cases like that of the leper of whom St Luke tells us, who was *full of leprosy*[5], terribly ill, but one day decided to approach Christ humbly and truthfully, and found healing. *They asked the Lover which was the fountain of love. He answered that it was the one where the Beloved had cleansed us from our sins, and from which he gives us, as a free gift, that living water which brings whoever drinks it to eternal life in endless love.*[6] Our Lord is always waiting for us in generous and sincere prayer and in the Sacraments.

---

[5] Luke 5:12-13
[6] R. Lull, *The Book of the Lover and the Beloved*, 115

13.2 Causes of lukewarmness.

Like winnowed chaff driven away by the wind. Weightless and fruitless ... Isolated faults do not lead necessarily to tepidity. This sickness of the soul *is characterized by the fact that one more or less deliberately treats venial sin lightly. It is a state in which one has neither zeal nor fervour. Being in a state of aridity, or of desolation, or even of feeling repugnance for the things of the spirit or of God, is not tepidity; for in spite of such feelings the ardour of the will and the determination to do right can remain strong and steadfast. Even if someone still frequently commits venial sins, it does not mean that he is tepid, provided he is sorry for them and fights against them. Tepidity is a state of conscious and deliberate lack of fervour, a state of enduring carelessness and half-heartedness, which pretends to justify itself with maxims like: 'one should not be petty'; 'God is too big and magnanimous to bother about such little things'; 'everybody else does the same', and so on.*[7]

Tepidity is the result of prolonged carelessness in the interior life. It usually follows a whole string of small infidelities, whose unrepented guilt has come between the soul and God. This carelessness is expressed in the habitual neglect of little things, in lack of contrition for one's personal faults, in failure to have specific aims for improving one's behaviour towards God. One has no definite spiritual objectives that attract or excite one. 'One gets by.' There is no struggle, or only a pretended and ineffectual struggle, to be better.[8] Mortification is abandoned, and *weighed down by the excessive demands of the body, the soul is ill-equipped for soaring towards*

---

[7] B. Baur, *Frequent Confession*
[8] F. Carvajal, *Lukewarmness – the devil in disguise*

the heavens.[9]

The state of tepidity is like a gentle slope down which the soul slips further and further from God. Almost without noticing, it becomes content with not going too far, with staying just within the boundaries which separate it from mortal sin, while becoming careless of venial sin and consenting to it without a struggle.

The tepid soul excuses itself for this easy-going, undemanding attitude by pleading its nature, its health, its work, its ineffectiveness and anything which will help it to indulge its small disordered inclinations, its attachment to people or things, its comforts which it describes to itself as necessities. And every time it does so, its strength diminishes.

Where there is tepidity, there is no true worship of God in the Holy Mass; lack of love and preparation make Holy Communion itself cold and indifferent. Prayer becomes vague, woolly and distracted; there is no real personal conversation with Our Lord. The examination of conscience, which calls for special sensitivity, is either abandoned altogether, or done as a matter of perfunctory and lifeless routine which produces no fruit.

In this sorry state the tepid soul loses all desire to get really near to God (which, it tells itself, is in point of fact impossible): *I'm sorry to see the danger of lukewarmness in which you place yourself when you do not strive seriously for perfection within your state.*[10]

To sum up: *You are lukewarm if you carry out lazily and reluctantly those things which have to do with God; if deliberately or 'shrewdly', you look for some way of cutting down your duties; if you think only of yourself*

---

[9] St Peter of Alcantara, *Treatise on Prayer and Meditation*, 2,3
[10] St. J. Escrivá, *The Way*, 326

*and of your comfort; if your conversations are idle and
vain; if you do not abhor venial sin; if you act from
human motives.*[11]

Let us put up a real struggle against ever falling
victim to this sickness of the soul; let us be on the alert to
recognize its first symptoms; let us go instantly to Our
Lady. She always increases our hope, and renews in us
the joy of Our Lord's birth: *Rejoice and be glad,
daughter of Jerusalem: behold, your King is coming;
fear not, Sion, your salvation is at hand.*[12]

Our Lady, when we go to her, always brings us to
her Son.

13.3 How to prevent this serious spiritual illness.

If we increase our determination to struggle against
tepidity, this will involve taking great care with our daily
examination of conscience. We shall often discover some
point in which to try to do better next day, and shall be
moved to make an act of contrition for the ways in
which, in the course of the day that has passed, we have
not been wholly faithful to Our Lord.

This watchful love, this active desire to look for Our
Lord in all the happenings of the day, is at the opposite
pole from tepidity, which is carelessness, lack of interest,
laziness and disinclination in fulfilling our duties towards
him.

This desire to struggle will not always ensure
victory: there will be failures, but contrition and
reparation will still bring us nearer to God. Contrition
makes the soul young again.

*When we are faced with weaknesses and sins, with
our mistakes – even though, by God's grace, they be of*

---

[11] *ibid*, 331
[12] *Divine Office, Second Antiphon of the Readings*

*little account – let us turn to God our Father in prayer,
and say to him, 'Lord, here I am in my wretchedness and
frailty, a broken vessel of clay. Piece me together again,
Lord, and then, helped by my sorrow and by your
forgiveness, I shall be stronger and better than ever!'
What a consoling prayer, which we can say every time
something fractures this miserable clay of which we are
made.*[13] Then, once more, close to Christ, with new joy,
with new humility – humility, sincerity, repentance ...
beginning again. We have to know how to begin yet
again once more every time we fall. God takes our frailty
into account.

God always forgives: but we must get up, repent,
and go to Confession whenever it is necessary. A deep,
incomparable joy will come from beginning again and
again. In the course of our life we shall have to do it
many times, because we shall always make mistakes, and
have our full share of deficiencies, frailty and sin.
Perhaps this present time of prayer may bring us to the
point of beginning once more. Our Lord takes our
failures into account, but he also expects from us many
little victories in the course of our days. Then we will
never fall into self-satisfied mediocrity, into carelessness,
into lovelessness.

---

[13] St. J. Escrivá, *Friends of God*, 95

14. EXAMINATION OF CONSCIENCE

14.1 The fruits of a daily examination of conscience.

Behold, I am coming soon and my recompense is with me, says the Lord, to bestow a reward according to the deeds of each.[1]

It was laid down in the Law that everyone had to pay tithes: one tenth of all corn, wine and oil was to be given for the support of the Temple and its worship. The Pharisees, strict observers of the Law but lacking in love, paid tithes even of *mint and dill and cumin*, which then as now were sometimes grown in gardens for use as flavourings. They interpreted the Law scrupulously, down to the tiniest detail.

St Matthew reports the very stern words in which Our Lord reproved the Pharisees for their hypocrisy and the double standards of their lives: *Woe to you, scribes and Pharisees, hypocrites! For you tithe mint and dill and cumin, and have neglected the weightier matters of the Law, justice and mercy and faith: these you ought to have attended to, without neglecting the others. You blind guides, straining at a gnat and swallowing a camel!*[2]

In their lives we can see, on the one hand, a stifling meticulousness; on the other, an enormous laxity in really important matters: they neglected *the weightier matters of the Law: justice, mercy and faith.* They failed to understand what God really wanted from them.

We too, in these days of Advent, by improving our examination of conscience, can make sure that we do not linger over things which are basically of little

---

[1] *Communion Antiphon of the Mass*
[2] Matt 23:23-24

consequence, while we fail to notice those that are really important. If we make a habit of examining our conscience every day – briefly, but thoroughly – we shall be safe from the hypocrisy and distorted vision of the Pharisees. We will see clearly the errors that draw our hearts away from God, and we will be able to react against them in time.

The examination of conscience is like an eye which can see into the innermost recesses of the heart and recognize all its deviations and attachments. *By it do I see and become enlightened, that I avoid dangers and correct faults, and that I set my ways right. By it do I flood my soul with light and bring light to bear upon everything; and thus I cannot abide in evil, but I am bound to do the truth, that is to say, to advance in piety.*[3]

If through laziness we neglect our examination of conscience, our errors and bad inclinations may put down deep roots into our souls. We will no longer be able to see the greatness to which we have been called. On the contrary, we will be left staring at *mint and rue and cumin,* at trivialities which are of little or no importance in the sight of God.

In the examination of conscience we will discover the hidden origins of our obvious failures in charity or in work, the hidden roots of our gloom and bad temper, or of our lack of piety, which perhaps crop up quite often in our lives, and we will see what remedies we need to apply to them. *Examine yourself: slowly, courageously. Is it not true that your bad temper and your gloominess, both without cause – without apparent cause – are due to your lack of determination in breaking the subtle but real snares laid for you – cunningly and attractively – by your*

---

[3] J. Tissot, *Interior Life*, Part III

concupiscence?[4]

The daily examination of conscience is an indispensable help if we are to follow Our Lord with sincerity of heart and integrity of life.

14.2 The examination of conscience as a meeting with Our Lord.

Everything we do – in our families, in our work, in our social life – is an opportunity for meeting God. Moreover, during the course of our day there are several very special meetings with Our Lord: in Holy Communion, in such times of prayer as this ..., and in the examination of conscience.

The daily examination of conscience is a thorough inspection of what we have written on the page of each unrepeatable day of our lives. Many an ill-written word can be corrected by means of contrition. A page of sheer horror can be turned into something good, even very good, by means of repentance and the resolution to begin again with renewed effort on the clean page which our Guardian Angel offers us on God's behalf – a unique and unrepeatable page, like each unique and unrepeatable day of our life. *And at the top of each of these blank pages which we begin to scribble each day,* says one writer of our own times, *I like to put as a heading just one word; 'Serviam.' I will serve. It is both a desire and a hope.*

After beginning in that way – with that desire and that hope – I try to write words and phrases and make paragraphs and fill the page with neat, clear, handwriting. That means work, prayer, apostolate – all my day's activity.

I try to pay a lot of attention to punctuation – which is the practice of keeping presence of God. These pauses

---

[4] St. J. Escrivá, *The Way*, 237

– commas, or semi-colons or colons – represent the silence of my soul and the aspirations I try to use to give meaning and supernatural outlook to everything I write.

I particularly like the full stops, because after every full stop I begin, in a way, to write again. They are a kind of indication that I am correcting my intention, saying to Our Lord that I'm going to start writing again: I'm going to start again with the right intention of serving him and dedicating my life to him, moment by moment, minute by minute.

I am also careful about dotting my "i's" and crossing my "t's" – the little mortifications which give my life and my work a truly Christian meaning. When I fail to dot an "i" or cross a "t" it means that I did not accept in a Christian way the mortification which Our Lord was sending me, which he had lovingly prepared for me and wanted me to recognize and receive with pleasure.

I try to see that there is nothing crossed out, no mistakes or blots, or irrelevant parentheses or big gaps; but ... there are so many! These are my imperfections, my infidelities, my sins ... and my omissions.

It hurts me to see that there is hardly a single page that has not got some sign of my awkwardness and clumsiness. But I quickly console myself and recover my serenity by remembering that I am just a little child who hasn't yet learned to write properly, and has to use a ruled sheet under the page to help him write straight, and needs a teacher to guide his hand to make sure he does not write nonsense: what a good Teacher God our Lord is; what infinite patience he has with me![5]

---

[5] S. Canals, *Jesus as Friend*

14.3 The examination. How to do it. Contrition and resolutions.

The purpose of the examination of conscience is to get to know ourselves better, in order to become more receptive to the graces the Holy Spirit pours out upon us, and to grow to resemble Christ himself.

The question to ask ourselves which will perhaps give us the most light of all is: On what have I set my heart? What takes up most room in it? Is it Christ? *At the very moment of putting this question, the answer comes within me. This question causes me to cast a rapid glance into the innermost centre of my being, and I at once see the salient points; I give ear to the tone echoed by my soul, and immediately catch the dominant note. It is an intuitive proceeding, and is quite instantaneous ... It is a glance, 'in ictu oculi' ... Sometimes I shall see that my dominant disposition is the want of approval or praise, or the fear of reproach. Sometimes, the bitterness that springs from some annoyance, from some harmful project or proceeding, or else the resentment caused by some remonstrance. Sometimes, the pain of being under suspicion, or the trouble felt through some aversion. Or, it may be the slackness induced by sensuality, or the discouragement resulting from difficulties or failure. At other times routine, the product of carelessness, or frivolity, the product of idle curiosity and empty gaiety, etc. Or else, on the contrary, it may be the love of God, the desire for sacrifice, the fervour kindled by some touch of grace, full submission to God, the joy of humility, etc. Whether it be good or bad, it is the main and dominant disposition that must be ascertained; for we must look at the good as well as the evil, since it is the state of the heart that it is important to know. I must go directly to the mainspring which sets all the wheels of the clock in motion.*[6]

When we are examining our consciences our aim is to discover whether that day we have fulfilled the will of God and carried out what was expected of us, or whether we have followed our own will. And then we should come down to specific details of our behaviour towards God; of how we have fulfilled our duties towards him in our plan of life, in our work, in our relationships with other people. Let us examine how much determination we have put into struggling against our tendencies to love of comfort and to the creation of imaginary necessities for ourselves. Let us look at how much effort we have made, for example, to lead a life which even on social occasions is sober and temperate in eating and drinking, and in the use of earthly goods. We have to see if we have filled the day which has just passed with the love of God, or if, unhappily, we have let it remain empty for all eternity (something which will not happen if we allow ourselves to be helped by grace), or if it has been defiled by sin. It is like a miniature judgement to which we submit ourselves beforehand.

We will detect some things which need to be borne in mind for our next Confession. We must always finish with an act of contrition, because if there is no repentance the examination will have been useless. We should make some small resolution, which we can renew at the beginning of the next day, either in our morning offering, in our personal prayer, or in the Holy Mass. And finally we should give thanks to Our Lord for all the good things which he has given us that day.

---

[6] J. Tissot, *op cit*

THIRD SUNDAY OF ADVENT

15. THE JOY OF ADVENT

15.1 Advent: a time of happiness and hope. What happiness is – being near Jesus: unhappiness – losing him.

The liturgy of today's Mass repeats the words of St Paul in which he urges the first Christians of Philippi: *Rejoice in the Lord always; again I say, rejoice.*[1] And the Apostle goes on to give the basic reason for this profound happiness: *the Lord is at hand.*

This is also the joy of Advent, and that of every day: Jesus is very near us. He is nearer every day. And St Paul gives us the key to understanding the origin of any unhappiness we may feel: it comes from our putting a distance between ourselves and God, through our sins, through tepidity.

Our Lord always brings us joy and not affliction. His mysteries are all joyful mysteries, the sorrowful mysteries we bring on ourselves.[2]

Hail, full of grace, the Lord is with you,[3] said the Angel to Mary. It is the nearness of God which makes the Virgin rejoice. And the nearness of the Messiah will make the unborn Baptist show forth his joy in the womb of Elizabeth.[4] And the Angel will say to the shepherds: *Be not afraid; for behold, I bring you good news of a great joy which will come to all the people; for to you is born this day a Saviour ...*[5] Joy is to possess Jesus;

---

[1] Phil 4:4
[2] P. A. Reggio, *Supernatural Spirit and Good Humour*
[3] Luke 1:28
[4] Luke 2:4
[5] Luke 2:10-11

unhappiness is to lose him.

The people followed Our Lord and the children gathered around him (children do not gather round gloomy people), *and all the people rejoiced at all the glorious things that were done by him.*[6]

After the dark days that follow his Passion, the risen Jesus will appear to his disciples on various occasions. And the Evangelist will be pointing out over and over again that the Apostles *were glad when they saw the Lord.*[7] They will never forget those meetings which filled their souls with such indescribable joy.

Rejoice, says St Paul to us today. And we have good reason for doing so, and one surpassing reason, above all: *The Lord is at hand.* We can come close to him whenever we want to. In a few days it will be Christmas, a great feast for us Christians, but also for the whole human race, which, without knowing it, is looking for Christ. Christmas is coming, and God wants us to be joyful, like the shepherds, like the wise men, like Mary and Joseph.

We shall be full of joy if Our Lord is really present in our life, if we have not lost him, if we have not allowed our sight to be clouded by tepidity or lack of generosity. When one attempts to discover happiness along other paths which lead away from God, all one finds in fact is sorrow and misery. All those who, in one way or another, ever turned their backs on God have had the same experience: they have proved that apart from God there is no true happiness. There can be none.

To find Christ, and to remain in his company, is to possess a deep happiness which is new every day.

---

[6] Luke 13:17
[7] John 20:20

15.2 Christian happiness. Its foundation.

Sing for joy, O heavens, and exult, O earth. Break forth, O mountains into singing, for our Lord is coming![8] In his days, justice and peace shall flourish.[9]

Happiness should be essential to the Christian. Ours, however, is not just any sort of happiness. It is the happiness of Christ, which brings justice and peace. Only he can give it and preserve it, because the world does not possess its secret.

Worldly happiness leads inevitably to its own loss ...; it arises precisely when man contrives to escape from himself, when he looks outward, when he manages to turn his gaze away from his meaningless and solitary interior life. The Christian carries his joy within himself, because he meets God in his soul in grace. This is the unfailing spring of his happiness.

It is not difficult to imagine Our Lady, in these days of Advent, radiant with joy at carrying the Son of God beneath her heart.

The world's happiness is a poor and transitory thing. The Christian's happiness is profound and can exist in the midst of difficulties. It is compatible with pain, with illness, with failures and contradictions. Our Lord has promised: *Your hearts will rejoice, and no one will take your joy from you.*[10] Unless we separate ourselves from its source, nothing and nobody can take away this joyful peace.

To have the certainty that God is our Father and wants all that is best for us gives us a serene and joyful confidence even in the face, sometimes, of unexpected hardships. In those moments which a man without faith

---

[8] Is 49:13
[9] Ps 71:7
[10] John 16:22

would consider to be meaningless and deadly blows of fate, the Christian discovers God, and with Him a much greater good than he seems to have lost. *How many obstacles vanish, when in our hearts we place ourselves next to this God of ours, who never abandons us! Jesus' love for his own, for the sick and for the lame is renewed, expressed by different sufferers in different ways. 'What's the matter?' he asks; and we reply, 'It's my ...' At once there is light, or at least the acceptance of his will, and inner peace.*[11] 'What's the matter?' he asks us. And we look at him, and at once nothing at all is the matter. At his side we find our peace and joy again.

We will have difficulties, as everyone always has, but whether they are great or small these contradictions will never be able to destroy our happiness. We have to expect the setback as part and parcel of ordinary life, and we cannot put off being happy until some impossible time arrives in which there are no contradictions, temptations or sorrows. What is more, we should have no opportunities at all for growing in virtue if we had no obstacles to overcome.

We need a firm foundation for our happiness. It cannot depend exclusively on changeable circumstances like good news, good health, peace and quiet, enough money to bring up the family comfortably and having all the material possessions we would like. All these things are good in themselves if they do not separate us from God, but they are unable to provide us with real happiness.

Our Lord asks us to be happy always. *Let each man take care how he builds. For no other foundation can anyone lay than that which is laid, which is Jesus*

---

[11] St. J. Escrivá, *Friends of God*, 249

Christ.[12] Only he can be the support of our whole life. There is no sorrow which he cannot alleviate: *Do not fear, only believe,*[13] he says to us. He knows everything which is going to happen in our lives, including those things that will result from our stupidity and lack of sanctity. But he has the remedy for them all.

Very often, as we are doing now in this time of prayer, we shall have to come to him in the Tabernacle and have a conversation with him which is both serious and intimate. And we shall need to lay bare our soul in Confession, and in personal spiritual direction. There we shall find the source of happiness; and our gratitude will show itself in greater faith, in an ever-increasing hope which banishes all sadness, and in our care for other people. *For yet a little, just a very little while, and He that is to come will come, and shall not delay;*[14] and with him come peace and joy; with Jesus we find meaning in our life.

15.3 Bringing happiness to other people. Its indispensability in all apostolic work.

A gloomy soul is at the mercy of many temptations. How many sins have been committed in the shadow of that gloominess! When the soul is happy it spreads its happiness and is an encouragement to others. When it is downcast it spreads misery and does harm to others. Sad looks spring from egoism, from thinking about oneself to the exclusion of others, from laziness in one's work, from lack of mortification, from the search for small self-indulgences, from carelessness in one's relationship with God.

---

[12] 1 Cor 3:11
[13] Luke 8:50
[14] Heb 10:37

Unless we forget ourselves, and are not too much taken up with our own affairs, we will not be able to know and serve Christ, in whom is our true happiness. Anyone excessively self-centred will find it very difficult to discover the joy of opening himself out towards God and towards other people.

In order to reach God and to grow in virtue we must have joy. Moreover, if we fulfil our duties joyfully we will be able to give a great deal of help to those around us, for this is a happiness that draws many to God. St Paul instructs the first Christians: *Bear one another's burdens, and so fulfil the law of Christ.*[15] And we can often make life more pleasant for other people in little ways which have no apparent importance in themselves, but which show that we consider others and appreciate them: a smile, a friendly remark, a word of praise, not making a great fuss over unimportant things that would be better overlooked and forgotten. In these ways we can help to make life easier for the people around us. An important part of our Christian mission is to bring happiness to a world which is sad at heart because it is drifting away from God.

One can often follow a stream back to its source. The happiness they see in us may lead those who are frequently in our company to the source of all true happiness, Christ our Lord.

Let us get ready for Christmas by being close to Our Lady. Let us try, as well, to get ready for the Holy Season by encouraging an atmosphere of Christian peace where we live and work, and by doing all we can in small ways to bring pleasure and affection to those around us. People need to be convinced that Christ has really been born in Bethlehem, and few things are more convincing

---

[15] Gal 6:2

than the habitual happiness of the Christian, even in the midst of pain and contradictions. Our Lady knew many such contradictions when she came to Bethlehem tired out and after such a long journey, and unable to find a place fit for the birth of her Son. But these problems did not cause her to lose her joy when God *became Man, and dwelt amongst us*.

16. PURITY OF HEART

16.1 The purity of heart that Christmas calls us to. The fruits of this virtue. Internal acts.

Shower, O heavens, from above, and let the skies rain down righteousness; let the earth open, that salvation may spring up.[1]

Christmas is a light in the darkness, a light that will never go out. Everyone who looks towards Bethlehem can contemplate the baby Jesus, with Mary and Joseph; that is to say, everyone who looks with a pure heart, because God shows himself only to the *pure in heart*.[2]

Christmas is a summons to purity of heart. Perhaps many men see nothing wonderful when this feast comes around because they are blind to what is truly important: their hearts are full of material things, or of filth and misery. Uncleanness of heart produces insensitivity to the things of God, and to much that is humanly good as well, including compassion for the unhappiness of other people. But from a pure heart spring joy, the ability to see the divine, trust in God, sincere repentance, recognition of ourselves and our sins, true humility, and a great love for God and for other people.

Some scribes and Pharisees once asked Jesus: *Why do your disciples transgress the tradition of the elders? For they do not wash their hands when they eat.* Our Lord took the opportunity to show them that they were disregarding more important precepts. *Hypocrites!* he said to them. *Well did Isaiah prophesy of you when he*

---

[1] Is 45:8
[2] Matt 5:8

said: This people honours me with their lips, but their hearts are far from me.[3] Then Jesus called the people together, because he was going to say something important. It was not to be a question of yet another interpretation of a point in the Law, but something fundamental. Our Lord was about to explain what really makes someone pure or impure in God's eyes.

And he called the people to him and said to them, *Hear and understand: it is not what goes into the mouth that defiles a man, but what comes out of the mouth; this defiles a man.*[4] And a little later he explained to his disciples on their own: *What comes out of the mouth proceeds from the heart, and this defiles a man. For out of the heart come evil thoughts, murder, adultery, fornication, theft, false witness, slander. These are what defile a man; but to eat with unwashed hands does not defile a man.*[5] What comes out of the mouth proceeds from the heart. The whole man is defiled by what happens in his heart – evil desires and intentions, envy, spite ... These external sins which Our Lord enumerates, before ever they are committed externally, have already been committed interiorly in the sinner's heart. This is where God is loved or offended.

It is true that sometimes the external action increases the goodness or the sinfulness of the interior act, through a greater intensity of determination, of the harm caused to other people, and so on. But it is the heart which must be kept healthy and clean, and then all the rest will be pure and pleasing to God.

Our Lord describes as blessed and happy those who guard their hearts, and we have to work at this every day.

---

[3] Matt 15:2,7-8
[4] Matt 15:10
[5] Matt 15:18-20

16.2 Guarding one's heart.

Keep custody of your heart with all vigilance; for from it flows the springs of life,[6] says the book of Proverbs. And from it too flow joy and peace, the ability to love, and to do apostolate ... How carefully we must guard our hearts! Because otherwise they always tend to attach themselves in the wrong way to people and to things.

Among all the aims of our lives, there is only one which is truly necessary: it is to reach the goal which God has set for us; to attain to heaven, by living our own individual vocation to the full. In order to achieve this we have to be ready to lose everything else, to clear away anything which would obstruct our way. Everything must be a means for reaching God, and if anything whatever proves not to be a means but an obstacle, then we must put it right or give it up in sacrifice. Our Lord's words are clear: *If your right eye causes you to sin, pluck it out and throw it away ... And if your right hand causes you to sin, cut it off and throw it away; it is better that you lose one of your members than that your whole body go into hell.*[7] By *right eye* and *right hand* Our Lord means anything that at a given moment seems indispensably precious and valuable. Sanctity, salvation – one's own and one's neighbour's – has to come first.

If thy right eye scandalize thee ..., pluck it out and cast it from thee! – poor heart! For this it is that scandalizes you ... Press it, squeeze it tight in your hands! Give it no consolations. And when it asks for them, say to it slowly and with a noble compassion – in confidence, as it were: Heart, heart on the Cross! Heart on the Cross![8]

---

[6] Prov 4:23
[7] Matt 5:29-30
[8] St. J. Escrivá, *The Way*, 163

The things we need to abandon, or to cut out of our lives, can be of many very different sorts. Sometimes they will even be things that are good in themselves but which our own egoism, or our failure to rectify our intention, has turned into obstacles to our sanctity. Very often they will not be anything of great importance, but mere whims, habitual minor self-indulgences, failures in complete self-control, excessive pre-occupations with material things, and so on. *Observe,* says St Augustine, *how the sea comes in through any leaky places in the hull, and little by little fills the hold of the boat. Unless it is expelled, the ship goes down ... . Imitate the sailors: their hands never rest until they have baled her out thoroughly; let yours never rest from doing good. In spite of everything however, the bottom of the ship will fill with water again, because the weak points of our human nature are always there; and you will have to man the pumps again.*[9]

These obstacles and tendencies which we cannot succeed in getting rid of with one determined effort, but which demand of us a continual confident and cheerful struggle, give us great help towards becoming more humble.

Love of frequent confession and persistence with the daily examination of conscience help us to keep our souls clean and ready to contemplate Jesus in the cave at Bethlehem, in spite of our obvious daily weaknesses.

16.3 The pure of heart will see God even in this life, and fully in the life to come.

'The pure in heart shall see God.' It is with good reason that the beatitude of seeing God is promised to the pure in heart. A life that is defiled can never

---

[9] St Augustine, *Sermon 16,* 7

contemplate the splendour of the true Light, because the very same thing which is the joy of pure souls will be the punishment of those that are defiled.[10]

If our hearts are pure they will know how to recognize Christ in the intimacy of silent prayer, in the busy middle of our work, in the everyday events of our ordinary life. He lives and goes on acting within us. A Christian who sincerely searches for Our Lord will find him, because it is this same Lord who is looking for us.

If we lack inner purity the clearest signals will mean nothing to us, and we shall interpret them all wrong, as the Pharisees did, even to the point of being scandalized by them. God himself and his works in the world can only be seen by those whose dispositions are good.

If we want to contemplate God while we live on earth, we are under the blessed obligation of developing our interior life, of keeping watch over our senses, and of persevering in the little mortifications which we can offer to God every day. This state of interior recollection is perfectly compatible with hard work, and with the normal social relationships proper to someone who has to live in the middle of the world.

How is that heart of yours getting along? – Don't worry; the saints (who were perfectly ordinary, normal beings like you and me) also felt those 'natural' inclin-ations. In fact, if they had not felt them, their 'supernatural' reaction of keeping their heart – their soul and body – for God, instead of giving it to creatures, would have had little merit. Once the way is seen therefore, I think the heart's weakness need be no obstacle for a determined soul, for a soul in love.[11]

This contemplative life is within the reach of every

---

[10] St Leo the Great, *Sermon 95, On the Beatitudes.*
[11] St. J. Escrivá, *op cit*, 164

Christian. But there has to be a firm, serious decision to look for God in every circumstance, to purify oneself and to make reparation for one's sins and errors. It is always a grace from God, and he does not deny it to anyone who humbly asks for it. Advent is an especially propitious time to ask for this gift.

Then, if we have been faithful, we will attain to a knowledge of God as perfect, immediate, clear and thorough as is possible for man's created and limited nature. We shall see him *when the time has come,* as perhaps it may for us quite soon. We shall know God as he knows us, directly and face to face: *we know that when He appears we shall be like him, for we shall see him as He is.*[12] Man will then be able to gaze upon God without being blinded and without dying. We shall at last be able to contemplate the God we have tried to serve throughout our lives.

Let us contemplate God the Father, God the Son, and God the Holy Spirit. And, very close to the Blessed Trinity, let us contemplate Our Lady, Daughter of God the Father, Mother of God the Son, Spouse of God the Holy Spirit.

---

[12] 1 John 3:2

17. 'WHO' JESUS IS

17.1 Jesus, the Only-Begotten Son of the Father.

You are my son: today I have begotten you,[1] we read in the Entrance Antiphon for Christmas Midnight Mass, words from the second Psalm. *The advent 'today' speaks of eternity, the 'today' of the Blessed and Glorious Trinity.*[2]

During his public life Jesus frequently spoke of the fatherhood of God in relation to men, using the numerous expressions found in the Old Testament. However, *for Jesus, God is not merely 'the Father of Israel, the Father of mankind', but 'my Father'! 'My': precisely because of this the Jews wished to kill Jesus, for 'he called God his father' (John 5:18). 'His' in a very literal sense: he whom only the Son knows as Father and by whom alone he is reciprocally known ... 'My Father' is the Father of Jesus Christ: the origin of his being, of his messianic mission, of his teaching.*[3]

When, in the district of Caesarea Philippi, Simon Peter confesses: *You are the Christ, the son of the living God, Jesus answers, Blessed are you ... for flesh and blood have not revealed this to you, but my Father ...*[4] for *no one knows the Son except the Father just as no one knows the Father except the Son.*[5] Only the Son can make the Father known: the visible Son enables us to see the

---

[1] Ps 2:1
[2] John Paul II, *General audience*, 16 October 1985
[3] *ibid*, 23 October 1985
[4] Matt 16:16-17
[5] Matt 11:27

invisible Father. *He who has seen me has seen the Father.*[6]

The baby who will be born in Bethlehem is the only-begotten Son of God, consubstantial with the Father, eternal, having his own divine nature and also the human nature which he has assumed in Mary's virginal womb. When we look at him this Christmas and see him helpless in the arms of his mother, we must not forget that this is God, made man for love of us, every single one of us.

During these days when we read with profound wonder the words of the Gospel *and dwelt among us,* or when we say the *Angelus*, we shall have a good opportunity for making a deep and grateful act of faith, and for adoring the sacred Humanity of Our Lord.

17.2 Perfect God and perfect Man. He became a child so that we could go to him without fear. Special relationships with Jesus.

Jesus came to us from the Father, but he was born for us of a woman: *when the time had fully come God sent forth his Son, born of woman,*[7] says St Paul. The prophets announce that the Messiah will come down from heaven like rain and grow from the earth like a seed.[8] He will be *mighty God* and, at the same time, *a child, a son.*[9] *I am from above,*[10] Jesus says of himself; at the same time he is born *from the seed of David:*[11] *there shall come forth a shoot from the stump of Jesse and a*

---

[6] John 14:9
[7] Gal 4:4
[8] Is 44:8
[9] Is 9:6
[10] John 8:23
[11] Rom 1:4

branch shall grow out of his roots.[12] He will be born on earth, on this earth of ours.

In the Gospel for the Mass of Christmas Eve we read the human genealogy of Jesus.[13] The Holy Spirit wants to show us how the Messiah is related to one family and one people, and through them to the whole of humanity. In her womb, Mary shared her own blood with Jesus, the blood of Adam, of Phares, of Solomon.

The Word of God became flesh and dwelt amongst us;[14] he became man, but that does not mean that he stopped being God. Jesus Christ is perfect man and perfect God.

When, after his Resurrection, Our Lord miraculously entered through closed doors and appeared so inexplicably, a disciple might have thought that Jesus was a kind of spirit, so he himself dispelled such doubts for ever. He said to them: *Handle me and see; for a spirit has not flesh and bones as you see that I have.*[15] And then *they gave him a piece of broiled fish, and he took it and ate before them.* John was there and, as on so many other occasions, saw him eat. After that he could never lose his overwhelming certainty of that flesh *which we have seen with our eyes, which we have looked upon and touched with our hands.*[16]

God became man in Mary's womb. He did not suddenly appear on earth like a heavenly vision, but became a real man like us, taking our human nature in the pure womb of a woman. In this way his eternal generation (his divinity, the pre-existence of the Word) is

---

[12] Is 11:1
[13] Matt 1:1-25
[14] John 1:14
[15] Luke 24:39
[16] 1 John 1:1

distinguished from his birth in time. Jesus in his divinity is mysteriously begotten, not made, by the Father through all eternity. In his humanity, however, he was born, 'was made' from the Blessed Virgin Mary at one definite moment in human history. Because of this, the Blessed Virgin, being the Mother of Jesus Christ, who is God, is truly the Mother of God, as the Council of Ephesus defined as a Dogma of the Faith.[17]

We look at the baby who will be born in a few days in Bethlehem of Judaea, and we know very well that he is *the key, the centre and the purpose of the whole of man's history.*[18] On this child depends our whole existence, on earth and in heaven. And he wants us to treat him with friendship and complete confidence. He became so small in order that we should not be afraid to come close to him.

17.3 The most holy Humanity of Our Lord is the way to the Trinity. Imitating Jesus. Getting to know him better by reading the Gospels. Meditating on his life.

God the Father predestined humanity to be conformed to the image of his Son, *in order that he might be the first-born among many brethren.*[19] Our life has to be a continual imitation of his life here on earth. He is our Model for all the virtues and our relationship with him is different from that which we have with the other two Persons of the Blessed Trinity. The grace bestowed upon man through the sacraments is not merely 'the grace of God', (like that which filled the soul of Adam before the Fall) but, in a true and accurate sense, 'the grace of Christ'.

---

[17] *Dz-Sch*, 252
[18] Second Vatican Council, *Gaudium et spes*, 10
[19] Rom 8:29

Christ was a real man, an individual man, with his own family and his own country, with his own customs, with his own trials and personal preferences; one specific individual, *this Jesus*.[20] But at the same time, because of the supremacy of his divine Person, he could and can receive into himself everything which is truly human, everything which properly belongs to human nature. We cannot experience a single good thought or feeling which he cannot make his own, nor is there any thought or feeling of his which we ought not to do our best to make ours. Jesus has a deep love for all that is truly human – work, friendship, the family – and above all for men, with their defects and miseries. His most holy Humanity is our way to the Trinity.

By his example Jesus teaches us how we must serve and help the people around us: *I have given you an example*, he tells us, *that you also should do as I have done to you*.[21] Charity is to love *as I have loved you*.[22] *Walk in love, as Christ loved us*,[23] says St Paul. And when he wanted to exhort the first Christians to charity and humility he said simply: *Have this mind among yourselves which was in Christ Jesus*.[24]

We must take Christ as our Model in the way we practise the virtues, the way we treat other people, the way we do our work, in everything. To imitate him is to be filled with a spirit and a way of reacting which ought to direct the life of every Christian, whatever his qualities, his state in life, or his place in society.

To imitate Our Lord, really to be his disciples, we

---

[20] Acts 2:32
[21] John 13:15
[22] John 13:34
[23] Eph 5:1
[24] Phil 2:5

must *see ourselves in him*. It's not enough to have a general idea of the spirit of Jesus; we have to learn the details of his life and, through them, his attitudes. Especially must we contemplate his life, to derive from it strength, light, serenity and peace.

When you love someone, you want to know all about his life and character, so as to become like him. That is why we have to meditate on the life of Jesus, from his birth in a stable right up to his death and resurrection.[25] Only in this way will our mind and our heart draw nearer to Christ.

During these days it will be easy for us, by reading and meditating on the gospel, to contemplate the baby Jesus with Mary and Joseph in the manger at Bethlehem. We will learn important lessons about detachment, humility and concern for other people. The shepherds will teach us the joy of finding God, and the wise men how we must adore him; we will feel that we have been given new strength to persevere in the following of our way.

If we make a habit of attentively reading and meditating on the Holy Gospel every day we shall, in a sense, take part in the life of Christ; we shall get to know him better every day; and, perhaps without our realising it, our life in the world will come to be a reflection of his.

[25] St. J. Escrivá, *Christ is passing by*, 107

THIRD WEEK OF ADVENT – WEDNESDAY

18. THE SIGNS

18.1 Our Lord makes himself known to us by giving sufficiently clear signs.

In that hour he cured many of diseases and plagues and evil spirits and on many that were blind he bestowed sight.[1] Then he replied to those who had been sent, *Go and tell John what you have seen and heard: the blind receive their sight, the lame walk ... You do not have to look for another: I am the Lord, and there is no other,*[2] he declares in today's first reading. He brings us the happiness that we are hoping for; he satisfies all the aspirations of the soul. *He who finds Jesus finds a good treasure ... And he who loses Jesus loses a great deal, more than if he lost the whole world. He who lives without Jesus is poor indeed, and he who is with Jesus is rich indeed.*[3] There is nothing greater to search for. And he comes as *a hidden treasure,*[4] as *a pearl of great value,*[5] whose value we must learn to appreciate.

Hidden from the eyes of men who are waiting for him, he is born in a cave, and some simple shepherds are the first to adore him. It was the simplicity of these men that would enable them to see the Child who had been announced to them. It enables them to surrender themselves to Him and adore Him. Others who find Him are the Magi, old Simeon who was *looking for the*

---

[1] Luke 7:19-23
[2] Is 45:7
[3] T. à Kempis, *The Imitation of Christ* II
[4] Matt 13:44
[5] Matt 13:45-46

consolation of Israel, and the prophetess Anna. And John himself who points him out: *This is the Lamb of God ...* Likewise did a good number of His disciples, and all those who throughout the centuries have made their whole lives revolve around him. Many have given their lives for him. We too have found him and this discovery is the most extraordinary part of our poor existence. Without Our Lord our lives would be worthless. He makes himself known to us with clear signs. We do not need any more proofs in order to see him.

God always gives us sufficient signs to discover Him. But we need good interior dispositions to see Our Lord who is passing by alongside us. Without humility and purity of heart it is impossible to recognise him, although he may be very close.

We ask Jesus now, in our personal prayer, for good interior dispositions and for supernatural outlook so that we may find him in the things around us – in nature itself, in suffering, in work, in what appears to be failure. Our own personal history is full of signs so that we do not mistake the way. We too will be able to say to our brothers, to our friends, *We have found the Messiah,* with the same certainty and conviction as that with which Andrew told his brother Simon.

18.2 Supernatural outlook so as to understand the happenings in our life and the events around us. Humility. A clean heart. Presence of God.

To have supernatural outlook means seeing things as God sees them – learning to interpret and judge events from the angle of faith. Only in this way will we understand our lives and the world around us.

Sometimes we hear people say, 'If only God would work a miracle, then I would believe, then I would take Him seriously'. Or, 'If God gave me more convincing proofs of my vocation, I would give myself to Him completely and without reserve'.

Our Lord gives us sufficient light to follow the way, light in our souls and light through the people He has placed beside us. But our will, if it is not humble, has a tendency to ask for new signs, and even then would want to judge whether they were sufficient. Sometimes this apparently sincere desire for further proof, before making the decision to give oneself more fully, can hide a type of laziness or conceal a lack of correspondence to grace.

At the beginning of one's call to the faith (or to one's vocation), God generally lights a little lamp which illumines just the first steps that we have to take. Beyond these first steps is darkness. But as we correspond with deeds, so the light and the certainty become greater. God always shows himself clearly to a soul which is sincere and humble and is seeking the truth. *Go and tell John what you have seen ...*

God has to find us with that humble disposition which is fully authentic and which excludes pre-conceived ideas and enables us to listen. God's language, although adapted to our way of being, can be difficult to accept at times because it goes against our plans or our fancies. Sometimes his words may not be precisely the ones we were expecting or the ones we wanted to hear ... Sometimes the atmosphere of materialism which surrounds us can present us with false reasons, contrary to the language by which God makes himself known. Then it is like listening to two different languages; God's language and the world's language, the latter presenting us with reasons which are apparently 'more human'. This is why the Church invites us to pray: *Almighty and merciful God, may no earthly undertaking hinder those who set out in haste to meet your Son, but may our learning of heavenly wisdom gain us admittance to his company.*[6]

18.3 The soul's conversion in order to find God in our daily duties.

You do not have to look for another. Jesus Christ is among us and he calls us. *Behind him on this earth of ours he has left the clear outlines of his footprints. They are indelible signs which neither the erosion of time nor the treachery of the evil one have been able to erase. Jesus Christus 'heri, et hodie; ipse et in saecula'. How I love to recall these words! Jesus Christ, the very Jesus who was alive yesterday for his Apostles and the people who sought him out; this same Jesus lives today for us, and will live forever. Yet, at times, we poor men fail to recognise his ever-present features, because our eyes are tired and our vision clouded.*[7]

It was with that clouded vision and lack of faith that the fellow-countrymen of Jesus looked at him the first time he went back to Nazareth. Those Jews saw in Jesus only *the son of Joseph,* [8] and in the end they rudely turned him out. They could not see any deeper. They did not discover the Messiah who was visiting them.

We want to *see the Lord.* We want to get to know him, love him and serve him, and to make this the primary objective in our life. We have no more important objective than this. What a great mistake it would be if we were to haggle, to lack generosity in carrying out the things that refer to God. *Open the gates wide to Christ!,* his Vicar here on earth encourages us. *Have confidence in Him. Take the risk of following him. Obviously this demands that you should come out of yourselves, or your*

---

[6] *Collect of the Mass for the Second Sunday of Advent*
[7] St. J. Escrivá, *Friends of God*, 127
[8] Luke 4:22

*own way of reasoning, or your prudence. It demands that
you leave behind your indifference, your self-sufficiency,
those un-Christian habits that you have perhaps
acquired. Yes; that demands renunciation, a conversion,
which first of all you must want to want; want to pray for
in your prayer, and want to put into practice. Let Christ
be for you the way, the truth and the life. Let Him be your
salvation and your happiness. Let him take over the
whole of your life so that with Him you can live it in all
its dimensions. Let all your relationships, activities,
feelings, thoughts, be integrated in Him, or, so to speak,
'Christified'. I wish,* said the Pope, *that with Christ you
may come to recognise God as the beginning and end of
your existence.*[9]

Once again we must want a new conversion – that
turning towards God just before Christmas, so as to
contemplate him with a clearer look, and never with *tired
eyes or clouded vision.* This is why with the Church we
beg, *Keep us alert, O Lord our God, as we await the
advent of Christ your Son, so that when he comes and
knocks, he may find us watchful in prayer and exultant in
his praise.*[10]

The Blessed Virgin will help us in our struggle
against all that separates us from God; we will be able to
prepare our soul during the feasts that we are about to
celebrate, and we will be better able to guard our senses,
which are, as it were, the doors of the soul. *Nunc coepi!*
Now, Lord, I begin again, with the help of your Mother.
We turn to her *because it is the will of God that we
should have nothing which has not passed through the
hands of Mary.*[11]

---

[9] John Paul II, Parc des Princes, 1 June 1980
[10] *Collect of the Mass for Monday of the First Week of Advent*
[11] St Bernard, *Sermon 3, Christmas Eve, 10*

As a resolution from this time of prayer, we can offer Our Lord our desire to carry out faithfully the plan of life that we have agreed on with our spiritual director, even though for some reason it may seem difficult. The fortitude of our Mother, the Blessed Virgin, will help our weakness, and will make us experience that *with God nothing is impossible.*[12]

---

[12] Luke 1:37

THIRD WEEK OF ADVENT – THURSDAY

19. WATCHFUL FOR OUR LORD'S COMING

19.1 Our Lord invites us to be watchful. To be watchful is to love. *Come Lord Jesus.*

Behold, the Lord will come descending with splendour to visit his people with peace, and he will bestow on them eternal life.[1]

Our Lord is coming to visit us, to bring us peace, and to give us the eternal life promised from of old. He has to find us like the good servant[2] who does not fall asleep during his master's absence but, rather, when the master returns is found at his post, devoted to his duty.

What I say to you, I say to all; watch.[3] These words are addressed to men of all times. They are words that the Lord speaks to each one of us, because we men tend towards drowsiness and comfort-seeking. We cannot allow our hearts to *become dulled with gluttony and drunkenness, and the cares of this life.*[4] In this way we would lose that supernatural outlook that should give life to everything we do.

Our Lord is coming to us and we must await his arrival with a vigilant spirit. We should not be fearful, like people caught doing wrong. We should not be distracted like those who have placed their heart entirely in earthly goods. We should be attentive and cheerful like

---

[1] *Entrance Antiphon of Friday of the Third Week of Advent;* cf Mark 13:34-37
[2] Mark 13:37
[3] Luke 21:34
[4] cf 1 Thess 5:4-11

eager people who expect a long-awaited loved one.

Keeping watch is above all a matter of loving. We may have difficulties in keeping our love awake: selfishness, a lack of mortification and temperance always threaten to extinguish the flame that Our Lord lights time and again in our hearts. That is why we need constantly to revive the flame, to shake ourselves out of any repetitive routine, to struggle. St Paul compares this watchfulness to the well-armed soldier on guard duty who does not allow himself to be taken by surprise.[5]

The first Christians repeated frequently and lovingly the aspiration, *Come, Lord Jesus.*[6] Through practising their faith in this way, those faithful members of the Church found the interior strength and optimism that they needed if they were to fulfil their family and social duties. At the same time they detached themselves interiorly from earthly goods, with the mastery that comes from the hope of eternal life.

This meeting with Our Lord will not come unexpectedly for the Christian who has been on the watch. For him He will not come *like a thief in the night.*[7] There will be no surprises, because there will already have been many meetings with Him each day; meetings in the Sacraments and in ordinary happenings of the day which have been full of love and friendship. So the Church prays, *Hear in kindness, O Lord, the prayers of your people, that those who rejoice at the coming of your Only Begotten Son in our flesh may, when at last he comes in glory, gain the reward of eternal life.*[8]

---

[5] 1 Cor 16:13
[6] *The Navarre Bible*, note to Mark 13:33-37
[7] 1 Thess 5:2
[8] *Collect, Mass for 21 December*

19.2 Vigilance has to be in the little things of each day. Daily prayer, examination of conscience, small mortifications which keep us alert.

We need to be on guard not only against God's enemies but also against the complicity proffered by our evil inclinations: *Watch and pray that you may not enter into temptation; the spirit indeed is willing, but the flesh is weak.*[9]

We are alert when we make an effort to improve our personal prayer, which in turn increases our desire for sanctity and helps us to avoid lukewarmness. We will also stay awake to the things of God by living a spirit of mortification. We strengthen our vigilance through doing a careful examination of conscience so that we do not fall into the situation described by St Augustine, as though spoken by God: *For whilst you give yourself up to evil, you come to consider yourself good, because you do not take the trouble to look at yourself. You reproach others and you do not take stock of yourself. You accuse others and you do not examine yourself. You place them before your very eyes and you place yourself behind your back. So when the time comes for me to reckon with you I shall do the opposite; I will turn you around and confront you with yourself. Then you will see yourself and you will weep.*[10]

Our vigilance has to be in the little things that fill up our day: *That supernatural mode of conduct is a truly military tactic. You carry on the war – the daily struggles of your interior life – far from the main walls of your fortress.*

And the enemy meets you there: in your small mortifications, your customary prayer, your methodical

---

[9] Matt 26:41
[10] St Augustine, *Sermon 17*

*work, your plan of life: and only with difficulty will he
come close to the easily-scaled battlements of your
castle. And if he does come, he arrives exhausted.*[11]

If in our examination of conscience we consider *the
little things of each day*, we will find the true way and
will discover the root causes of our failings in love of
God. Little things generally open the way to big things.

Our daily meditation will keep us on the look-out for
the enemy, who never sleeps, and will give us strength to
bear and to overcome temptations and difficulties. In that
meditation we will find too the means to struggle against
the 'old man', those less than upright tendencies that
remain latent within us.

To achieve this necessary interior purification we
need to practise constant mortification of the memory
and the imagination. If we do this we will be able to
eliminate from our understanding those troublesome
things that prevent us from carrying out God's will to the
full. During these days before Christmas then, let us tone
up our interior purification so that we can receive Christ
with a clean mind. We will try to get rid of anything that
goes against, or does not belong to our way. Then our
mind will no longer have in it anything that does not
belong to Our Lord. *That joke, that witty remark held on
the tip of your tongue; the cheerful smile for those who
annoy you; that silence when you're unjustly accused;
your friendly conversation with people whom you find
boring and tactless; the daily effort to overlook one
irritating detail or another in the persons who live with
you ... this, with perseverance, is indeed solid interior
mortification.*[12]

---

[11] St. J. Escrivá, *The Way*, 307
[12] *ibid*, 173

19.3 Interior purification.

That purification of the soul through interior morti-fication is not something merely negative. It is not just a matter of avoiding what borders on sin; quite the opposite, it consists of knowing how to deprive oneself, for love of God, of things that it would be quite licit to have.

This mortification, which tends to purify the mind of everything that is not God, aims in the first place at freeing the memory from recollections that would oppose the way that leads to heaven. Those recollections can assault us during our work or our rest, and even whilst we are praying. Without violence, but promptly, we will apply the means to get rid of them. We will struggle to make the effort which is necessary for our mind to fill itself once more with love, and a longing for the things of God.

Something similar can happen to the imagination. It can often upset us by inventing all kinds of novels, weaving fantastic fictions which are quite useless. *Get rid of those useless thoughts which, at best, are but a waste of time.*[13] Then, as well, we have to react quickly and return serenely to our ordinary task.

In any case, interior purification does not end with emptying the understanding of useless thoughts. It goes much further; the mortification of our potencies opens up to us the way to contemplative life, in whatever circumstances God has wanted to place us. With that interior silence towards everything that goes against God's wishes and is improper to his children, the soul finds itself well disposed for a continuous and intimate dialogue with Jesus Christ. In this dialogue our imagination helps contemplation – for example, when we

---

[13] *ibid*, 13

contemplate the Gospel or the mysteries of the Holy Rosary. It is then that our memory recalls the wonders God has done for us, and his abundant goodness; and this will cause our hearts to burn with gratitude and ardent love.

The Advent liturgy repeats the urgent message many times: The Lord is coming and we have to prepare a broad path for him; a clean heart. *Create in me a clean heart, O God,*[14] we beg him.

Today in our prayer we make specific resolutions to empty our hearts of anything displeasing to God. We make the resolution to purify our hearts through mortification and to fill them with love of God whilst constantly showing our affection for Our Lord. We do this in the same way as Our Lady and St Joseph did, by saying aspirations and making spiritual communions, and in making many acts of love and atonement.

Many other souls can benefit from the effort we make to prepare a worthy dwelling place for Our Lord. We can say to many of those who walk along the same paths as we do, what is so simply expressed in that old folk rhyme:

I know of a smooth path
by which we can reach God
holding tight Our Lady's hand.

We ask her to let us walk throughout our lives, as St Paul asked the first Christians at Ephesus to do, *to walk in love.*[15]

---

[14] Ps 50:10
[15] cf Eph 5:2-5

20. OUR LORD'S SECOND COMING

20.1 All men will go towards Christ triumphant. Signs that will accompany Our Lord's second coming. The sign of the Cross.

We await a saviour, the Lord Jesus Christ, who will change our mortal bodies, to conform with his glorified body.[1]

The season of Advent also prepares our souls for the expectation of the second coming of Christ at the end of time. Then the world will see *the Son of Man coming in a cloud with power and great glory*[2] to judge the living and the dead in a universal judgement, before the coming of *new heavens and a new earth in which righteousness dwells.*[3] Meanwhile, *the pilgrim Church, in its sacraments and institutions, which belong to this present age, carries the mark of this world which will pass, and she herself takes her place among the creatures which groan and travail yet and await the revelation of the sons of God.*[4]

Jesus Christ will come as the Redeemer of the World, as King, Judge and Lord of the whole Universe. He will take men by surprise as they busy themselves about their own affairs. He will not give any warning of the imminence of his coming: *For as the lightning comes from the east and shines as far as the west, so will be the coming of the Son of Man.*[5]

Men, both good and evil, living and dead, will gather

---

[1] *Communion Antiphon of the Mass*
[2] Luke 21:27
[3] Pet 3:13
[4] Second Vatican Council, *Lumen gentium*, 48
[5] Matt 24:27

to him; all men will turn irresistibly towards Christ triumphant, some attracted by love, others forced by justice.[6]

Then there will appear in heaven *the sign of the Son of Man – the Holy Cross*.[7] That Cross so often despised, so often abandoned, *a stumbling block to Jews and folly to Gentiles*,[8] which had been considered as something senseless; that Cross will appear before the astonished gaze of men as the sign of salvation.

Jesus Christ will show Himself in all his glory to those who have rejected Him – in his person or in his Church. He will show himself to those who, not satisfied with rejecting him, persecuted him; to those who lived without ever coming to know him. He will also show himself to those who loved him with deeds. The whole of humanity will realise that God *has highly exalted him and bestowed on him the name that is above every name, that at the name of Jesus every knee should bow, in heaven and on earth and under the earth, and every tongue confess that Jesus Christ is Lord, to the glory of God the Father.*[9]

Then we will consider as well used, all our effort, all those good works that we did for God, although perhaps nobody in this world was aware of them. Then we will feel great joy as we see that Cross, which we tried to seek out throughout our lives; that Cross that we wanted to place at the summit of all the activities of men. And we will have the joy of having played our part as good servants in the kingdom of that King, Jesus Christ, who now appears filled with majesty, in all his glory.

---

[6] *The Navarre Bible*, note to Matt 24:23-28
[7] Matt 24:30
[8] 1 Cor 1:23
[9] Phil 2:9-11

20.2 The universal judgement. Jesus our Friend.

And he will send out his angels with a loud trumpet call and they will gather his elect from the four winds, from one end of heaven to the other.[10] All men since Adam will be there. And now they will all understand with complete clarity the value of self-denial, of sacrifice, or surrender to God and to other people. At Christ's second coming the honour and glory of the saints will publicly be made known; for of these many died unknown, despised, misunderstood, and now they will be glorified in the sight of all.

The spreaders of heresy will receive the punishment that they accumulated throughout the centuries, as their errors passed from one person to another, and were an obstacle that prevented many from finding salvation. Likewise, those who gave the faith to other souls and enflamed others with the love of God will receive the reward for the fruits that their prayer and sacrifice produced down the ages. They will see the results that the good each one of their prayers, their sacrifices and their vigils produced.

We will see the true value of men considered as wise, but in fact teachers of error, whom many generations surrounded with praise and esteem. We will see the value of others who were relegated to oblivion when they should have been highly esteemed and heaped with honours. It is then that these forgotten men and women will receive the reward for their work, which the world denied to them.

The judgement of the world will serve for God's glorification.[11] Then will be revealed His Wisdom in his government of the world; his Goodness and his Patience

---

[10] Matt 24:31
[11] cf Thess 1:10

with sinners, and above all, his retributive Justice. The glorification of the God-man, Jesus Christ, will culminate in the exercise of his judicial power over the Universe.

The particular judgement of individuals will not be revised or amended in the universal judgement, but it will be confirmed and made known publicly. In the universal judgement each man will be judged in the sight of the whole human race and as a member of human society. Then reward and punishment will complement each other as they are extended to the body after its resurrection.[12]

20.3 Preparing for our judgement. Examination of Conscience. The practice of frequent Confession.

Before Our Lord's second coming in glory, each one's particular judgement will take place, immediately after death. *It is in regard to death that man's condition is most shrouded in doubt. Man is tormented not only by pain and by the gradual breaking-up of his body but, also, and even more, by the dread of forever ceasing to be. But a deep instinct leads him rightly to shrink from and to reject the utter ruin and total loss of his personality. Because he bears in himself the seed of eternity, which cannot be reduced to mere matter, he rebels against death.*[13] Revelation teaches us that death is a step, a passage to eternal life. Between life here on earth and eternal life, the particular judgement of each one will take place. This will be carried out by Jesus Christ himself, when each one will be judged according to his works, *for we must all appear before the judgement seat of Christ, so that each one may receive good or evil, according to what he has done in the body.*[14]

---

[12] cf St Thomas, *Summa Theologica*, suppl 88,1
[13] Second Vatican Council, *Gaudium et spes*, 18
[14] 2 Cor 5:10

Nothing will fail to be presented to the divine tribunal: thoughts, desires, words, actions and omissions. Each human act will then acquire its true dimension – the dimension that it has before God, not that which it had before men.

There will appear all the thoughts, imaginings and desires ... all those internal weaknesses that perhaps it is difficult for us to recognise now. Jesus Christ *will bring to light the things now hidden in darkness and will disclose the purposes of the heart.*[15] The words too that we have sometimes used to prop up our own excellence; at others as the instrument of lies; sometimes a lack of understanding, charity or justice. And our deeds. We will be judged too by our deeds: *For I was hungry and you gave me food ...*[16] Christ will look at our lives, examining how we have behaved towards him, or towards our fellow men, his brothers.

All the opportunities that we had to do something for other people will appear very clearly. Each of our days is full of possibilities for doing good, in whatever circumstances we may be. It would be sad if our life was like a great avenue of wasted opportunities. All this could happen through letting negligence, laziness, comfort-seeking, selfishness and a lack of love creep into us.

However, for those of us who are close to him throughout our lives Jesus Christ will not be a judge who is a stranger to us, because we try to serve him every day of our existence on earth. We can be intimate friends of him who has to judge us. That friendship must increase each day that passes. *I was amused to hear you speak of the 'account' that Our Lord will demand of you. 'No, for none of you will he be a judge – in the harsh sense of the*

---

[15] 1 Cor 4:5
[16] cf Matt 25:35

word; he will simply be Jesus.' These lines, written by a good bishop, have consoled more than one troubled heart, and could well console yours.[17]

It would help us to meditate fairly frequently on the particular judgement towards which we are striding. All the time we are coming closer to it. Then we will see Christ – our judge and friend – glancing at our lives. This will encourage us to fill our lives with little things which are not unnoticed by Him, although generally they will not be perceived by men, nor will men give them any great value.

A daily examination of conscience and the practice of frequent Confession are very important means of preparing each day for that definitive meeting with Our Lord, which will take place, perhaps sooner than we expect. They are also excellent means of preparing for this new meeting with Our Lord at Christmas, which is coming close: *Come quickly, we pray, Lord Jesus, and do not delay, that those who trust in your compassion may find solace and relief in your coming.*[18]

---

[17] St. J. Escrivá, *The Way*, 168
[18] *Collect, Morning Mass of 24 December*

FOURTH SUNDAY OF ADVENT

21. ADVENT: A TIME OF HOPE

21.1 Mary, teacher of hope. The origin of discouragement and dejection. Jesus Christ the supreme good.

The spirit of Advent largely consists in living close to Our Lady during this time when she is carrying Jesus in her womb. We can think of the whole of our life as a somewhat longer *advent*, a time of waiting for that definitive moment when we will at last find ourselves with God forever. The Christian knows that he has to live this *advent* beside Our Lady every day of his life if he wants to be certain of attaining the only thing in the whole of his existence that is really important – finding Christ in this life, and afterwards being with him in eternity.

There is no better way of preparing for Christmas, which is now so close, than by keeping Mary company, getting to know her and deepening our love and trust in her.

Mary imparts a great joy to our souls, because when we turn to her she leads us to Christ. *Mary teaches us to hope. 'All generations will call me blessed', she proclaimed. Humanly speaking, how could she hope for such a thing? Who was she, in the eyes of her contemporaries? The great heroines of the Old Testament – Judith, Esther, Deborah – won a measure of human renown even here on earth ... What a contrast between Our Lady's hope and our own impatience! We call so often upon God to reward us at once for any little good we may have done. For us, no sooner does the very first difficulty appear than we begin to complain. Often we find ourselves incapable of sustaining our efforts, of keeping our hope alive.*[1]

The ones who become discouraged are not those who undergo difficulties and feel pain. It is those, rather, who do not aspire to sanctity and eternal life, those who despair of ever reaching them, who buckle and give up. The attitude of the former is shaped by a lack of faith, by comfort-seeking, lukewarmness and an excessive attachment to earthly goods, which they consider to be the only good things worth having. Discouragement, if it is not remedied, paralyses any effort to do good and overcome difficulties. Sometimes discouragement over one's own failure to advance in sanctity comes about through lack of will-power, through fear of the effort the ascetical struggle entails, and of having to give up disordered attachments of the senses. Not even *apparent* failures in our interior struggle, or in our concern to do apostolate should be cause for dismay. Whoever does things for love of God and for His Glory *never fails. Convince yourself of this truth: your success – this time, in this matter – was to fail. Give thanks to our Lord ... and try again!*[2] *You haven't failed; you have gained experience. On you go!*[3]

In a few days' time we shall see Jesus in the Crib. The sight will be a proof of God's mercy and love. We will be able to say: *On this Christmas night everything inside me stops. I am face to face with Him; there is nothing but this Child in the whole of that huge white expanse. He does not say anything, but He is there ... He is God loving me.*[4] And if God becomes man and loves me, how am I going to refuse to seek Him? How am I

---

[1] St. J. Escrivá, *Friends of God*, 286

[2] *idem*, *The Way*, 404

[3] *ibid*, 405

[4] J. Leclerq, *A Year with the Liturgy*

going to give up hope of finding Him, if He is searching for me? Let us rid ourselves of any suggestion of discouragement. Neither external difficulties nor our personal wretchedness can do anything to quell the joy of the Christmas which is approaching.

21.2 The object of our hope.

Hope is recognised clearly throughout the Old Testament as one of the most essential characteristics of the true people of God. All eyes are fixed on the distant future when the Messiah will arrive one day. *The books of the Old Testament describe the history of salvation in the course of which the coming of Christ into the world was slowly prepared.*[5]

In *Genesis* we already hear about the victory of the Woman over the powers of evil, about a new world.[6]

The prophet *Hosea* announces that Israel will return to its ancient love and will blossom in it.[7] *Isaiah*, in the midst of the tribulations of the chosen people during the ministry of Ezechiel, announces the coming of the Messiah.[8] *Micah* will point to Bethlehem of Judah as the place of His birth.[9]

There are only a few days left before we see Our Lord lying in the manger: *For all the oracles of the prophets foretold him, the Virgin Mother longed for him with love beyond all telling, John the Baptist sang of his coming and proclaimed his presence when he came. It is by his gift that already we rejoice at the mystery of his Nativity, so that he may find us watchful in prayer and*

---

[5] Second Vatican Council, *Lumen gentium*, 55
[6] cf Gen 3:15
[7] Hos 2:16-25
[8] Is 7:9-14
[9] cf Mic 5:2-5

exultant in his praise.[10]

From the stable at Bethlehem to the moment of his ascension into Heaven, Jesus Christ proclaims a message of hope. Jesus himself is *our only hope.*[11] He is the firm pledge that we will attain to the marvellous future we have been promised. We look towards the cave at Bethlehem *in watchful hope*, understanding that it is only in his company that we can *boldly approach God the Father.*[12]

Our Lord himself points out to us that the principal objects of Christian hope are not the good things of this life which *moth and rust consume, and which thieves can break in and steal*,[13] but the treasures of the 'incorruptible heritage' and, above all, the supreme happiness of the eternal possession of God.

We confidently hope that one day He will give us eternal blessedness, and here and now, pardon for our sins, and his grace. As a consequence, hope offers to everyone the means necessary to achieve what has been promised. Seen in this light, the good things of earth can also find a place within the scope of things to be legitimately hoped for, but only insofar as God orders them to our salvation.

We are going to struggle with all our strength, today and always, against those lesser forms of despair which we can experience as loss of heart and dejection, and an excessive concentration on and a nearly exclusive concern with material things and their possession.

Hope leads us to abandon ourselves in God and to do all that we can to undertake a deliberate ascetical

---

[10] *Second Preface of Advent*
[11] cf 1 Tim 1:1
[12] 1 Tim 3:12
[13] Matt 6:19

struggle. This struggle will move us to begin again many times, to be constant in the apostolate and patient in adversity; to have a more supernatural outlook on life and its vicissitudes.

In proportion as the world grows weary of its Christian hope, the alternative is materialism, of a type with which we are already familiar – that and nothing else. The world's experience of Christianity has been like a great love, the love of a lifetime ... No new voice ... will have any appeal for us, if it does not bring us back to the stable at Bethlehem – there to humble our pride, and enlarge our charity, and deepen our sense of reverence with the sight of a dazzling purity.[14]

21.3 Trust in our Lord. Jesus never too late to give us the help and graces we need.

Hearken to me, you stubborn of heart, you who are far from deliverance. I bring near my deliverance; it is not far off, and my salvation will not tarry.[15]

Our hope in God has to be all the greater, the less plentiful the means at our disposal or the more apparently insurmountable the difficulties. On a certain occasion when Jesus returned to Capharnaum, St Luke tells us, *They were all waiting for him.*[16] In the thick of that crowd one person is singled out by the Evangelist, who identifies him as a *ruler of the synagogue*; this man begs Jesus to cure his daughter. *He fell at his feet.* He has no hesitation in giving that public proof of his humility and of his faith in Him.

Immediately, at an indication from Our Lord, they all move off in the direction of Jairus' house. The girl,

---

[14] R. A. Knox, *Sermon on Christmas*
[15] cf Is 46:12-13
[16] Luke 8:40-56

twelve years of age, is dying. She must be in her death throes by this time. Just at this very moment, when they have gone part of the way, inconspicuous in the middle of the jostling crowd, a woman who suffers from a haemorrhage that makes her unclean according to the Law, comes up behind Our Lord and touches the edge of his cloak. She too is a woman full of deep humility.

Jairus has demonstrated his hope and his humility by prostrating himself before Jesus in front of everyone. This woman wants to pass undetected. She is anxious not to take up any of the Master's time. She considers herself too unimportant to be noticed by Our Lord. It is enough if she can touch his cloak.

Both miracles are to be fully accomplished. The woman, for whom the skill of so many doctors has been unavailing, will be cured forever. Jairus' daughter will go on to live a completely healthy life even though when the retinue arrives, after the delay to their journey, she has breathed her last.

Whilst the encounter with the woman with the issue of blood is taking place, what has become of Jairus? It seems he has fallen into the background, and it is not too difficult to imagine him somewhat distraught, because his daughter had been already on the point of death when he left her to seek out the Master. Jesus, on the other hand, does not appear to be in any hurry. He does not even seem to attach much importance to whatever is happening in Jairus' house.

When Jesus arrives the girl has already died. There is no longer any possibility of preventing her death. It seems that Jesus has arrived too late. And precisely now, when as far as human intervention is concerned nothing can be done, when all natural hope is gone and everything calls for collapse into grief, the moment has come to awaken supernatural hope.

Jesus never arrives too late. He only demands greater faith. He waited until it was 'too late' in this instance in order to teach us that supernatural hope remains, like a solid foundation, amid the ruins of human hope, and all we need is unlimited trust in him who can do anything He wills at any moment.

This passage reminds us of our own lives. When it seems sometimes that Jesus has not intervened to meet our need, He then gives us a much greater grace than we have been beseeching him for. It reminds us of so many occasions in front of the tabernacle when we have been aware in our heart of words very similar to these: *Do not be afraid; only believe.* To hope in Jesus is to trust in him and to let him act, to let him do what He will. The greater the trust, the fewer the elements we should need to rely on in human terms.

Devotion to the Blessed Virgin is the greatest guarantee of our achieving the means necessary for our salvation and the eternal happiness for which we have been destined. Mary is truly 'the port in a storm for those who are shipwrecked.' She is *the consolation of the world, ransom of captives, joy of the sick.*[17] During these days that precede Christmas, and always, let us ask her to teach us how to hope in her son Jesus Christ, the Messiah whose advent was foretold by the Prophets. *She shines forth on earth, until the day of the Lord shall come, a sign of sure hope and comfort to the pilgrim People of God.*[18]

---

[17] St Alphonsus Liguori, *Visit to the Blessed Sacrament*, 2
[18] Second Vatican Council, *Lumen gentium*, 68

22. THE NATIVITY: AT ST JOSEPH'S SIDE

22.1 Joseph's mission

And Jacob was the father of Joseph the husband of Mary, of whom Jesus was born, who is called Christ.[1]

The Gospel of today's Mass gives us the genealogy of Jesus on Joseph's side. Among the Jews, as among other peoples of nomadic origin, the genealogical tree was of capital importance. A person was known fundamentally by the clan or tribe to which he belonged rather than by the place where he lived.[2]

Among the Hebrews we have the added circumstance of belonging to the chosen people through ties of blood, a person's ancestry being traced through the male line. Joseph, as the husband of Mary, was the legal father of Jesus and, as such, carried the duties of a true father.

Joseph, like Mary, was *of the house and family of David,*[3] of whom would be born the Messiah, according to God's promise: *When your days are fulfilled and you lie down with your fathers, I will raise up your offspring after you, who shall come forth from your body, and I shall establish his kingdom. He shall build a house for my name, and I will establish the throne of his kingdom for ever.*[4] Thus, Jesus, who was a descendant of David through Mary, was registered in the royal house through

---

[1] Matt 1:16
[2] cf *The Navarre Bible*, notes to Matt 1:1 and Matt 1:6
[3] Luke 2:4
[4] 2 Sam 7:12-13

Joseph, *since he who came into the world ought to be registered according to the custom of the world.*[5]

It would also be Joseph's responsibility to give his name to the Word incarnate, in accordance with the instructions given him by the angel: *You shall call his name Jesus.*[6]

God had foreseen that his Son would be born of the Virgin Mary, in a family just like any other, and that in her he would develop in his humanity. The life of Jesus had to be in this respect the same as that of other men. He was to be born defenceless, in need of a father who would protect him and teach him the things that all fathers should teach their sons.

The essence and ultimate meaning of Joseph's life had to lie in the fulfilment of his mission as Mary's husband and as the father of Jesus. He was born into the world to act as the father of Jesus and to be Mary's most chaste spouse, in the same way that every person who comes into the world has a specific vocation from God, in which is rooted the whole meaning of his life.

When the angel revealed to him the mystery of the virgin birth of Jesus, Joseph fully accepted his vocation, to which he was to remain faithful until death. His worldly mission was to be the head of the Holy Family.

St Joseph's whole glory and happiness lay in his knowing how to understand what God wanted of him and in his having faithfully carried it out to the end.

Today in our prayer let us contemplate Joseph at the side of the Blessed Virgin, who is with child and soon to give birth to her only begotten Son. And let us resolve to spend the time of Christmas at St Joseph's side, a place as unnoticed as it is privileged: *How good Joseph is! He*

---

[5] St Ambrose, *Commentary on the Gospel of St Luke*, 1-3
[6] Matt 1:21

treats me like a son. He even forgives me if I take the child in my arms and spend hour after hour saying loving things to him.[7]

22.2 Joseph's relations with Jesus

Joseph, we read in a sermon of St Augustine, *not only claims the name of father, but has a greater claim to it than any other.*[8] And then he adds: *How was he a father? All the more effectively, the more chaste the paternity. Some thought that he was the father of our Lord Jesus Christ in the same way as other fathers, who beget sons of the flesh and do not receive them only as the fruit of a spiritual love. This is why St Luke says: 'he was thought to be the father of Jesus.' Why only thought to be? Because thought and human judgement refer to what is usual among men. And our Lord was not born of Joseph's seed. Yet of the piety and love of Joseph a son – who was the Son of God – was born to him of the Virgin Mary.*[9]

St Joseph was deeply in love with Mary. *He must have loved her so much and with such generosity of heart that, when he learned of her desire to preserve the consecration she had made to God, he agreed to marry her. He would rather renounce having children than live apart from the woman he loved.*[10] His was a pure, refined and deep love. It was full of respect with no hint of selfishness. God himself had definitively sealed their union with a new and even stronger bond, which was their joint earthly mission of bringing up the Messiah. And they had already been betrothed, which was why the angel had said: *Do not be afraid to take Mary to be 'your*

---

[7] St. J. Escrivá, *Holy Rosary*, Third Joyful Mystery
[8] St Augustine, *Sermon 51, 26*
[9] *ibid*, 27-30
[10] F. Suarez, *Joseph of Nazareth*

wife'. What kind of relationship would Joseph have had with Jesus? *Joseph loved Jesus as a father loves his son and showed his love by giving him the best he had. Joseph, caring for the child as he had been commanded, made Jesus a craftsman, transmitting his own skill to him. So the neighbours in Nazareth would call Jesus both 'faber' and 'fabri filius', the craftsman and the son of the craftsman (Mark 6:3; Matt 13:55). Jesus worked in Joseph's workshop and by Joseph's side.* What sort of man must Joseph have been, and how must grace have been active in him, that he was able to carry out the task of bringing up the Son of God?

For Jesus must have resembled Joseph: in his way of working, in the traits of his character and in his way of speaking. Jesus' realism, his eye for detail, the way he sat at table and broke bread, his preference for using everyday situations in his teaching – all this reflects his childhood and the influence of Joseph.[11]

We stay close to Joseph as we meditate on the approaching Nativity. He only asks us to be simple and humble in our contemplation of Mary and her son. There is no room for the proud in that little group in Bethlehem.

22.3 Go to Joseph, so that he may teach us to live side by side with Jesus and Mary

In the words of Blessed John Paul II, in his homily at a Midnight Mass: *Weariness fills men's hearts and makes them sleep, as the shepherds slept nearby in the fields of Bethlehem. What happened in that stable, in that cavern of rock, has a dimension of profound intimacy. It is something that only happens between a mother and a child about to be born. No one else is present. Even Joseph, the carpenter of Nazareth remains – outside – as*

---

[11] St. J. Escrivá, *Christ is passing by*, 55

a silent witness. She alone is fully aware of her maternity. And only she sees the Child's face when he utters his first cry. The birth of Christ is before all else her mystery, her great day. It is the mother's festival.[12] And only she truly grasped the meaning of this mystery of Christ's birth and the Redemption.

Between Mary and Jesus there exists an absolutely unique and special relationship shared by no one else – not even Joseph by himself who, in the Pope's words, is only *a silent witness*. Joseph, full of admiration, unspeaking and respectful, contemplates the child and its mother. After Mary, he was the first person to see the Son of God made man. No one could have experienced more happiness than he when he took in his arms the Messiah, who in no visible way could be distinguished from any other child.

Nevertheless, the mystery which Joseph contemplated imposed on him certain limits which he would never cross. With Mary it is different, *because the great event concerned, above all else, the mother and her son. Joseph was to participate shortly afterwards, when the profound and mysterious relationship had already been established between Jesus and his mother. Initially, Joseph's participation in the mystery had come about through the knowledge given him by the angel's revelation of the mission he was to carry out for these two exceptional people.*[13]

St Joseph was present later when the shepherds arrived. *He saw them approach the cave, timid and curious, to see for themselves the 'babe wrapped in swaddling clothes'. He heard them explain to Mary about the apparition of the heavenly messenger who had told them about the birth of the Saviour in Bethlehem and*

---

[12] John Paul II, *Homily during Midnight Mass in 1978*
[13] F. Suarez, *op cit*

*about the sign by which they would recognise him,
describing how a multitude of angels had gathered with
this first herald envoy, glorifying God and promising
peace on earth to men of good will ... Joseph also
contemplated the radiant happiness of the woman who
was his wife, this marvellous lady who had been
entrusted into his keeping. Enthralled by the way she
gazed at her son, he saw her own unspeakable joy, her
own overflowing love, her every gesture so full of
exquisite tenderness and meaning.*[14]

If we stay close to Joseph during these few days
between now and Christmas, he will help us to
contemplate this tremendous mystery of which he was a
silent witness and to gaze lovingly at Mary as she holds
in her arms the Son of God made man.

From the very start Saint Joseph grasped the fact that
his whole reason for living was this child, precisely
because he was a child, and as such, in need of help and
protection, as Mary was too, for God himself had com-
missioned him to take her into his home and give her
protection. How grateful Jesus would be for all the
vigilance and attention that Joseph paid to Mary! It is
not surprising that, after the Blessed Virgin, Joseph is the
person most endowed with grace. That is why the Church
has always paid him great tribute and been fervent in his
praise, having recourse to him in times of greatest
difficulty. *Sancte Joseph, ora pro eis, ora pro me. Saint
Joseph, pray for them* (for our loved ones), *pray for me*
(for I too need your help). In whatever need, the Holy
Patriarch, together with the Blessed Virgin, will hear our
prayers. Today, we ask him to make us simple of heart so
that we will know how to show our love for the child
Jesus as he did.

---

[14] *ibid*

23. MARY'S VIRGINITY: OUR PURITY

23.1 Virginity, apostolic celibacy and marriage.

Mary's virginity is a privilege intimately united with her divine maternity, which is in perfect harmony with her Immaculate Conception and her glorious Assumption. Mary is Queen of virgins: *the dignity of virginity stems from the Mother of God.*[1]

The Blessed Virgin is the most perfect example for every life that is completely dedicated to God.

The renunciation of human love for God's sake is a divine grace which drives and encourages a person to surrender body and soul to Our Lord with all the possibilities that the heart possesses. God is thus the one and only focus of this unshared love. It is in God that the heart finds its fulfilment and its perfection, without the intervention of any earthly love. The result is that God grants a bigger heart which, in him, is capable of loving all creatures.

The vocation to apostolic celibacy, *for the love of the Kingdom of Heaven,*[2] is a special grace from God and one of his greatest gifts to his Church. In the words of John Paul II, *virginity keeps alive in the Church the awareness of the mystery of marriage and defends it against all attempts to impoverish it or reduce its importance. It frees the heart of man in a special way ... bearing witness to the fact that the Kingdom of God and its justice is a pearl of great price to be preferred to any other treasure however great its value may be. Moreover,*

---

[1] St Augustine, *Sermon 51*
[2] Matt 19:12

virginity should be sought as the only real object of value. The Church, therefore, throughout its history, has defended the superiority of this divine gift over matrimony, because of its particular link with the Kingdom of God.

Even though a person has renounced physical parenthood, as a virgin he or she can assume a spiritual parenthood towards many by co-operating in the development of the family according to God's plan.[3]

From those who are called by a specific vocation to renounce human love, God asks that they give their whole heart, and they find in him the fulfilment of loving. To live virginity or apostolic celibacy means to live the perfection of love. *Celibacy and perfect chastity give the soul, the heart and the external life of those who profess them that freedom which the apostolate needs so much if it is to serve with maximum generosity the good of other souls. This virtue which makes men spiritual and strong, free and agile, helps them to see around them other souls and not merely bodies, souls who hope for the light of their word and of their prayer, and the charity of their time and of their affection. We should have a great love for celibacy and chastity, because they are concrete and tangible proofs of our love of God, and are at the same time sources which make us grow continuously in that same love.*[4]

Virginity and apostolic celibacy not only do not contradict the dignity of marriage but presuppose and confirm it.[5]

The Church always needs people who offer to God an undivided heart as a *living sacrifice, holy and*

---

[3] John Paul II, Apostolic Exhortation, *Familiaris consortio*

[4] S. Canals, *Jesus as Friend*

[5] cf John Paul II, *ibid*

acceptable.[6] The Church also needs saintly families, Christian homes, which will be the true leaven of Christ and be themselves the source of many vocations of complete self-surrender to God.

23.2 Holy purity in and outside marriage. The fruits of this virtue. Purity is necessary for love.

For both single and married people, Mary's virginity is also a call to live with finesse the virtue of holy purity, which is essential if we are to see God and serve our fellow men. Perhaps this virtue will clash with our environment and be misunderstood by many, blinded as they will be by a materialistic outlook. In fact, it will be scorned and its utility called into question. Nevertheless, holy purity is absolutely necessary for us, even from the point of view of being a little more human, and of being able to look at God. Without the virtue of purity it is simply impossible to be a contemplative soul.

The Holy Spirit acts in a special way on the soul that is refined in its chastity. Holy purity produces rich fruit in the soul. It enlarges the heart and helps in the normal growth of the affections. It gives rise to deep internal happiness even in the midst of many obstacles. It makes apostolate possible. It makes us more human, with a greater capacity for understanding and sympathising with other people's problems.

On the other hand, impurity gives rise to insensitivity of heart, to mediocrity and selfishness. It makes a person incapable of real love and produces in the soul all the necessary conditions for it to germinate like weedy growths and nurture every kind of vice and unfaithfulness. *Don't forget that when someone is corrupted by concupiscence of the flesh, he cannot make*

---

[6] Rom 12:1

any spiritual progress. He is unable to do good works. He is a spiritual cripple, fit to be cast aside like an old rag. Have you ever seen patients suffering from a progressive paralysis and unable to help themselves or even to get up? Sometimes they cannot as much as move their heads. Well, in the spiritual order, the same thing happens to people who are lacking in humility and have made a cowardly surrender to lust. They don't see, or hear, or understand anything of primary importance. They are, as it were, paralysed. They are like men gone mad. Each of us here ought to invoke Our Lord, and his Blessed Mother, and pray that He will grant us humility and the determination to avail ourselves frequently and devoutly of the divine remedy of confession.[7]

Today let us ask Our Lord in our prayer to have mercy on us and to help us have a more purely refined attitude towards him. *Jesus, guard our hearts! Make them big and strong and tender hearts, affectionate and sensitive, overflowing with love for you and ready to serve all mankind.*[8]

23.3 How to live this virtue.

Today we can offer our hearts to Our Lady and resolve to strive for greater care in living this virtue. Holy purity is so pleasing to her, and produces so many fruits in our interior life and in the apostolate.

The Church has always taught that, with the help of grace, and especially in this case with the help of the sacraments of the Eucharist and Penance, it is possible to live this virtue at every moment and in all the circumstances of life. All we have to do is make use of the appropriate means at our disposal. *What do you want*

---

[7] St. J. Escrivá, *Friends of God*, 181
[8] *ibid*, 177

us to do? Go up into the mountains and become monks? – St John Chrysostom was asked. What you say is enough to make me weep, he replied. That you should think modesty and chastity proper only to monks! No. Christ laid down the same laws for everyone. So when he said 'every one who looks at a woman lustfully' he wasn't speaking to monks, but to men everywhere ...[9]

Holy purity entails a daily self-conquest, for it is not acquired once and for all. There may be times when the struggle becomes more intense, so that it is necessary to have more frequent recourse to the Blessed Virgin and to use, perhaps, some more unusual remedy.

To acquire this virtue it is first necessary to be very humble, a condition clearly shown by sincerity in spiritual direction, for sincerity itself leads to humility. *Remember the poor boy who was possessed by a devil, and was unable to be helped by the disciples. Only Our Lord could free him, by prayer and fasting. On that occasion the Master worked three miracles. The first enabled the boy to hear, because, when the dumb devil gets control, the soul refuses to listen. The second made him speak and the third expelled the devil.*[10]

Other ways of caring for and cultivating this virtue are those small, customary mortifications which help to keep the body under control. *If we want to keep intact the most beautiful of all the virtues, which is chastity, we must realise that it is a rose that only blooms in the midst of thorns, for which reason it is only to be found, as are the other virtues, in a mortified person.*[11]

Take very special care of the virtue of chastity and also of the virtues which accompany it – modesty and

[9] St John Chrysostom, *Homilies on St Matthew*, 7,7
[10] St. J. Escrivá, *op cit*, 188
[11] St Jean Vianney, (The Curé d'Ars), *Sermon on penance*

refinement. They are, as it were, the safeguard of chastity. Don't take lightly those norms of conduct which help so much to keep us worthy in the sight of God: keeping a watchful guard over our senses and our hearts; the norm of courage – the courage 'to be a coward' – to flee from the occasions of sin; of going to the sacraments frequently, particularly to the sacrament of Confession; of complete sincerity in our own spiritual direction; the norms of sorrow, contrition and reparation after one's falls. And let all this be imbued with a tender devotion to Our Lady, so that she may obtain for us from God the gift of a clean and holy life.[12]

We carry this great treasure of purity in *vessels of clay*, fragile and vulnerable. But we have all the weapons needed to conquer temptation, so that with the passage of time this virtue may go on increasing in its refinement, that is, in a greater tenderness towards God. *Let us end this period of conversation in which you and I have been praying to Our Father, asking him to grant us the grace to live the Christian virtue of chastity as a joyful affirmation.*

We ask this of him through the intercession of Our Lady, she who is immaculate purity itself. Let us turn to her, 'tota pulchra', all beautiful, taking to heart that advice I gave many years ago to those who felt uneasy in their daily struggle to be humble, pure, sincere, cheerful and generous. 'All the sins of your life seem to be rising up against you. Don't give up hope! On the contrary, call to your holy Mother Mary, with the faith and abandonment of a child. She will bring peace to your soul.'[13]

---

[12] St. J. Escrivá, *op cit*, 185
[13] *ibid*, 189

24. SPIRITUAL CHILDHOOD

24.1 Becoming like children before God.

St Mark tells us that *they were bringing children to him, that he might touch them; and the disciples rebuked them.*[1]

Behind those children we can see their mothers gently pushing their little ones in front of them. Jesus must have created around himself an atmosphere of goodness and attractive simplicity. The mothers feel glad to see Jesus blessing their children and edged closer to him.

The conflict between these women and the disciples, who were obviously concerned to keep some sort of order in the throng, is the prologue to a profoundly significant lesson from Christ. In the midst of the striving and pushing forward of some and the resultant protests of those who want them to take the children away, Jesus takes the disciples to task. He is happy to be with these little ones. *Let the children come to me; do not hinder them; for to such belongs the kingdom of God. Truly, I say to you, whoever does not receive the kingdom of God like a child shall not enter it. And he took them in his arms and blessed them, laying his hands upon them.*[2] The children and their mothers had gained the day and went home happy.

We have to approach Bethlehem with the dispositions of children – simply, that is, without prejudice and with our souls wide open to grace. More

---

[1] Mark 10:13
[2] Mark 10:14-16

than that, it is necessary to become completely child-like in order to enter the kingdom of heaven: *unless you turn and become like children, you will never enter the kingdom of heaven,*[3] Our Lord says on another occasion, as he places a little one in their midst.

Our Lord is not recommending childishness, but innocence and simplicity. He sees in children traits and attitudes that are essential in anyone if he is to gain heaven, and, even in this life, if he is to enter the kingdom of faith. A child is devoid of even the slightest feeling of self-sufficiency. It is in constant need of its parents, and knows it. A child is fundamentally a being in need, and this is what a Christian should be before his Father God, a being in total need. A child lives fully in the present and nothing more. The adult's less admirable predisposition is to look restlessly to the future, ignoring the here and now, the present moment, which ought to be lived to the full.

This gesture of Our Lord towards their little ones must have won over those women who, perhaps, in their eagerness to get their children to the front, had not been paying much attention to the words addressed by Jesus to his audience. In this passage Jesus shows us the way of spiritual childhood, so that we can open wide our hearts to God and be fruitful in the apostolate.

Be a little child: the greatest great daring is always that of children. Who cries for the ... moon? Who is blind to dangers in getting what he wants?

To such a child add much grace from God, the desire to do his Will, great love for Jesus, all the human knowledge he is capable of acquiring, and you will have a likeness of the apostles of today such as God undoubtedly wants them.[4]

---

[3] Matt 18:3
[4] St. J. Escrivá, *The Way*, 857

24.2 Spiritual childhood and divine filiation. Humility and abandonment in God.

A few days before the Passion *the chief priests and the scribes saw the wonderful things that he did, and the children crying out ..., and they were indignant; and they said to him, 'Do you hear what these are saying?' And Jesus said to them, 'Yes; have you never read, "Out of the mouth of babes and sucklings thou hast brought perfect praise"?'*[5] Throughout the whole of the Gospel we come across this same idea: that which is little is chosen so as to confound the great. Open the mouths of those who know least, and close the lips of those who seem to be wise.

Jesus openly accepts the Messianic confession of these children. They are the ones who see clearly the mystery of God there present. Only with this attitude can we receive the kingdom of God.

We Christians, recognising Jesus in the stable at Bethlehem as the long-promised Messiah, must react with the mind, the simplicity and the daring of children. *Child, enkindle in your heart an ardent desire to make up for the excesses of your grown-up life.*[6] What 'excesses' we commit when in the hardness of our heart we lose interior simplicity and the clear vision of Jesus Christ, withdrawing from Him our praise when He most desires our open confession of faith in an environment of such blindness to the things of God!

To become like children at heart while remaining adults can be costly. It requires real determination and strength of will, and a total abandonment to God. *To become children we must renounce our pride and self-sufficiency, recognising that we can do nothing by*

---

[5] Matt 21:15-16
[6] St. J. Escrivá, *The Way*, 861

ourselves. We must realise that we need grace and the help of God our Father to find our way and keep to it. To be little, you have to abandon yourself as children do, believe as children believe, beg as children beg.[7]

24.3 The virtues proper to this path of childhood: docility and simplicity.

This life of childhood is possible if we have a deep-rooted awareness of being children of God. The mystery of divine filiation, founded on our spiritual life, is one of the consequences of the Redemption. *We are God's children now*[8] and it is very important that we become clearly aware of this marvellous reality so that we can approach God with the childlike spirit of a good son. Divine adoption implies a transformation that greatly surpasses the changed circumstances of ordinary human adoption. Divine adoption is more real than its human counterpart: *through the gift of grace, God makes man worthy to be adopted so that he may receive a heavenly inheritance. On the other hand, man does not make the person he adopts worthy of his adoption, but rather adopts someone who is already deserving of it.*[9]

As children of God we are heirs of glory. Let us try to be worthy of such an inheritance, and have for God a filial, tender and sincere piety.

The way of spiritual childhood presupposes a limitless confidence in God our Father. In a family, the father explains the great big world to his little one. The child feels its weakness, but knows its father will protect it, and because of this lives and walks confidently. The child knows that when its father is there, nothing can go

---

[7] *idem, Christ is passing by,* 143
[8] 1 John 3:2
[9] St Thomas, *Summa Theologica,* 3,q.23,a.1,c

wrong and nothing bad can happen to it. The child's soul and mind are open to its father's voice without fear or distrust. The little one knows that, even though others may deceive it, when it goes home its father will never be unfriendly or hostile, because he understands.

Children are not unduly sensitive to the fear of ridicule which paralyses so many undertakings. Nor do they tend to be inordinately concerned about that false human respect born of pride and the apprehensive dread of what others may think.

Children often tumble down, but they quickly pick themselves up again. And in the life of spiritual childhood those very same falls and weaknesses are means of sanctification. For in it love is always young, and unpleasant experiences are easily forgotten; not dwelt and brooded upon as so often happens with those who have 'grown-up' souls.

They are called children, St John Chrysostom comments, *not because of their age, but because of their simplicity of heart.*[10]

Simplicity is perhaps the virtue which summarises and co-ordinates all the other aspects of this life of childhood that Our Lord asks of us. As St Jerome says, we have to be *like the child whom I propose to you as an example ... He does not think one thing and say another, behaving as you also must behave, for if you did not have such innocence and purity of intention you would not be able to enter the kingdom of heaven.*[11]

Simplicity is shown in our sincere, friendly and unaffected dealings with others. It is a much appreciated virtue in human relations, but not always easy to find.

Another consequence of spiritual childhood is the

---

[10] St John Chrysostom, *The Golden Chain*, vol III, p.20
[11] St Jerome, *Commentary on St Matthew's Gospel*, 3,18,4

gentle virtue of meekness. *Child, abandonment demands docility.*[12] Etymologically, a person is 'docile' when he is disposed and prepared to be taught. This is how the Christian should be when faced with the mysteries of God and the things that refer to him, keeping the mind open to a correct formation and always full of desire to know the truth. The person with an 'adult' soul assumes that he knows many things, but in reality is ignorant. He thinks he knows, but has in fact not penetrated beyond external appearances, and has failed to get to the bottom of things in such a way that what is true could have a direct influence on his actions. When God looks at such a person, he sees him totally lacking in awareness of reality and shut off from knowledge of the truth.

How wonderful it would be if, some day, having finally become like children, we were to grasp the true meaning of things as familiar to Christians as the Our Father, for example, or of really taking part in the Holy Mass, or of sanctifying each day's work, or of seeing in the people around us souls that must be saved, or ... of so many things that too often we take for granted!

Let us learn to be children in the sight of God. *And we learn all this through contact with Mary ... Because Mary is our mother, devotion to her teaches us to be authentic sons: to love truly without limit; to be simple without the complications which come from selfishly thinking only about ourselves; to be happy, knowing that nothing can destroy our hope. The beginning of the way, at the end of which you will find yourself completely carried away by love for Jesus, is a trusting love for Mary.*[13]

---

[12] St. J. Escrivá, *The Way*, 871
[13] idem, *Christ is passing by*, 143

25. MARY'S VOCATION – OUR VOCATION

25.1 The Blessed Virgin chosen from eternity. Her vocation.

We are now very close to Christmas. The prophecy of Isaiah is now about to be fulfilled: *the maiden is with child and will soon give birth to a son whom she will call Emmanuel, a name which means 'God is with us'.*[1]

The Hebrew people were familiar with the prophecies which singled out the descendants of Jacob, through David, as bearers of the Messianic promises. But they could not imagine that the Messiah would be God himself made man.

But when the time had fully come, God sent forth his Son, born of woman.[2] And this woman, chosen and predestined from all eternity to be the mother of the Saviour, had consecrated her virginity to God, renouncing the honour of counting the Messiah among her direct descendants. And she is prefigured in the Book of Proverbs: *Ages ago I was set up, at the first, before the beginning of the earth.*[3]

We can obtain great benefits at this time by keeping close to Our Lady and showing our love for her. She herself tells us: *Like a vine I caused loveliness to bud, and my blossoms became glorious and abundant fruit. I am the mother of all love, all reverence, all true knowledge, and the holy gift of hope.*

---

[1] *First reading of the Mass*, Is 7:14
[2] Gal 4:4
[3] Prov 8:23-31

Come to me, you who desire me, and eat your fill of my produce. For the remembrance of me is sweeter than honey and my inheritance sweeter than the honeycomb.[4]

Mary appears as the virgin Mother of the Messiah, she who will give all her love to Jesus, with an undivided heart, as the prototype of that self-surrender that Our Lord will ask from many souls.

In the fulness of time, God sent the Angel Gabriel to Nazareth where Our Lady dwelt. In popular devotion Mary is represented as recollected in prayer while she hears, most fervently, of God's plan for her and learns her vocation. The Angel says to her: *Hail, full of grace, the Lord is with you,*[5] as we read in today's Gospel.

The Virgin gives her full consent to the divine will: *Be it done unto me according to your word.*[6] From this moment on, she accepts her vocation and begins to put it into practice. Her vocation is to be *Mother of God and Mother of men.*

Unknown to anyone, the hub of human history and the centre of all mankind is now the little village of Nazareth. Here lives the woman most loved by God, she who is to be the most loved human being in the whole world, the most frequently invoked and called upon of all time. And we, in the intimacy of our heartfelt prayer, say: 'Mother! Blessed art thou among all women.'

In the exercise of her Motherhood she was adorned with all the graces and privileges which made her a worthy abode for the Most High. God chose his Mother and put in her all his love and power. He did not permit there to be in her the least taint of sin, neither original nor personal. She was conceived Immaculate, without any

---

[4] Sir 17:20
[5] Luke 1:28-33
[6] Luke 1:38

stain at all. And He granted her so much grace that under God, it would be impossible to conceive of anyone greater than she: such was to be her state that *no one, apart from God, could even begin to comprehend it.*[7] Her dignity is almost infinite.

All these privileges and graces were given to her so that she could carry out her vocation. As with each individual, her vocation was the central moment of her life: She was born to be the Mother of God, chosen by the Blessed Trinity from all eternity.

She is our Mother too, a fact which, in this season, we want constantly to keep in mind. In the words of an ancient prayer, which we have made our own, we can say to her: *Remember, O most holy Virgin Mother of God, ever before the Lord, to say good things of me.*

25.2 Our vocation. Correspondence to it.

For each one of us, our vocation is the central theme of our lives. It is the axis around which everything else turns. Everything, or almost everything, depends on our knowing and carrying out what God asks of us.

To follow and to love one's own vocation is the most important and joyously fulfilling thing in life. But in spite of its being the key that opens the door to happiness, there are many who do not want to know what their vocation is. They prefer to do what pleases them, to do their own will instead of God's will, to remain in a state of culpable ignorance instead of seeking in all sincerity the road that will lead them to happiness and enable them to reach heaven in safety as well as to bring this same joy to many others.

Our Lord calls every one of us by our own name, today as much as ever. He needs us, it seems.

---

[7] Pius IX, Bull, *Ineffabilis Deus*

Furthermore He calls all of us to a holy vocation, a vocation to follow him in a new life whose secret He alone possesses: *if any man would come after me ...*[8] Through Baptism we have all received a vocation to seek God in the fulness of love. *For the ordinary life of man among his fellows is not something dull and uninteresting. It is there, in their ordinary lives, that God wants the vast majority of his children to achieve sanctity.*

It is important to keep reminding ourselves that Jesus did not address himself to a privileged set of people; he came to reveal to us the universal love of God. God loves all men, and he wants all men to love him – everyone, whatever his personal situation, his social position, his work. Ordinary life is something of great value. All the ways of the earth can be an opportunity to meet Christ, who calls us to identify ourselves with him and carry out this divine mission – right where He finds us.

God calls us through what happens in the ordinary course of our day: through the sorrows and joys of the people we live with, through the human interests of all our colleagues and the things that go to make up our family life. He also calls us through the great problems, conflicts and challenges of each period of history, the portentous events that attract the interest and idealism of a large part of mankind.[9]

The call of Our Lord urges us to a greater self-giving, for among other reasons, *the harvest is plentiful, but the labourers are few.*[10] And there are harvests which perish daily because there is no one to gather them in.

---

[8] Matt 16:24
[9] St. J. Escrivá, *Christ is passing by*, 110
[10] cf Matt 9:37

Be it done unto me according to your word,[11] says Our Lady. And we contemplate her, radiant with joy. As we raise up our minds and hearts in prayer, we can enquire of ourselves: Am I seeking God in my work or in my study, in my family, out in the street ... in everything? Am I *daring* in doing apostolate? Does Our Lord want more of me?

25.3 Imitating Our Lady in her spirit of service to others.

To God's will, Our Lady has but one reaction: to love it. Proclaiming herself *the handmaid of the Lord*, she accepts his plans without any reservation whatever. In the world of antiquity, in which slavery, the lot of the servant, was a common condition, this expression of Mary is seen in all its force and depth. The slave, one can say, did not have a will of his own, nor could he have any desire independent of his master's. Our Lady agrees with the greatest joy and with all her heart to have no other wish than that of her Master and Lord. She gives herself to him unreservedly, without condition.

We also, in imitation of Our Lady, do not want to have any other will, or any plans other than those of God. And we want this in the things that are obviously of transcendent importance for us, that is, in our vocation to sanctity, and also in what immediately relates to it – in the ordinary little things of every day, the mundane details of our work, our family life and our social relations.

One of the mysteries of Advent is that on which we meditate in the second Joyful Mystery of the Rosary, namely, the Visitation. Let us focus in our consideration of it on one specific aspect of service to others which is

---

[11] Luke 1:38

part of our vocation: the order of charity.

This visit of our Mother to her cousin St Elizabeth presents one outstanding manifestation of the order of charity. We must love all men because they are all, or can be, sons of God. But we must love in the first place those who are closest to us, those with whom we have special ties, such as members of our families. This *caritas* must be shown by deeds, not only by affection or fondness. Let us think now of our dealings with our family, of the numberless opportunities that come our way of exercising, quite normally and naturally, our love and spirit of service.

We would like to live these days of Advent with the same spirit of service as our Mother had during her time of expectant waiting. Supported by the humble self-giving of Mary, let us ask her (like good children) to help us, so that when Our Lord comes our hearts may, with complete generosity, be ready to receive his commands, his counsels and his suggestions.

Let us ask the blessed Virgin to make us contemplatives, to teach us to recognise the constant calls from God when he knocks at the door of our heart. Let us ask her now: Mother, you brought into the world Jesus, who reveals to us the love of our Father God. Help us to recognise him in the midst of the cares of each day. Stir up our minds and our wills, so that we may be ready to listen to the voice of God, to the calls of grace.[12]

---

[12] St. J. Escrivá, *ibid*, 174

26. GENEROSITY AND SPIRIT OF SERVICE

26.1 Mary's generosity and a spirit of service.

In those days Mary arose and went with haste into the hill country, to a city of Judah, and she entered the house of Zachariah and greeted Elizabeth.[1]

Our Lady puts all she has at God's disposal. In an instant, all her personal plans – and no doubt she had many – were discarded so that she could do everything God wanted her to. She made no excuses, had no reservations. From the very first moment, Jesus is the one great ideal of her life.

Throughout her life on earth Our Lady showed limitless generosity. Among the few episodes of the Gospel that refer to her, two of them speak directly of her attention to the wants of others. She generously gave of her time to look after her cousin St Elizabeth until the birth of her son, John,[2] and she was solicitous for the well-being of the young couple and their guests at the wedding reception in Cana of Galilee.[3] Such attitudes were second nature to her. Her neighbours in Nazareth would have much to tell us about Mary's innumerable little services to them in their everyday lives.

The Blessed Virgin never thought of herself, but of others. She did her household chores with the greatest simplicity and happiness while maintaining the deepest interior recollection, for she knew that God was within

---

[1] *Gospel of the Mass*
[2] Luke 1:31
[3] John 2:1

her. In Elizabeth's house everything was sanctified by
Our Lady and the Child she carried in her womb.

In Mary we confirm the truth that generosity is a
virtue of great souls, who know how to find their reward
in the act of giving: *you received without pay, give
without pay.*[4] A generous person knows how to be loving
and understanding and how to give material help –
without demanding love, understanding or help in return.
He gives and forgets he has given, and in this lies his
riches. He has understood that *it is better to give than to
receive.*[5] He realises that to love *is in its essence to give
oneself to others. Far from being an instinctive
inclination, love is a conscious decision of the will to
draw close to other people. To be able to love truly it is
important to be detached from everything and,
especially, from self, to give gratuitously ... This
detachment from self is the source of a balanced
personality. It is the secret of happiness.*[6]

Giving enlarges the heart and makes it youthful, with
an ever greater capacity for loving. Selfishness, on the
other hand, impoverishes the heart and narrows its
horizons. The more we give, the richer we become.

Today let us ask the Blessed Virgin to teach us to be
generous, first of all with God and then with other
people, those we live or work with and those we meet in
all the varied circumstances of our lives. She will show
us how to give ourselves in the service of our fellow-men
in the ordinary course of each day.

---

[4] Matt 10:8

[5] Acts 20:35

[6] John Paul II, *Address*, 1 June 1980

26.2 Our need to imitate the Blessed Virgin. Details of generosity and service in our relations with others.

If we feel that in spite of our struggle we are still unable to rid ourselves of selfishness, we will look again at Our Lady with the desire of imitating her in her generosity and to know the joy of giving ourselves to others. We need to have a better understanding of the way generosity enriches and widens the heart, need to be sure that we can attain it. And we must realise that selfishness is like a slow-acting poison that acts insidiously but with deadly effect.

Close to Mary, we perceive that God has made us for himself and that each time we give ourselves exclusively to our own plans, concentrating on ourselves and our personal affairs while ignoring him, we die a little more. *The Kingdom of Heaven is beyond price, and yet it costs what you have to give ... It cost Peter and Andrew the price of a boat and some nets. It cost the widow two little coins ...*[7] It cost them everything they had as it will do in our case too.

What we are and what we have are saved at the moment we surrender them. *Your boat (your talents, your hopes, your achievements) is worth nothing whatsoever, unless you leave it in Christ's hands, allowing him the freedom to come aboard. Make sure you don't turn it into an idol. In your boat, by yourself, if you try to do without the Master, you are – supernaturally speaking – heading straight for shipwreck. Only if you permit and seek his presence and captaincy will you be safe from the storms and contrary currents of life. Put everything in the hands of God. Let your thoughts, the brave adventures you have imagined, your lofty human ambitions, your noble loves, pass through the heart of Christ. Otherwise, sooner or*

---

[7] St Gregory the Great, *Homily 5 on the Gospels*

later, they will all sink to the bottom together with your selfishness.[8]

Everyone, no matter where or how he is called by God, must do as that woman of Bethany did, who showed her great love for Our Lord by breaking open for him a jar of *pure nard of great price.*[9] It was an exterior manifestation of that love. This woman did not want to keep back anything for herself or for anyone else. Hers was a gesture of self-giving without reservations, of unalloyed friendship, of deep tenderness towards Christ. *The house was filled with the fragrance of the perfume.* Like hers, our demonstrations of love and self-giving to Christ will remain like perfume. Just that. Everything else will be evanescent and pass on and away like the waters of a stream.

Generosity to God must be shown by generosity to our fellow-men: *as you did it to one of the least of these my brethren, you did it to me.*[10]

A characteristic of generosity is knowing how to forget quickly those little irritations that can crop up in daily life. It is knowing how to smile and make life more agreeable for those around us, even though they may be suffering setbacks; to give others the benefit of the doubt; to do the least pleasant tasks first in our work or in family life; to accept people as they are, without attaching too much importance to their defects; to be ready with a pat on the back for a job well done; to give a positive tone to our conversation and, if the occasion arises, to a possible correction that we ought to make; to avoid negative criticism, which is often useless and unfair; to open up wider horizons, both human and supernatural, for our

---

[8] St. J. Escrivá, *Friends of God*, 21
[9] John 12:3
[10] Matt 25:40

friends. All these betoken generosity of spirit, but above all, if we are to be really generous in loving our neighbour, we must do our best to make it easier for those around us to come closer to Christ. That is the best thing we can do.

Every day we have a treasure to distribute. If we don't give it, we lose it. If we share it, Our Lord multiplies it. If we are attentive, if we contemplate his life, He will find for us opportunities of serving voluntarily where, perhaps, few people would wish to do so. Like Jesus who, at the Last Supper, *washed the feet of his disciples*,[11] we will not be deterred by the lowliest chores, which are often the most necessary and will involve us in the most thankless of tasks. We will learn that the occasions of serving are turned to reality through sacrifice, as the fruit of an interior attitude of abnegation and renunciation. We will realise that to find these opportunities of service it is necessary to look for them, thinking of the personalities of the people with whom we live or work, of what they need, of how we can be helpful or useful to them. The selfish person, who lives far away from God is aware only of his own needs and whims.

Our Lady was not only generous with God in the highest degree, but also with everyone she encountered throughout her life on earth. Of her, too, it can be said that she *went about doing good*.[12] It ought to be possible to say the same about each one of us.

26.3 The reward for generosity.

God rewards here and in the life hereafter our poor little demonstrations of generosity, and always above

---

[11] cf John 13:4-17
[12] Acts 10:38

measure. He is so grateful that whoever so much as raises his mind to think of him will not miss his reward.[13]

In Sacred Scripture we come across many examples of God's supernatural generosity in relation to man's. The widow of Sarepta gave a handful of flour... and a little oil,[14] only to receive an inexhaustible supply of both. The poor widow in the Temple gave two little coins and Jesus said she *has put in more than all those who are contributing to the treasury.*[15] The servant who has succeeded in making a profit with the talents he has received will hear from the mouth of his Lord: *Because you have been faithful in very little, you shall have authority over ten cities.*[16]

One day Peter said to Jesus: *Lo, we have left our homes and followed you.* And Jesus answered him: *Truly, I say to you, there is no man who has left house or wife or brothers or parents or children for the sake of the Kingdom of God, who will not receive manifold more in this time, and in the age to come eternal life.*[17]

How will he, who takes into account the least of our actions, be able to forget the faithfulness of one day after another? He who multiplied the loaves and fishes for the crowds that followed him for a few days, what will he not do for those who have left all to follow him always? If these should one day beg from him a special grace to keep moving forward, how could Jesus deny them? He is a good paymaster.

God gives a hundredfold for each thing left behind for love of him. Furthermore, whoever follows Jesus in

---

[13] St Teresa of Avila, *The Way of Perfection*, 23,3
[14] 1 Kings 17:10
[15] Mark 12:43
[16] Luke 19:16-17
[17] Luke 18:28-30

this way is not only enriched a hundredfold in this life, but is also predestined to a reward the munificence of which beggars the imagination. At the end he will hear the voice of Jesus, whom he has served all his life: *Come, O blessed of my Father, inherit the kingdom prepared for you from the foundation of the world.*[18] On hearing these words of welcome into eternity, generosity will have been well recompensed. The faithful servant will enter into everlasting life hand in hand with Jesus and Mary.

---

[18] Matt 25:34

27. THE *MAGNIFICAT:*
THE HUMILITY OF MARY

27.1 The humility of the Blessed Virgin. The meaning of humility.

O gates, lift high your heads; grow higher, ancient doors. Let him enter, the king of glory![1]

Wherever she went, the Blessed Virgin was a bringer of joy: *For behold, when the voice of your greeting came to my ears, the babe in my womb leaped for joy,*[2] says St Elizabeth, referring to John the Baptist with whom she was then with child. Hearing such praise from her cousin, Our Lady replied with words which have become that most beautiful hymn of jubilation: *My soul magnifies the Lord, and my spirit rejoices in God my Saviour.*

In the *Magnificat* is to be found the deepest meaning of true humility. Mary considers that God has regarded *the low estate of his handmaiden.* Thus, *He who is mighty has done great things* in her.

On this scale then, one of grandeur and humility, is passed Our Lady's entire life. *What humility, that of my holy Mother Mary! She is not to be seen amidst the palms of Jerusalem, nor – excepting the first one at Cana – at the hour of the great miracles. But she doesn't flee from the degradation of Golgotha: there she stands, 'juxta crucem Jesu', by the Cross of Jesus – His Mother.*[3] She never sought the slightest personal glory.

The virtue of humility, so evident in Our Lady's life,

Antiphon of the Mass

·ivá, *The Way*, 507

is truth,[4] the true recognition of what we are and are worth in the eyes of God and of our fellow men. It is also an emptying of ourselves to allow God to work in us with his grace. *It is the rejection of appearances and of superficiality; it is the expression of the depth of the human spirit; it is a condition for its greatness.*[5]

Humility is founded on the awareness of our position in the eyes of God and on the wise moderation of our always excessive desires for glory. It should never be confused with timidity, faint-heartedness or mediocrity.

It is not opposed to our awareness of the talents we have received, nor to the full use of them with rectitude of intention, for humility does not diminish, but broadens one's outlook. Humility recognises that all the good in us, whether in the order of nature or in that of grace, belongs to God alone; *for of his fulness we have all received.*[6] God is all that is great in us; of ourselves we are defective and weak. We come before God as *debtors who do not know how to discharge our debts,*[7] and for this reason we go to Mary as the Mediatrix of all graces, to the Mother of mercy and tenderness to whom no one has ever had recourse in vain: *abandon yourself full of confidence in her maternal womb; ask her to obtain for you this virtue which she prized so dearly. Don't worry about not being heard. Mary will ask it for you from that God who exalts the humble and crushes the proud, and, since Mary is all-powerful with her Son, you will most certainly be heard.*[8]

---

[4] cf St Teresa of Avila, *Sixth Mansion*, ch 106

[5] John Paul II, *Angelus*, 4 March 1979

[6] 1 Cor 1:4

[7] cf Matt 18:23-35

[8] J. Pecci (Leo XIII), *Practice of humility*, 56

27.2 The foundation of charity. Fruits of humility.

Humility is at the root of all the virtues, and without it none of them can be developed. Without humility *everything else is like a huge heap of hay which we have piled up, but which with the first gust of wind is blown over and scattered far and wide. The devil has little respect for those devotions which are not founded on humility, because he knows well that he can get rid of them whenever he pleases.*[9] There is no possibility of sanctity without an effective struggle to acquire this virtue; without it, it is not even possible to develop an authentic human personality. Furthermore, a humble person has a special facility for making friends, even with people of very different tastes and of varying age-groups, which is a great help in all kinds of personal apostolate.

Humility is, in a very special way, the basis of charity. It gives it consistency and makes it possible: *the dwelling place of charity is humility,*[10] says St Augustine. To the extent that a person can forget about self, he can take an interest in other people and attend to their needs. Many sins against charity have been provoked by previous faults of vanity, pride, selfishness and the desire to stand out from among others. And thus these two virtues, humility and charity, *are the mother virtues; the others follow as chickens do the mother hen.*[11]

A humble person hates to put on airs, 'to show off'. He knows well that he is not in the position he occupies, whatever it is, in order to shine or to receive compliments, but to serve, to carry out a mission. *Do not sit down in a place of honour ..., but when you are*

---

[9] St Jean Vianney, (The Curé d'Ars), *Sermon on humility*
[10] St Augustine, *On Virginity*, 51
[11] St Francis de Sales, *Letters*

invited, go and sit in the lowest place.[12] And if a Christian is to be found among *the places of honour*, occupying a pre-eminent position, he knows that *this position of excellence has been given to him by God so that he may become useful to others, from which it follows that in as much as the witness of others ought to be pleasing to him, so much the more should he contribute to their good.*[13]

We ought to be in our proper place, always conscious that we are in the presence of God and resolutely refusing to allow our judgement to be distorted by ambition. Much less should we let ourselves be propelled by vanity into a mad scramble for higher and higher positions for which, perhaps, we have not the competence, and which later on will lead to humiliation, thereby creating in ourselves the dismaying conviction that we have got ourselves into a situation for which our gifts have not fitted us. This does not mean that God has not called us to make the best use of our talents and to make many sacrifices in using our time well.

On the contrary, humility is opposed to a lack of the right intention in one's work, a lack that is a clear symptom of pride. The humble person knows his place, however exalted or lowly it be. He feels he belongs there and is happy in his work. He knows his limitations and possibilities, and does not allow himself to be deceived by mere ambition. His qualifications are the right ones for his job, to a greater or lesser degree: he is never a dead weight, holding others back. He carries out his work as well as he might, as a member of a team.

Another manifestation of humility is the avoidance of negative judgements about other people. The

---

[12] Luke 14:7
[13] St Thomas, *Summa Theologica*, II-II, q131

knowledge of our own weakness will prevent us from
entertaining *a bad thought about anyone, even if the
words or conduct of the person in question give good
grounds for doing so.*[14] We look on others with respect
and understanding which, when necessary, will naturally
and normally lead to fraternal correction.

27.3 Ways of acquiring this virtue.

Among the ways of attaining humility is, in the first
place, ardently to desire it, to value it and to ask God for
it. Then our aim should be to foster docility in resolutely
carrying out the advice received in spiritual direction, to
receive fraternal correction joyfully and thankfully, to
accept humiliation in silence for love of God, to obey
quickly and wholeheartedly and, above all, to strive to
attain this precious virtue through the exercise of charity
in continual details of cheerful service to others. Jesus is
the supreme example of humility. No one has ever had a
dignity comparable to his and no one has ever served
mankind with such tender care as He: *I am among you as
one who serves.*[15] If we imitate Our Lord, we will accept
others as they are and pay no attention to all those little
annoyances which, in themselves, are of little
importance. Humility disposes us to patience, and helps
us to be patient with our own defects and with the defects
of the people around us. We will render many little
services in the course of our daily lives without expecting
anything in exchange; and we will learn from Jesus and
Mary how to get along with everyone and to understand
other people, defects and all. If we try to see others as
Our Lord sees them, it will be easy to accept them as he
accepts them.

---

[14] cf St. J. Escrivá, *The Way*, 442
[15] Luke 22:27

When we meditate on those passages of the Gospel that show the shortcomings of the apostles, we will learn not to be impatient with our own failings. Our Lord takes them into account just as He also takes into account time, grace and our own desires to improve in this or that virtue or in some particular aspect of our character.

Let us finish our prayer in contemplation of our holy mother Mary by asking that she will obtain for us from her Son the virtue of humility which we need so much. *Turn your eyes towards Mary. No creature ever surrendered herself to the plans of God more humbly than she. The humility of 'ancilla Domini', the handmaid of the Lord, is the reason we invoke her as 'causa nostrae laetitiae', cause of our joy ... Mary, in confessing herself the handmaid of the Lord, becomes the Mother of the Divine Word, and is filled with joy. May the rejoicing that is hers, the joy of our good Mother, spread to all of us, so that with it we may continually go to her and greet her, our Holy Mother Mary, and thus become more like Christ, her Son.*[16]

---

[16] St. J. Escrivá, *Friends of God*, 109

28. CHRISTIAN DETACHMENT AND POVERTY

28.1 The Christmas call on us to live poverty as it was preached and lived by Christ.

An effective detachment from everything we have and are is necessary if we are to follow Jesus, if we are to open our hearts to Our Lord who is passing by and calls out to us. On the other hand, attachment to earthly things closes our doors to Christ and closes the doors to love and to any possibility of understanding what is most essential in our lives. *So, therefore, whichever of you does not renounce all that he has cannot be my disciple.*[1]

The birth of Jesus, and his whole life, is an invitation to us to examine, these days especially, the attitude of our hearts towards earthly goods. Our Lord, the Only-Begotten of the Father, the Redeemer of the world, was not born in a palace, but in a cave; not in a great city, but in an unknown village, in Bethlehem. He did not even have a cradle, but rather a manger. The hasty flight into Egypt was for the Holy Family the experience of being exiled to a foreign land, with few means of subsistence other than Joseph's hands, which were accustomed to work. During his public life, Jesus was to suffer hunger,[2] he would not have even the two small coins of paltry value needed to pay the temple tribute.[3] He himself would say that *the Son of man has nowhere to lay his head.*[4] His death on the Cross is the great sign of supreme detachment.

Our Lord wanted to undergo the rigours of extreme poverty – a real lack of necessities – especially during the most noteworthy hours of his life.

The poverty lived by a Christian must be real poverty. It should be bound up with his work, with cleanliness, with order in the care of the house and the condition of the implements he works with, with the way he helps others, and with sobriety of life. That is why it has been said that *The best examples of poverty are those mothers and fathers of large and poor families who spend their lives for their children and who through their effort and their constancy – often without complaining of their needs – bring up their family, creating a cheerful home in which everyone learns to love, to serve and to work.*[5]

If material goods do come our way it will still be possible *to live like mothers and fathers of large and poor families,* and to do good by means of them, *because It is this sort of poverty, made up of detachment, trust in God, sobriety and a readiness to share, that Jesus declared blessed.*[6]

The poverty that God asks of all of us is not a matter of squalor, meanness, slovenliness or idleness. Virtue does not reside in these things. In order to learn to live detachment from things in the midst of the world of men, we have to look at our Model, Jesus Christ, who *for your sake ... became poor, so that by his poverty you might become rich.*[7]

---

[4] Matt 8:20
[5] *Conversations with Monsignor Escrivá,* 111
[6] Sacred Congregation for the Doctrine of the Faith, *Instruction on Christian freedom and liberation,* 66, 22 March 1986
[7] 2 Cor 8:9

28.2 What evangelical poverty consists in.

The poor to whom Our Lord promises the kingdom of Heaven[8] are not just those who happen to suffer need, but those who, whether or not they have possessions, are detached from them and do not find themselves imprisoned by them. Such poverty of spirit must be lived in all life's circumstances. *I know,* said St Paul, *how to have to do without, and how to abound. I have learned the secret of facing plenty and hunger, abundance and want.*[9]

Man can direct his life towards God, whom he can reach by using material things as means; or he can have as his end money with its many manifestations, such as the desire for luxury, unrestrained comfort, ambition and greed. The two ends are irreconcilable. *No one can serve two masters.*[10] Love for riches leaves no room for love of God; it is not possible for God to dwell in a heart which is filled with a different kind of love from his. God's word is stifled in the heart of a rich man, like *the seeds that fell upon thorns.*[11] That is why we are not surprised to hear Our Lord teach that *it is easier for a camel to pass through the eye of a needle than for a rich man to enter the Kingdom of God.*[12] How easy it is, if we are not vigilant, for the spirit of riches to enter our hearts!

The Church has kept on reminding us, from the beginning up to our own times, that the Christian has to be on guard when it comes to his use of material things, and she admonishes her children to *see that they direct their affections rightly, lest they be hindered in pursuit of perfect love by the use of worldly things, and by an*

---

[8] Matt 5:3
[9] Phil 4:12
[10] Matt 6:24
[11] Matt 13:7
[12] Matt 19:24

adherence to riches which is contrary to the spirit of evangelical poverty, following the apostle's advice: Let those who use this world not fix their abode in it, for the form of this world is passing away (cf 1 Cor 7:31 – Greek text).[13] The person who puts his heart into worldly goods not only distorts their right use and destroys the order established by God, but his soul grows dissatisfied, becoming a prisoner of those material things, which render it incapable of really loving God.

The Christian way of life demands a radical change in attitude towards earthly things; they should be procured and used, not as an end in themselves, but as a means of serving God. Because they are only a means they are not worth putting our hearts into; true goods are something else altogether.

We have to recall in our prayer that effective detachment from things demands sacrifice. Detachment which we do not find hard is not detachment. Real detachment will show itself frequently in generous almsgiving, in knowing how to do without anything superfluous, in fighting against a disordered tendency to well-being and comfort, in avoiding the indulgence of unnecessary whims, in the renunciation of luxury or the spending of money out of vanity etc.

This virtue of poverty is so important for a Christian that we can well say, *those who do not love and practise the virtue of poverty do not have Christ's spirit. This holds true for everyone, for the hermit who retires to the desert, to the ordinary Christian who lives among his fellow men whether he enjoys the use of this world's resources or is short of many of them.*[14]

---

[13] Second Vatican Council, *Lumen gentium*, 42
[14] *Conversations with Monsignor Escrivá*, 110

28.3 Poverty's detail and ways of living it.

The human heart tends to give excessive importance to its search for earthly goods. If there is no positive struggle to become detached from things, we can affirm that man, more or less consciously, has set his sights on an objective here below. A Christian, however, must never forget that he is journeying towards God.

Therefore he should examine himself frequently and ask himself whether he loves the virtue of poverty, and whether he is living it. Is he alert to the danger of falling into a desire for comfort, or for the easy life which is incompatible with being a disciple of Christ? Is he detached from earthly things? Finally, does he possess things as a means for doing good and for living ever closer to God? *In the course of history we are reminded that the use of temporal things has been tarnished by serious defects ... . Again, in our own days not a few ... deviate into a kind of idolatry of the temporal; they become the slaves of it rather that its masters.*[15]

We always can and should be sparing in the supplying of our personal needs, curbing superfluous expenditure, not giving in to frivolous cravings, being aware of the tendency we all have to create false needs, being generous in almsgiving or in assisting with the upkeep of good works. The same reasons should lead us to look after our possessions in our homes. Indeed we should consider all the things we have and use as being on loan, and remind ourselves that we are simply their administrators. *Poverty lies in being truly detached from earthly things and in cheerfully accepting shortage or discomfort if they should arise ... . We must live thinking of others and using things in such a way that there will be something to offer them. All these are dimensions of a*

---

[15] Second Vatican Council, *Apostolicam actuositatem*, 7

poverty that guarantees an effective detachment.[16]

In this and other ways we will show our resolve not to have our heart set on riches. We will show it too when our work puts us in a position to make personal use of things that belong to other people. The sobriety we show then will be the *bonus odor Christi*, 'the sweet fragrance of Christ' which must always accompany the life of a Christian.

Speaking to men and women striving to reach sanctity in the midst of the world – businessmen, academics, agricultural labourers, office-workers, mothers and fathers – St Josemaría Escrivá said: *The ordinary Christian has to reconcile two aspects of his life that can at first sight seem contradictory. There is on the one hand 'true poverty' which is obvious and tangible and made up of definite things. This poverty should be an expression of faith in God and a sign that the heart is not satisfied with created things and aspires to the Creator; that it wants to be filled with love of God so as to be able to give this same love to everyone. On the other hand, the ordinary Christian 'is and wants to be one more among his fellow men', sharing their way of life, their joys and their sorrows, working with them, loving the world and all the good things that exist in it, using all created things in order to solve the problems of human life and to establish the kind of spiritual and material environment that will foster personal and social development.*

Achieving a synthesis between these two aspects is to a great extent a personal matter. It requires interior life, which will help us assess in every circumstance what God is asking of us.[17]

If we struggle effectively to live detached from the

---

[16] *Conversations with Monsignor Escrivá*, 111
[17] *ibid*, 110

things we have and use, Our Lord will find our hearts
clean and wide open to him when he comes to us again
on Christmas Night. What happened in the inn at that
time will not happen in our hearts: it was full, and they
had no room for him there at all.

29. WAITING FOR JESUS

29.1 Mary. Spirit of Recollection. Spirit of Prayer.

Through the tender mercy of our God, when the day shall dawn upon us from on high to give light to those who sit in darkness and in the shadow of death, to guide our feet into the way of peace.[1] Jesus is the Dawn who gives light to our existence. If we want everything we do to have any meaning, it must be done with reference to him.

In a very special and extraordinary way Our Lady's life centres around Jesus. And especially so on this, the eve of her son's birth. We can hardly begin to have any idea of what the spirit of recollection within her soul was like.

She was always recollected. And that is how we must learn to be; we, whose thoughts are so dissipated and so distracted by things of little importance! Only one thing is really important in our lives: Jesus, and everything that refers to him.

But Mary kept all these things, pondering them in her heart.[2] *And his mother kept all these things in her heart.*[3] Twice the evangelist refers to Our Lady's attitude towards events as they occurred.

The Virgin ponders and meditates. She understands that interior spirit of recollection which enables her to evaluate and to keep in her heart all the happenings of her life, whether they be great or small. Deep within her,

---

[1] Luke 1:78-79
[2] Luke 2:19
[3] Luke 2:51

enriched by the fullness of grace, reigns that praeternatural harmony for which man was created. There is no better place to preserve and to ponder on that exceptional divine action in the world to which she bears witness.

After original sin, the soul lost its dominion over the senses and its natural orientation towards the things of God. It was not so in Our Lady: but it is in us. In her, who had been preserved from original sin, all was harmony, as at the beginning of creation. Moreover, she was adorned by the presence, altogether singular and extraordinary, of the Blessed Trinity in her soul.

Mary is always at prayer because she does everything with reference to her Son: when she talks to Jesus she prays *for prayer is 'to talk to God'*. She prays each time she looks at Him *that is prayer too – to look with faith at Jesus in the Blessed Sacrament, truly present in the tabernacle.* She prays when she asks him for something or whenever she smiles at him *so often!* or when she thinks about him. Her life was determined by Jesus, and her thoughts were set permanently on him.

Her interior spirit of recollection was constant. Her prayer blended with her very life, with her work and with her attention towards others. Her interior silence was richness, fullness and contemplation.

Today we ask her to give us this interior spirit of recollection, which is necessary if we are to see and to talk to God, who is also very close to our lives.

29.2 Our prayer. Learning to talk to Jesus. Need for prayer.

Today you will know that the Lord will come, and he will save us, and in the morning you will see his glory.[4]

---

[4] *Entrance Antiphon, Evening Mass of 24 December*

Our Lady encourages us, on this eve of her Son's birth, never to neglect prayer, which is conversation with Our Lord. Without prayer we are lost; with it we are strong and are able to carry out our tasks.

Among other reasons, we must pray too because we are fragile and culpable. We need to admit humbly and truly that we are poor creatures, with confused ideas ... We are fragile and weak, and in constant need of interior strength and consolation. Prayer gives us strength for great ideals, for keeping up our faith, charity, purity, generosity; prayer gives us strength to rise up from indifference and guilt, if we have had the misfortune to give in to temptation and weakness. Prayer gives light by which to see and to judge from God's perspective and from eternity. That is why you must not give up praying! Don't let a day go by without praying a little! Prayer is a duty, but it is also a joy because it is a dialogue with God through Jesus Christ![5]

We have to learn to come closer to Our Lord through mental prayer – those moments which we dedicate to talking to him quietly about our concerns, thanking him, asking for his help – simply being with Him! Through vocal prayer, too, perhaps sometimes through prayers we learned as children. Never in our lives will we meet anyone who listens with as much interest or as much attention as Jesus. Nobody has ever taken our words as seriously as he has. He looks at us. He pays attention to us. He listens to us with the greatest interest when we pray.

Prayer always enriches us – even in that silent dialogue before the tabernacle in which we do not use any words. It is enough to watch and to feel ourselves watched. How different from the verbosity of many men,

---

[5] John Paul II, *Audience with Young People*, 14 March 1979

who say nothing because they have nothing to
communicate! *From the abundance of the heart, the
mouth speaks.* If our heart is empty, what can our lips
say? If we are sick with envy or sensuality, what content
will the dialogue have? Nevertheless we always come
away from our prayer with more light, greater joy, more
strength. Being able to pray is one of the greatest gifts a
man has. To talk to and to be listened to by his Creator!
To talk to him and call him Friend!

In our prayer we have to talk very simply to Our
Lord. *To think and to understand what we are saying,
and to whom we are saying it. Who are we who dare to
speak to such a great Lord, to think these and other
similar things about how little we have served Him and
how much we are obliged to serve, is mental prayer.*[6]

Some may think that prayer is something extra-
ordinarily difficult, or that it is just for special people. In
the Gospels we see people of very different backgrounds
approaching Our Lord with confidence: Nicodemus,
Bartimeus, the children whom Our Lord particularly likes
to be with – a mother, a father who has a sick child, a
thief, the Wise Men, Anna, Simeon, his friends in
Bethany. All of them, and now we, speak to God.

29.3 Humility. Talking to Jesus. Ejaculatory prayers. Turning to St Joseph, teacher of the interior life.

What matters in prayer is perseverance and good
dispositions; amongst them faith and humility. We
cannot come to our prayer like the pharisee in that
parable meant for *some who trusted in themselves ... and
despised others.*[7] The pharisee *stood and prayed thus
with himself, 'God I thank thee that I am not like other*

---

[6] St Teresa of Avila, *The Way of Perfection*, 25:3
[7] Luke 18:9

men, extortioners ... . I fast twice a week ...'. We realise straightaway that the Pharisee has entered the Temple without any love. He is the centre of his thoughts and the object of his own estimation. Consequently, instead of praising God, he praises himself. There is no love in his prayer, no charity, no humility. He does not need God.

On the other hand we can – with our mind fixed on the person we are talking to – learn a lot from the prayer of the tax collector, who is humble, attentive and confident. We endeavour not to make it a monologue in which we just think about ourselves, recalling situations without referring them to God, failing to control our imagination and so on.

Because he lacked humility, the Pharisee left the Temple without having prayed. Even in that his hidden pride manifested itself.

Our Lord asks us for simplicity, to acknowledge our faults, and to talk about what is of interest to us and to Him. *You write: 'To pray is to talk with God, but about what?' About what? About Him, about yourself; joys, sorrows, successes and failures, noble ambitions, daily worries, weaknesses! And acts of thanksgiving and petitions: and Love and reparation. In a word: to get to know him and to get to know yourself: to get acquainted.*[8]

'Et in meditatione mea exardescit ignis.' And in my meditation a fire shall flame out. That is why you go to pray: to become a bonfire, a living flame giving heat and light. So, when you are not able to go on, when you feel that your fire is dying out, if you cannot throw on it sweet-smelling logs, throw on the branches and twigs of short vocal prayers and ejaculations, to keep the bonfire burning. And you will not have wasted your time.[9]

---

[8] St. J. Escrivá, *The Way*, 91
[9] *ibid*, 92

Particularly at the beginning, and again at certain times, it will be helpful to use a book, as a cripple uses crutches, so as to make progress in prayer. Many saints did just that. *If it was not just after receiving Holy Communion, I never dared to start the prayer without a book; my soul feared being at prayer without a book, as though I were going to fight a great crowd of people. With this remedy, which was like a companion or a shield which could receive the blows of so many thoughts, I felt consoled.*[10]

We should habitually conclude our prayer with definite resolutions to improve. We will ask Our Lord sincerely: What do you want of me in this particular thing that I have been considering? How can I improve now in this virtue? What resolution should I make to carry out your Will in the next few months?

Nobody in this world has known how to talk to Jesus as his Mother did and, next to his mother, St Joseph who must have spent long hours gazing on him, talking to him, simply being in his company and venerating Him. So, *if anyone cannot find a teacher to teach him how to pray, let him take this glorious saint as his teacher and he will not stray from the path.*[11]

As we finish our prayer, we contemplate Joseph very close to Mary. He is full of consideration and attention towards her. Jesus is about to be born. He has prepared that cave as well as he could. We ask him to help us to prepare our souls so that we are not dissipated and distracted when we have Jesus so close to us.

---

[10] St Teresa of Avila, *Life*, 4:7
[11] *ibid*, 6:3

CHRISTMAS DAY – 25 DECEMBER

30. CHRISTMAS MEDITATION

30.1 In Bethlehem they did not want to receive Christ. Today, too, many people do not want to receive him.

In those days a decree went out from Caesar Augustus that all the world should be enrolled.[1]

Now we can see clearly that this decree of the Roman Emperor's was part of God's providence. It is the reason why Mary and Joseph went to Bethlehem, and Jesus was born there as had been prophesied many centuries before.[2]

Our Lady knew that Jesus' birth was about to take place and she set out on that journey with her thoughts centred on the Child who was to be born of her in the town of David.

They came to Bethlehem, both with the joy of having reached the place of their ancestors and with the tiredness caused by travelling along badly-made roads for four or five days. In her condition, Our Lady must have been very tired when she arrived. And in Bethlehem they could not find anywhere to stay. *There was no place for them in the inn,*[3] says St Luke briefly. Perhaps Joseph judged that the crowded inn was not a suitable place for Our Lady, especially in those circumstances. St Joseph must have knocked on many doors before taking Mary to a stable on the outskirts of the town. We can well imagine the scene: Joseph explaining time and again with growing anxiety, the same story, *that they had come from*

---

[1] Luke 2:10
[2] Mic 5:2
[3] cf Luke 2:7

..., and Mary a few feet away seeing Joseph and hearing the refusals. They did not let Christ in. They shut the doors on him. Mary feels sorry for Joseph and for those people. How cold the world is towards its God!

Perhaps it was Our lady who suggested to Joseph that they could stay provisionally in one of those caves, which served as stables outside the town. She probably encouraged him, telling him not to worry, that they would manage ... Joseph would feel comforted by Mary's words and her smile. So they made their lodging there with the few belongings they had been able to bring from Nazareth: the swaddling clothes, some items that she herself had prepared with that joy that only mothers can experience when they prepare for their first child.

It was there that the greatest event of humanity's history took place, with the utmost simplicity. *And while they were there,* St Luke tells us, *the time came for her to be delivered.*[4] Mary lovingly wrapped Jesus *in swaddling clothes and laid him in a manger.*

The Virgin had a more perfect faith than any other before her or since. All her gestures were an expression of her faith and her tenderness. She would have kissed his feet because he was her Lord, his cheek because he was her Son. She would have remained quietly contemplating him for a very long time.

Later Mary placed the Child in Joseph's arms. Joseph well knows that this the Son of the Most-High, whom he must care for, protect and teach a trade. Joseph's whole life centres around this defenceless Child.

Jesus, newly born, does not speak; but he is the eternal Word of the Father. It has been said that the manger is a Chair of learning. Today we should *learn the lessons which Jesus teaches us, even when he is just a*

---

[4] Luke 2:6

newly born child, from the very moment he opens his eyes on this blessed land of men.[5]

He is born poor, and he teaches us that happiness is not to be found in an abundance of earthly goods. He comes into the world without any ostentation, encouraging us to be humble and not to depend on the applause of men. *God humbled himself to allow us to get near him, so that we could give our love in exchange for his, so that our freedom might bow, not at the sight of his power merely, but before the wonder of his humility.*[6]

We make a resolution to live the virtues of detachment and humility. We look at Mary and we see her filled with joy. She knows that a new era has begun for humanity – that of the Messiah, her Son. We ask her never to let us lose the joy of being beside Jesus.

30.2 The Messiah's birth. The 'Chair' of Bethlehem.

Jesus, Mary and Joseph were alone. But God sought out simple people as their companions: some shepherds, perhaps because, as they were humble, they would not be dismayed at finding the Messiah in a cave, wrapped in swaddling clothes.

It is to the shepherds of that district that the prophet Isaiah referred: *those who dwelt in a land of deep darkness, on them light has shone.*[7]

On this first night it is in them alone that the prophecy is fulfilled, *And an angel of the Lord appeared to them and the glory of the Lord shone around them.*[8] *And the angel said to them, 'Be not afraid; for behold I bring you good news of a great joy which will come to all*

---

[5] St. J. Escrivá, *Christ is passing by*, 14
[6] *ibid*, 18
[7] Is 9:2
[8] Luke 2:9

the people; for to you is born this day in the city of David, a Saviour who is Christ the Lord'.[9]

That night they are the first and only people to learn the news. *On the other hand, today, millions of men throughout the world know of it. The light of that night in Bethlehem has reached many hearts, but nevertheless, at the same time, darkness remains. Sometimes it even seems more intense ... The men of that night welcomed the news; they experienced great joy – the joy that comes forth from light. The world's darkness overcome by the light of the birth of God ...*

It does not matter that on this first night, the night of God's birth, the joy of that event should have reached only a few hearts: it does not matter. It is destined for every human heart! It is the joy of the whole human race, a superhuman joy! Could there be any greater joy than this, any greater Good News than this: man has been accepted by God so as to become his son in this Son of God who has become man?[10]

God also wanted those shepherds to be the first bearers of the news: they would go around telling *all they had heard and seen. And all who heard it wondered at what the shepherds told them.*[11] In the same way Jesus reveals himself to us in the midst of the ordinary incidents of each day; and we need the same dispositions of simplicity and humility in order to reach him. It is possible that throughout our lives he gives us signs that mean nothing to us if we see him merely humanly. We have to be alert so as to discover Jesus in the simplicity of ordinary life, *wrapped in swaddling clothes and laid in a manger*, without any showy manifestations. Everyone

---

[9] Luke 2:10

[10] John Paul II, *Homily of the Mass of Christmas Night*, 1980

[11] Luke 2:18

who sees Christ feels moved to make him known straight away. He cannot wait.

Naturally, the shepherds would not have set out without taking gifts for the baby. *In the eastern world of those days it was inconceivable that anybody should present himself before a respected person without a gift. They would take what they had; a lamb, cheese, butter, milk, curd.*[12]

Doubtless it is not far removed from reality to imagine the scene as it is portrayed in the countless cribs of our days and in the Christmas carols which Christians sing with simplicity and which many of us may have made the theme of our prayer.

Mary and Joseph, surprised and delighted, invite the shy shepherds to come in and see the Child, to kiss him, to sing to him, and to leave their gifts beside the manger. Nor can we go to the cave of Bethlehem without taking our gift.

Perhaps what Our Lady would thank us for is that our heart be more devoted, more pure, more cheerful because it is conscious of its divine filiation: a heart which we have made better disposed through a contrite Confession, so that Our Lord can live more fully in us. The confession that perhaps for some time now, God has been waiting for ...

Mary and Joseph are inviting us to go in. And once inside we say to Jesus with the Church: *King of the universe, whom the shepherds found wrapped in swaddling clothes, help us always to imitate your poverty and your simplicity.*[13]

---

[12] F. M. Willan, *Life of Mary*, p 110
[13] *Divine Office, Lauds, Prayers, 5 January*

30.3 Adoration of the shepherds. Humility and simplicity in order to recognise Christ in our lives.

Let us all rejoice in the Lord, for our Saviour has been born in the world. Today true peace has come down to us from heaven.[14] *We have heard, my brethren, the announcement, full of sweetness and 'worthy of all acceptance' that 'Jesus Christ, the Son of God, is born in Bethlehem of Judah'. My very soul has melted at the sound of these words and my spirit is burning in my bosom, eager with its constant ardour of desire to communicate to you its own joy and exultation.*[15]

Let us all set out to contemplate and adore Jesus, for we all need him. He is the only one we really need.

There is no journey so great as that of seeking Christ
There is no journey so great as that of looking for Christ
There is no journey so great

go the words of a popular Spanish carol, telling us that no path is worth following unless it leads us to the Baby Jesus.

Today our Saviour is born. There can be no room for sadness when Life has just been born; that Life which overcomes all fear of death and fills us with the joy of the pledge of eternity.

Nobody should feel excluded from sharing in such joy. Our reason for rejoicing is common to all, because Our Lord, destroyer of sin and death, not finding anyone free of sin has come to free us all. Let the just man rejoice, as victory approaches. Let the Gentile rejoice, for he is called to life.

For the Son, in the fulness of time ... assumed our human nature in order to reconcile the human race with

---

[14] *Entrance Antiphon, Midnight Mass*
[15] St Bernard, *Sermons for Christmas Eve*, 6:1

its Creator.[16] Hence springs the joy of these feast-days, like a river overflowing its banks.

During these days of Christmas we sing with exultation because love will be among us till the end of time. The presence of the Child is Love among men; the world is no longer a place of darkness; those who seek for love know where to find it. It is essentially love that each man needs – even those men who claim to be already fully satisfied.

Today, whenever we go to kiss an image of the Child Jesus, or contemplate a crib or meditate on this great mystery, let us thank God for having wanted to come down to us so that we could understand him and love him. Let us make up our minds to become as little children so as to enter one day into the kingdom of heaven. We will finish our prayer asking our Father God, *that we may share in the divinity of Christ, who humbled himself to share in our humanity.*[17]

Holy Mary, Mother of God, pray for us.

---

[16] St Leo the Great, *Sermon on the Birth of Our Lord*, 1:3
[17] *Collect, Christmas Day*

FIRST SUNDAY AFTER CHRISTMAS
– FEAST OF THE HOLY FAMILY

31. THE HOLY FAMILY OF NAZARETH

31.1 Jesus wanted to launch the Redemption of the world from the heart of a family.

And when they had performed everything according to the law of the Lord, they returned into Galilee, to their own city, Nazareth. And the Child grew and became strong, filled with wisdom; and the favour of God was upon him.[1]

The Messiah wanted to start his redemptive task in the bosom of a simple, ordinary family. The first thing that Jesus sanctified with his presence was a home. Nothing extraordinary happened during those years in Nazareth where Jesus spent the greater part of his life.

Joseph was the head of the family. He was a father according to the law and it was he who supported Jesus and Mary with his work. It is he who received the message as to what name he must give the Child: *And you shall call his name Jesus*, and heard the words of those who wanted to protect the Child: *Rise, take the Child and his Mother and flee to Egypt* (Matt 2:13). *Rise, take the Child and his Mother and go to the land of Israel. Do not go to Bethlehem, but to Nazareth* (cf Matt 2:20-23). It was from Joseph that Jesus learned his trade, which was to be his means of earning a living. Jesus must often have shown his admiration and affection for him.

From Mary, Jesus learned certain turns of phrase, popular expressions full of wisdom which he was later to

---

[1] Luke 2:39-40

use in his preaching. He saw how she kept back a little dough from one day to the next, so that it could act as leaven; she added water and mixed it with the new dough, leaving it to rise, well covered with a clean cloth. When his mother mended their clothes, the Child used to watch her. If a garment was torn she would look for a piece of cloth to match. Jesus, with a child's curiosity, would ask her why she did not use a new piece of cloth. Our Lady explained to him that when new patches are washed they pull on the old cloth and tear it; that was why she had to make a patch out of used cloth ... The best clothes, the ones they wore on feast days, were kept in a chest. Mary also took great care to place certain aromatic plants between them so as to prevent moths from damaging them. Years later these occurrences will appear in Jesus' preaching. We never forget this teaching which is fundamental to ordinary life. *Mary spent nearly every day of her life like millions of other women who look after their families, bring up their children and take care of the house. Mary sanctifies the ordinary everyday things – what some people wrongly regard as unimportant and insignificant: everyday work, looking after those closest to you, visits to friends and relatives. What a blessed ordinariness, that can be so full of love of God!*[2]

Between Joseph and Mary there existed a holy affection, a spirit of service, and a mutual desire for each other's happiness. This is Jesus' family: sacred, holy, exemplary, a model of human virtues, ready to carry out God's will exactly. A Christian home must be an imitation of the house of Nazareth: a place where there is plenty of room for God so that He can be right at the centre of the love that members of the family have for one another.

---

[2] St. J. Escrivá, *Christ is passing by*, 148

Is our home like this? Do we dedicate to it the time and attention that it deserves? Is Jesus its centre? Do we live only for the others? These are some questions which we could ask in our prayer today, whilst we contemplate Jesus, Mary and Joseph on the feast that the Church dedicates to them.

31.2 The mission of parents. The example of Mary and Joseph.

In the family, *The parents by word and example are the first heralds of the faith with regard to their children.*[3] In the case of the Holy Family this was achieved in a most singular manner. Jesus learned the meaning of the things around him from his parents.

The Holy Family would have devoutly recited the traditional prayers which were said in every Jewish home. In that house, however, everything that referred particularly to God had a new meaning and content. How keenly and fervently, and with what a spirit of recollection, would Jesus have repeated the verses of Sacred Scripture which all Hebrew children had to learn.[4] He would often recite these prayers learned from his parents' lips.

When they contemplate these scenes, parents should frequently consider the words of Pope Paul VI, recalled for us by Blessed John Paul II, *Do you teach your children the Christian prayers? Do you prepare them, in conjunction with the priests, for the sacraments that they receive when they are young – Confession, Communion and Confirmation? Do you encourage them, when they are sick, to think of Christ suffering, to invoke the aid of the Blessed Virgin and the saints? Do you say the family*

---

[3] Second Vatican Council, *Lumen gentium*, 11
[4] cf Ps 55:18; Dan 6:11; Ps 119

Rosary together ...? Do you pray with your children, with the whole domestic community, at least sometimes? Your example of honesty in thought and action, joined to some common prayer, is a lesson for life and an act of worship of singular value. In this way you bring peace to your homes: Pax huic domui. Remember, it is thus that you build up the Church.[5]

If Christian homes imitate that home formed by the Holy Family of Nazareth, they will be *bright and cheerful homes*[6] because each member of the family will struggle first of all to get to know God and, with a spirit of sacrifice, will endeavour to make life more pleasant for those around him.

The family is a school of virtues and the ordinary place for us to find God. *Husbands and wives will achieve this aim by exercising the virtues of faith and hope, facing serenely all the great and small problems which confront any family, and will be persevering in the love and enthusiasm with which they fulfil their duties. They will learn to smile and forget about themselves in order to pay attention to others. Husband and wife will listen to each other and to their children, showing them that they are really loved and understood. They will forget about the unimportant little frictions that selfishness can magnify out of all proportion. They do lovingly all the small acts of service that make up their daily life together.*

The aim is this: to sanctify family life, while creating at the same time a true family atmosphere. Many Christian virtues are necessary in order to sanctify each day of one's life. First, the theological virtues and then all the others: prudence, loyalty, sincerity, humility,

---

[5] John Paul II, Apostolic Exhortation, *Familiaris consortio*, 60
[6] cf St. J. Escrivá, *Christ is passing by*, 22

industriousness, cheerfulness ...[7]

These virtues will strengthen the unity that the Church teaches us to pray for: *You, who by being born into a family, strengthen family bonds, let there be an increase in unity within the family.*[8]

31.3 The Holy Family, an example for all families.

United to Christ, a family is a member of his Mystical Body, and has been called the *domestic Church.*[9] That community of love and faith has to manifest itself in all circumstances, as the Church herself does, as a living witness to Christ. *The Christian family proclaims aloud both the present power of the kingdom of God and the hope of the life to come.*[10] The faithfulness of the spouses to their matrimonial vocation will lead them, among other things, to pray for vocations for their children so that they may dedicate themselves fully to God's service with a spirit of self-denial.

In the Holy Family, every Christian home finds its most perfect exemplar; in it the Christian family can discover what it should do and how it should behave so as to bring about the sanctification and full human development of each one of its members. *Nazareth is the school where we begin to understand Jesus' life; it is the school where we begin to get to know his Gospel. Here we learn to observe, to listen, to meditate, to penetrate the mysterious depths of this simple, humble and charming manifestation of the Son of God among men. Here we learn too, perhaps without realizing it, to*

---

[7] ibid, 23
[8] *Divine Office, Prayers II, Vespers of 1 January*
[9] Second Vatican Council, *Lumen gentium*, 11
[10] ibid, 35

imitate that life.[11]

The family is the simplest and most basic form of society. It is the main *school of all the social virtues*. It is the seed-bed of social life. For it is in the family that we learn to practise obedience, a concern for others, a sense of responsibility, understanding and mutual help, a loving co-ordination of essentially different characters. This becomes a reality, particularly in large families, which have always been praised by the Church.[12] Indeed, it has been proved that the health of a society is measured by the health of its families. This is why direct attacks against the family (as happens with legislation allowing divorce) are direct attacks against society itself, whose results are not long in making themselves felt.

May the Virgin Mary, who is the Mother of the Church, also be the Mother of the 'Church of the home'. Thanks to her motherly aid, may each Christian family really become a 'little Church' in which the mystery of the Church of Christ is mirrored and given new life. May she, the Handmaid of the Lord, be an example of humble and generous acceptance of the will of God. May she, the Sorrowful Mother at the foot of the Cross, comfort the sufferings and dry the tears of those in distress because of the difficulties of their family life. May Christ the Lord, the Universal King, the King of Families, be present in every Christian home as he was at Cana, bestowing light, joy, serenity and strength.[13]

Today we pray to the Holy Family in a very special way for each member of our families and in particular for the one in most need.

---

[11] Paul VI, *Homily*, Nazareth, 5 January 1964
[12] cf Second Vatican Council, *Gaudium et spes*, 52
[13] John Paul II, *op cit*, 86

THE CHRISTMAS SEASON
– 26 DECEMBER

32. ST STEPHEN – THE FIRST MARTYR

32.1 Following Jesus Christ leads to many kinds of calumny and persecution.

The gates of heaven were opened for blessed Stephen, who was found to be first among the number of the Martyrs and therefore is crowned triumphant in heaven.[1]

We have only just celebrated the birth of Our Lord and already the liturgy presents us with the feast of the first person to give his life for this Baby who has been born. *Yesterday, we wrapped Christ in swaddling clothes; today, he clothes Stephen with the garment of immortality. Yesterday, a narrow manger cradled the baby Christ; today, the infinite heaven has received Stephen in triumph.*[2]

The Church wants to make us realise that the Cross is always very close to Jesus and his followers. As he struggles for perfect righteousness – sanctity – in this world, the Christian will meet difficult situations and attacks by the enemies of God. Our Lord has warned us: *If the world hates you, know that it has hated me before it hated you ... . Remember the word that I said to you; a servant is not greater than his master: If they persecuted me they will persecute you.*[3] Since the very beginning of the Church this prophecy has been fulfilled. And in our days too, if we really follow Our Lord, we are going to suffer difficulties and persecutions in one way or another

---

[1] *Entrance Antiphon of the Mass*
[2] St Fulgentius, *Sermon 3*
[3] John 15:18-20

and of different kinds. *Every age is an age of martyrdom,* St Augustine tells us. *Don't say that Christians are not suffering persecution; the Apostle's words are always true ... : All who desire to live a godly life in Christ Jesus will be persecuted.*(2 Tim 3:12) *All,* he says, *with no one being excluded or exempted. If you want to test the truth of this saying, you have only to begin to lead a pious life and you will see what good reason he had for saying this.*[4]

At the very beginning of the Church the first Christians in Jerusalem were persecuted by the Jewish authorities. The Apostles were flogged for preaching Christ Jesus and suffered it joyfully: *then they left the presence of the Council, rejoicing that they were counted worthy to suffer dishonour for the name of Jesus.*[5]

The Apostles must have remembered the words of Our Lord: *Blessed are you when men revile you and persecute you and utter all kinds of evil against you falsely on my account. Rejoice and be glad, for your reward is great in heaven, for so men persecuted the prophets who were before you.*[6] *Don't say that they didn't suffer, but that they rejoiced to suffer. We can see that by the use to which they instantly put their freedom: immediately after the flogging they gave themselves up to preaching with wonderful zeal.*[7]

A short while afterwards the blood of Stephen was the first to be poured out for Christ. And this has never ceased. In fact, when Paul came to Rome, Christians were already known by the unmistakeable sign of the Cross and of contradiction: *with regard to this sect* – said

---

[4] St Augustine, *Sermon 6, 2*

[5] Acts 5:41

[6] Matt 5:11-12

[7] St John Chrysostom, *Homily on the Acts of the Apostles*, 14

the Jews of Rome to Paul – *we know that every where it is spoken against.*[8]

Our Lord, when he calls us or asks us for something, knows all about our limitations and the difficulties which we shall meet on the way. When the time of difficulty arrives, Jesus will be at our side, helping us with his grace: *In the world you have tribulation; but be of good cheer, I have overcome the world,*[9] he tells us.

We shouldn't be disconcerted if sometimes on our journey towards sanctity we have to suffer some tribulation, trivial or serious, in a world with so many heathen characteristics. We should then ask Our Lord for the grace to imitate St Stephen, in his courage, in his joy and in his zeal for proclaiming the truth of Christ, even in these circumstances.

32.2 Persecution still goes on. How a Christian should react to it.

Persecution has taken many forms. During the first centuries it tried to destroy the Christian faith by physical violence. At other times Christians have also been – and are – deprived of their most elementary rights, or attempts are made to confuse simple people by campaigns aimed at undermining their faith. Even in countries with a great Christian tradition, every sort of obstacle and difficulty is put in the way of parents who wish to educate their children in a truly Christian way. Or Christians, simply because they are Christians, are denied a fair chance of advancing in their profession.

In societies which describe themselves as 'free' it is not unusual for a Christian to have to live in an obviously hostile atmosphere. Then there is hidden persecution, by

---

[8] Acts 28:22
[9] John 16:33

a sarcastic ridiculing of Christian values or by pressure of opinion which tries to frighten the 'weaker brethren' into conformity. It adds up to a bloodless but severe persecution which often makes use of calumny and slander.

In former times, says St Augustine, *Christians were incited to renounce Christ; now they are taught to deny Christ. Then they were forced, now they are taught; then violence was used, now it is deception; then one heard the shouts of the enemy; now, when he prowls around, gentle and insinuating, it is difficult to recognize him. Everyone knows how he tried to force Christians to deny Christ: he tried to attract them to himself so that they would renounce him; but they confessed Christ and were crowned by him. Now they are taught to deny Christ by trickery, because he doesn't want them to realise that he is drawing them away from Christ.*[10] The saint seems to be talking about our own times.

Our Lord also wished to warn his followers not to be disconcerted when they were misjudged, not by the heathen, but by their own brothers in the Faith and who, usually because of envy, stereotyped reactions, or lack of rectitude of intention, would think that they were *offering service to God* [11] by this unjust behaviour. All contradictions, but especially these last, must be endured in the company of Our Lord in the Tabernacle: there the apostolate in which we are working will acquire a special fruitfulness.

Circumstances like these mean that Our Lord is calling us in a special way to be united with him through prayer. They are times when we have to display great courage and patience, without ever returning evil for evil. What is more, our interior life has need of contradictions

---

[10] St Augustine, *Commentaries on the Psalms*, 39:1
[11] John 16:2

and obstacles in order to grow strong and consistent. With the help of Our Lord the soul comes out of these trials purified and more humble. We taste the joy of Our Lord in a special way and can say with St Paul: *I am filled with comfort, with all our affliction I am overjoyed.*[12]

Grant, Lord, we pray, that we may imitate what we worship, and so learn to love even our enemies, for we celebrate the heavenly birthday of a man who knew how to pray even for his persecutors.[13]

32.3 The reward for having suffered any kind of persecution for the sake of Jesus Christ. Strengthening the hope of Heaven.

The Christian who is persecuted for following Jesus will draw from this experience a great capacity for understanding other people and a firm resolution never to wound them, never to offend them, never to treat them badly. Our Lord asks us, as well, to pray for those who persecute us[14] *veritatem facientes in caritate* – speaking the truth in love.[15] These words of St Paul show us how to teach the doctrine of the Gospel without losing the charity of Jesus Christ.

The last beatitude finishes with a fervent promise from Our Lord: *Blessed are you when men revile you and persecute you and utter all kinds of evil against you falsely on my account. Rejoice and be glad, for your reward is great in heaven.*[16] Our Lord is always a generous paymaster.

Stephen was Christianity's first martyr and died for

---

[12] 2 Cor 7:4
[13] *Collect of the Mass*
[14] Matt 5:44
[15] Eph 4:15
[16] Matt 5:11

proclaiming the truth. We too have been called to spread Christ's truth without fear or concealment: *Do not fear those who kill the body but cannot kill the soul.*[17] Because of this, if it is a question of proclaiming Christ's saving doctrine, we cannot give in when we come up against obstacles. Rather we must follow the saying: *Don't be afraid of the truth, even though the truth might mean your death.*[18]

The day on which Christians are persecuted, slandered or ill-treated for being disciples of Jesus Christ is for them a day of victory and profit: *Your reward is great in heaven.* Even in this life Our Lord pays with interest; but it is in the next, we can hope, if we are faithful, for an enormous reward. Here, joy can never be perfect; but when we come close to Our Lord, through prayer and the sacraments, we enjoy a foretaste of eternal happiness. *I consider*, wrote St Paul to the first Christians in Rome, *that the sufferings of this present time are not worth comparing with the glory that is to be revealed to us.*[19]

The history of the Church shows that, at times, tribulation makes someone grow cowardly and cold in his relationship with God; at other times, on the contrary, it ripens sanctity in souls which take up the cross of every day and follow Christ, becoming identified with him. We always see this double possibility: the same difficulty – illness, misunderstandings, etc – has different effects according to the dispositions of the soul. If we want to be saints it is obvious that our disposition has to be that of always following Our Lord closely, in spite of all obstacles.

---

[17] Matt 10:28
[18] St. J. Escrivá, *The Way*, 34
[19] Rom 8:18

At times of setback, it is very helpful to foster the hope of heaven. It will help us to be firm in the faith when we are faced with any kind of persecution or attempts to confuse us. *If you always pursue this determination to die rather than fail to reach the end of the road, the Lord may bring you through this life with a certain degree of thirst but in the life which never ends, he will give you great abundance to drink and you will have no fear of its failing you.*[20]

In times of external difficulty we have to help our brothers in the faith to put up a firm resistance to all opposition. We can help them a great deal with our example, with our words, with our cheerfulness, with our faithfulness and with our prayer. And we have to take especial care to show them real brotherly love at such times, because *a brother helped by his brother is like a strong city;*[21] he cannot be taken by storm.

Mary, our Mother, is especially close to us in all difficult circumstances. Today we entrust ourselves in a particular way to the first martyr who gave his life for Christ in order that we may be strong in all tribulation.

---

[20] St Teresa of Avila, *The Way of Perfection*, 20:2
[21] Prov 18:19

33. THE DISCIPLE WHOM JESUS LOVED

33.1 The Apostle's vocation. His faithfulness. Our own vocation.

St John the Apostle was a native of Bethsaida, a Galilean town on the northern shore of the Sea of Tiberias. His parents were Zebedee and Salome and his brother was St James the Greater. They were a well-to-do family of fisherfolk who, when they met Our Lord, put themselves completely and unhesitatingly at his disposal. John and James, in reply to Jesus' call, *left their father Zebedee in the boat with the hired servants and followed him.*[1] Salome, their mother, also followed Jesus, helping him with her possessions in Galilee and Jerusalem, and accompanying him even to Calvary.[2]

John had been a disciple of the Baptist when he was baptizing in the Jordan, until one day Jesus passed close by and the Precursor pointed him out: *Behold the Lamb of God. The two disciples heard him say that and they followed Jesus ... and they stayed with him that day.*[3] St John never forgot that meeting. He hasn't told us what he talked about with the Master that day. We only know that he never left Him again. When, as a very old man, he wrote his Gospel he couldn't resist putting in the very hour of his first meeting with Jesus: *it was about the*

---

[1] Mark 1:20
[2] Mark 15:40-41
[3] John 1:35-39

tenth hour,[4] four o'clock in the afternoon by our time.

He went back to his home in Bethsaida, to his work as a fisherman. Soon afterwards Our Lord, having already prepared him at that first meeting, called him specifically to be one of the group of the Twelve. St John, by far the youngest of the Apostles – he was not yet twenty when he answered Our Lord's call[5] – did so with all his heart, with a love that was undivided, exclusively for Jesus.

For St John, as for everyone else, his vocation gave a new meaning even to the most ordinary things. The whole of life is affected by Our Lord's plans for each one of us. *The discovery of one's personal vocation, is the most important point in each person's existence. It changes everything without changing anything; just as a landscape, without changing, is different before and after the sun goes down, beneath the light of the moon, or wrapped in the darkness of night. Every discovery gives a new beauty to things, and a new light creates new shadows; one discovery is the prelude to other discoveries of new lights and more beauty.*[6]

John's whole life was centred on his Lord and Master; in his faithfulness to Jesus he found the meaning of his life. He put up no resistance of any kind to His call; he was found on Calvary when all the others had disappeared. This is what our life, too, has to be like, because even though Our Lord calls some people in a special way, all his preaching comprises a vocation, an invitation to follow him into a new life whose secret he possesses: *if any man would come after me ...*[7]

---

[4] John 1:39
[5] *The Navarre Bible*, St John, p 20
[6] F. Suarez, *Mary of Nazareth*, p 58
[7] Matt 16:24

Our Lord has chosen all of us[8] – some of us with a specific vocation – to follow him, to imitate him and to carry on in the world the work of his Redemption. And from all of us he expects a joyful and unshakeable faithfulness like St John's – even in the most difficult moments.

33.2 Details of our Lord's special love. Entrusted with the care of Our Lady.

This is John, who reclined at the Lord's breast at supper, the blessed Apostle, to whom celestial secrets were revealed and who spread the words of life through all the world.[9]

Our Lord showed St John, together with Peter, special marks of friendship and confidence. The Evangelist refers to himself discreetly as *the disciple whom Jesus loved.*[10] He lets us know that Jesus had a special affection for him. Thus, he has recorded that at the solemn moment during the Last Supper when Jesus announced that one of the Twelve was going to betray him, he didn't hesitate to ask the Lord, leaning against his breast, who it was who would be the traitor.[11] Our Lord's supreme expression of confidence in *the beloved disciple* took place when, from the Cross, he entrusted to him the greatest love that he had on earth: his most holy Mother. If the most outstanding moment in John's life was that in which Jesus called him to leave all things and follow him, there on Calvary he received a more refined and intimate charge: that of caring for the Mother of God.

---

[8] Rom 1:7; 2 Cor 1:1
[9] *Entrance Antiphon of the Mass*
[10] cf John 13:23; 19:26 etc
[11] John 13:23

When Jesus saw his mother, and the disciple whom he loved, standing near, he said to his mother, 'Woman, behold your son!' Then he said to the disciple, 'Behold your mother!' And from that hour the disciple took her to his own home.[12] *To John, as to no one else, Our Lady could talk about all those things which she kept in her heart.*[13]

Today, on his feast, let us look at *the disciple whom Jesus loved* with a holy envy for the immense gift which the Lord bestowed on him; and, at the same time, we have to thank him for the care which he took of her until the end of her days here on earth.

All Christians, represented by John, have become Mary's children. We have to learn from St John to treat her with trustful confidence. He, *the disciple whom Jesus loved, brought Mary into his home, into his life. Spiritual writers have seen these words of the Gospel as an invitation to all Christians to bring Mary into their lives. Mary certainly wants us to invoke her, to approach her confidently, to appeal to her as our mother, asking her to 'show that you are our Mother'.*[14]

We can also imagine the enormous influence which Our Lady must have had on the soul of the young Apostle. We can get a more adequate idea of it by remembering those periods in our life – perhaps the present is one of them – when we ourselves have turned to the Mother of God and had a specially close relationship with her.

---

[12] John 19:26-27
[13] cf Luke 2:51
[14] St. J. Escrivá, *Christ is passing by*, 140

33.3 John's faith and love made him recognize Christ in the distance; we must learn to recognize Him in our daily life. Petitions to St John.

A few days after our Lord's Resurrection some of his disciples met together by the Sea of Tiberias, in Galilee, obeying the instructions which the risen Jesus had given them.[15] They had gone back to their work as fishermen. Among them were John and Peter.

Our Lord went to look for his friends. The Gospel paints a moving picture of Jesus with the men who, in spite of everything, had remained faithful. *He passes by, close to his Apostles, close to those souls who have given themselves to him and they don't realise that he is there. How often Christ is not only near us, but in us; yet we still live in such a human way ...! The disciples recall what they have heard so often from their Master's lips: fishers of men, apostles. And they realise that all things are possible because it is He who is directing their fishing.*

'Whereupon the disciple whom Jesus loved said to Peter: "It is the Lord." 'Love is farsighted. Love is the first to appreciate kindness. The adolescent Apostle, who felt a deep and firm affection for Jesus, because he loved Christ with all the purity and tenderness of a heart that had never been corrupted, exclaimed: 'It is the Lord!'.

'Simon Peter, hearing him say that it was the Lord, girded up his fisherman's coat and sprang into the sea.' Peter personifies faith. Full of marvellous daring, he leaps into the sea. With a love like John's and a faith like Peter's, what is there that can stop us?[16]

It is the Lord! This cry has to rise from our hearts too, in the middle of our work, when we are ill, in all our

---

[15] cf Matt 28:7
[16] St. J. Escrivá, *Friends of God*, 265-266

dealings with the people who share our lives. We must ask St John to teach us to recognize Christ's face in the middle of all the realities which surround us, because he is very near to us and he alone is able to give meaning to all the things that we do.

In addition to what we learn from Sacred Scripture, Tradition hands down to us some details which confirm the great care which St John took to preserve the purity of doctrine and his faithfulness to the commandment of fraternal love.[17] St Jerome tells us that when John was a very old man he repeated again and again to the disciples who came to see him, *Little children, love one another.* They asked him why he always went on repeating the same thing. St John answered, *It is the Lord's commandment and, if that is kept, it is enough.*[18]

We can ask St John for many things today: especially that young people may search for Christ, meet him and have the generosity to follow him when he calls. We can ask him, too, to intercede with Our Lord so that we may be as faithful as he was; that we may show the Successor of Peter the same love and respect which he showed to the first Vicar of Christ on earth; that he may teach us to treat Mary, the Mother of God and our Mother, with more love and more confidence. We ask him that the people around us be able to tell that we are disciples of Jesus by the way in which we treat them. *O God, who through the blessed Apostle John have unlocked for us the secrets of your Word, grant, we pray, that we may grasp with proper undestanding what he has so marvellously brought to our ears.*[19]

---

[17] *The Navarre Bible*, St John, p 24
[18] St Jerome, *Commentary on Galatians*, 3:6
[19] *Collect of the Mass*

34. THE HOLY INNOCENTS, MARTYRS

34.1 Suffering, reality in our life. The sanctification of suffering.

Herod, when he saw that he had been tricked by the wise men, was in a furious rage, and he sent and killed all the male children in Bethlehem and in all that region who were two years old or under, according to the time which he had ascertained from the wise men.[1]

There is no easy explanation for suffering, least of all for the suffering of the innocent. St Matthew's narrative, which we read in today's Mass, shows us the suffering, apparently useless and unjust, of some children who gave their lives for a Person and for a Truth whom they didn't even know. Suffering is a frequent cause of scandal. For many people it is like a great wall which prevents them from seeing God and his infinite love for men. Why doesn't Almighty God prevent such apparently useless suffering?

Suffering is indeed a mystery. Yet, through faith, the Christian can discover in the darkness of his own or other people's suffering, the loving and provident hand of his Father God who knows so much more and sees so much further than he himself can. Then he begins to understand to some extent the words of St Paul to the first Christians in Rome: *We know that in everything God works for good with those who love him,*[2] including everything that

---

[1] Matt 2:16
[2] Rom 5:28

seems to us piercingly inexplicable or incomprehensible.

Nor must we forget that our greatest happiness and our most authentic good are not always those which we dream of and long for. It is difficult for us to see things in their true perspective: we can only take in a very small part of complete reality. We only see the tiny piece of reality that is here, in front of us. We are inclined to feel that earthly existence is the only real one and often consider our time on earth to be the period in which all our longings for perfect happiness ought to be fulfilled. *There is anguish for us, twenty centuries later, in thinking of the slain babies and their parents. For the babies the agony was soon over; in the next world they would come to know whom they had died to save and for all eternity would have that glory. For the parents, the pain would have lasted longer; but at death they too must have found that there was a special sense in which God was in their debt, as he had never been indebted to any. They and their children were the only ones who ever agonized in order to save God's life ...* [3]

Suffering comes in many forms. No one willingly looks for it in any of them. And yet, Jesus proclaimed as *blessed* [4] (privileged, happy, lucky) those who mourn, that is to say, those who in this life carry a heavier cross: illness, handicap, physical pain, poverty, slander, injustice ... Faith transforms the meaning of suffering. In union with Christ's suffering it is changed into a sign of God's love, into something very valuable and fruitful.

Behold those redeemed as the first fruits of the human race for God and the Lamb, and who follow the Lamb wherever he goes. [5]

---

[3] F. J. Sheed, *To Know Christ Jesus*, p 45-6
[4] Matt 5:5
[5] *Communion Antiphon of the Mass*

34.2 The cross of every day.

The Cross, pain and suffering, are the means which Our Lord used to redeem us. He could have used other means, but he chose to redeem us precisely by the Cross. Since then suffering has had a new meaning, which can only be understood when it is united to Him.

Our Lord did not change the laws of creation for his own benefit; he chose to be a man like us. He had the power to do away with suffering, but he never used that power for himself. Although he worked miracles to feed the crowds, he himself suffered hunger. He shared with us the experience of exhaustion and pain. His soul tasted every bitterness: indifference, ingratitude, betrayal, slander, moral agony in its highest degree when he took upon himself the sins of the world, the shameful death of the cross. His enemies were astonished by his incomprehensible behaviour: *He saved others* – they said mockingly – *he cannot save himself.*[6]

After the Resurrection the Apostles were sent to proclaim the benefits of the Cross to the whole world. *It was necessary that the Messiah should suffer like this,*[7] Christ himself explained to the disciples on the road to Emmaus.

Our Lord wants us to avoid pain and combat illness with all the means at our disposal. But he wants us to understand, at the same time, that our pain and suffering can have a redemptive meaning and lead to our personal purification, even in the case of those which seem unjust or out of all proportion. This doctrine filled St Paul with joy in his prison, as he explained to the first Christians of Asia Minor: *Now I rejoice in my sufferings for your sake and in my flesh I complete what is lacking in Christ's*

---

[6] Matt 27:42
[7] cf Luke 24:26

afflictions for the sake of his body, that is, the Church.[8]

Suffering is not sanctified by those who suffer in this life because of wounded pride, envy, jealousy etc. How much suffering we create for ourselves! This cross is not Christ's but comes precisely from being far away from him. This cross is one's own and it is heavy and fruitless. Let us examine ourselves now in our prayer to see if we are carrying Our Lord's Cross wholeheartedly.

This Cross often consists in the tiny irritations which turn up in our work and in our dealings with other people. It may be something unforeseen for which we were not prepared, or the character of someone with whom we have to live, or a plan that has to be changed at the last minute, or tools of our work which fail us at the worst possible moment, or extremes of heat or cold, or misunderstanding, or being sufficiently off-colour to feel incapable of doing our work properly.

But little or great, suffering accepted and offered to Our Lord produces peace and serenity. When it is not accepted, the soul is out of tune and its internal rebellion is shown externally in gloom or bad temper. We have to make a conscious decision to take up and carry the little Cross of every day with determination. Suffering can be sent to us by God to purify many things in our past life or to strengthen our virtues and to unite us to the sufferings of Christ our Redeemer, who, in his innocence, suffered the punishment due to our sins.

O God, whom the Holy Innocents confessed and proclaimed on this day, not by speaking but by dying, grant, we pray, that the faith in you which we confess with our lips may also speak through our manner of life.[9]

---

[8] Col 1:24
[9] *Collect of the Mass*

34.3 Those who suffer with the intention of co-redeeming are comforted by Our Lord. We must sympathize with and help our brothers to overcome their difficulties and sufferings.

The innocents were slaughtered as infants for Christ; spotless, they follow the Lamb and sing for ever: Glory to you, Lord.[10]

Those who suffer with Christ will be rewarded by having God as their comforter in this life and, afterwards, the infinite joy of eternal life. *Well done, good and faithful servant ... enter into the joy of your master,*[11] Jesus will say to us at the end of our life if we have managed to remain united to him through all its joys and sorrows.

God will wipe away every tear from the eyes of the blessed and death shall be no more, neither shall there be mourning, nor crying, nor pain any more, for the former things have passed away.[12] The hope of heaven is an inexhaustible source of patience and energy in the time of severe suffering. In the same way the knowledge, which faith gives us, that our pain and suffering are of enormous use to our brothers, helps us to bear suffering and exhaustion without complaint.

We ought to feel that the weight of our affliction is light, compared to the good things which God has prepared for us.[13] Moreover, those who offer up their suffering are co-redeemers with Christ, and God the Father always pours out on them such great comfort that they are filled with peace in the midst of their sufferings. *For as we share abundantly in Christ's sufferings, so*

---

[10] *Entrance Antiphon of the Mass*
[11] cf Matt 25:21
[12] Rev 21:3-4
[13] cf 2 Cor 4:17

through Christ we share abundantly in comfort too.[14] St Paul feels the consolation of the divine mercy and this enables him to console and support others. Our Father God is always very near his human children, but especially when they are suffering.

Human brotherhood moves us to practise this service of comfort and help with one another: *Comfort one another*[15] pleads St Paul. For there are a thousand things which tend to separate us, but suffering unites us.

But it does happen sometimes that a painful situation arises in which we don't know what is the right thing to do. Perhaps if we recollect ourselves in prayer for a moment, and ask ourselves what Our Lord would do in the same circumstances, we shall receive abundant light. Sometimes all we need to do will be to keep the suffering company, to talk to him in a friendly and positive way, to encourage him to offer his suffering for some specific intention, to help him recite some prayer such as the Holy Rosary, or simply to listen to what he wants to say.

Nowadays when so many people have forgotten the Christian meaning of feasts, we can add to them the light and the salt of little mortifications, realising that in this way we give joy to Our Lord and help other souls to come nearer to Bethlehem.

If we contemplate Mary at the foot of her Son's Cross we will learn to offer our pain and suffering to him and to have great sympathy for those who suffer. Let us ask her now to teach us to sanctify pain, uniting it to that of her Son Jesus. Let us ask the Holy Innocents to help us to love mortification and voluntary sacrifice, to offer up our own pain and to have great compassion for all who suffer.

---

[14] 2 Cor 1:5
[15] cf 1 Thess 4:18

35. MAKING A MORE JUST WORLD

35.1 The duty of Christians to create a more just and more human society.

For God so loved the world that he gave his only Son, that whoever believes in him should not perish, but have eternal life.[1] St John tells us at the start of today's Mass.

The Child we have been contemplating in the crib during the last few days is the Redeemer of the world and of every one in it. He has come in the first place to give us eternal life as something to be looked forward to in this life and to be fully possessed after death. He has become man to call sinners,[2] to save what was lost,[3] and to make divine life known to all men.[4]

During the years of his public life, Our Lord had little to say about the political and social situation of his people, and this in spite of their oppression by the Romans. On different occasions he makes it clear that he does not want to be a political Messiah nor a liberator from the yoke of Rome. He came to give us the freedom of the sons of God: *freedom from the sins* we had committed, which had reduced us to a state of slavery. He came to give us *freedom from eternal death,* another consequence of sin; *freedom from the dominion of the devil,* since man could now overcome sin with the help of grace. And finally, he gave us *freedom from life*

---

[1] John 3:16
[2] Luke 5:32
[3] Luke 19:10
[4] Mark 10:45

according to the flesh, which is opposed to supernatural life: *The freedom brought by Christ through the Holy Spirit has restored to us the capacity, of which sin had deprived us, of loving God above all and of remaining in contact with him.*[5]

Through his way of acting, Our Lord also pointed out the path his Church would take so as to continue his work here on earth until the end of time.

It behoves Christians, within the many opportunities we have for action, to contribute to a world order that is more just, more human and more Christian without in any way compromising the Church as such.[6] The Church's concern for social problems derives from her spiritual mission and is kept within the limits of that mission. The Church, of her very nature, does not fulfil her purpose in solving temporal problems.[7] She follows Christ when he declared that his kingdom was not of this world,[8] and absolutely refused to be considered a judge or a promoter of justice in purely human affairs.[9]

Nevertheless, no Christian should stand aside from the need to do everything in his power to solve the enormous social problems that now afflict mankind. *'Let each one examine himself,'* exhorted Paul VI, *'to see what he has done up to now and what more he ought to accomplish. It is not enough to cite general principles, make resolutions, condemn grave injustices, make denunciations with a certain prophetic daring. None of this will carry any weight unless accompanied in each*

---

[5] Sacred Congregation for the Doctrine of the Faith (SCDF), *Instruction on Christian Freedom and liberation,* 53, 22 March 1986
[6] cf Paul VI, Encyclical, *Populorum progressio,* 8
[7] SCDF, *ibid,* 80
[8] John 19:36
[9] cf Luke 12:13

person by a more lively realisation of his own responsibility and by effective action. It is too easy to make other people responsible for today's injustices, if, at the same time, we don't realise that we too are responsible and that a personal conversion is therefore the first necessity.[10]

We can ask ourselves in our prayer whether or not we are doing our best to become familiar with the social teachings of the Church. Do we make them a practical force in our personal lives? Do we try, insofar as we are able, to make the laws and customs of our society conform to those teachings on the family, education, wages, the right to work and so on? Our Lord, whom we now contemplate in the stable of Bethlehem, will be content with us if we are really trying to make a more just world in the big city or small village where we live: in the district and in the company where we work, in the life of our own family.

35.2 Some consequences of the personal commitment of Christians. and mercy.

In the final analysis, the establishment of justice and peace in the world finds its solution in the human heart. And, when the heart is not centred on God, man reverts to his original state of slavery and is subject to every kind of oppression from his fellow creatures.[11] Thus, we can never forget that when, through our personal apostolate, we try to make the world around us more Christian, we are also making it more human. And, to the extent that we succeed in this, by creating a more just and more human environment in social, family and working conditions, we are at the same time creating a climate in

---

[10] Paul VI, Letter, *Octogesima adveniens*, 48, 14 May 1971

[11] SCDF, *op cit*, 39

which Christ can be more easily known and loved.

A decision to put into practice the virtue of justice, without reservations, will lead us to pray daily for the leaders of government, business enterprises, welfare services etc. For the solution to the major social and human problems of today depends to a great extent on such people. And in doing so we must endeavour to live up to this standard, without inhibitions and without leaving to others the practice of justice which the Church urges upon us. This means full payment for services rendered. It entails a serious effort to improve the living conditions of people in need. It presupposes exemplary behaviour in carrying out our work competently and well, showing responsibility and initiative in the exercise of our rights and duties as citizens. Finally, the practice of justice will lead us to join movements in which, together with other people of good-will, we can foster more human and more Christian ideals. And all this, though it may seem to take up more time than is normally at our disposal, is not impossible; for if we really make an effort, God will enlarge our day.

Our Lord has left us a programme of life which, if put into practice, is capable of completely transforming mankind. He has told us that we are all children of God and therefore brothers. This has a profound impact on the relations between men. God has given the goods of the earth to all to administer them well. To all he has promised eternal life. The doctrine of Christ has, over the centuries, led to great achievements: the abolition of slavery, the recognition of the dignity of women, the protection of orphans and widows, the care of the sick and the handicapped. They are a consequence of the sense of the brotherhood of man resulting from the Christian faith. In our own professional and social surroundings, can it really be said that in word and deed we are truly contributing towards making the world more just and more human?

Let us recall the words of St Josemaría Escrivá: *Perhaps you bring to mind all the injustices which cry for redress, all the abuses that go uncorrected, the discrimination passed on from one generation to the next with no attempt to find permanent solutions.*

A man or a society that does not react to suffering and injustice and makes no attempt to alleviate them is still distant from the love of Christ's heart. While Christians enjoy the fullest freedom in finding and applying various solutions to these problems, they should be united in having one and the same desire to serve mankind. Otherwise their Christianity will not be the word and life of Jesus; it will be a fraud, a deception of God and man.[12] God so loved the world that he gave his only-begotten Son ...

35.3 The problems of mankind cannot be solved by justice alone. Justice

With justice alone we cannot solve the problems of mankind: *even if we achieve a reasonable distribution of wealth and a harmonious organisation of society, there will still be the sufferings of illness, of misunderstanding, of loneliness, of the death of loved ones, of the experience of our own limitations.*[13] Justice is enriched and complemented by mercy. What is more, strict justice *can lead to the denial and an extinction of itself if no allowance is made for that deeper kind, which is love, to form human life,*[14] and can end up *in a system of oppression of the weaker by the stronger or in an arena of permanent*

---

[12] St. J. Escrivá, *Christ is passing by*, 167
[13] *ibid*, 168
[14] John Paul II, Encyclical, *Dives in misericordia*, 12

struggle of the one against the other.[15]

Justice and mercy mutually sustain and fortify each other. *Justice alone is never enough to solve the great problems of mankind. When justice alone is done, don't be surprised if people are hurt. The dignity of man, who is a son of God, requires much more.*[16]

Charity without justice would not be real charity: rather would it simply be an attempt to anaesthetise one's conscience. Nevertheless, one meets people who call themselves 'Christians' but *leave aside justice and limit their actions to a bit of welfare work, which they define as charitable, without realising that they are doing only a small part of what in fact they have a strict duty to do.*

Charity, which is like a generous overflowing of justice, demands first of all the fulfilment of one's duty. The way to start is to be just; the next step is to do what is most equitable ..., but in order to love, great refinement is required, and much thoughtfulness, and respect, and kindliness in rich measure.[17]

The best way of promoting justice and peace in the world is the commitment to live like true children of God. If we Christians really decide to practise the demands of the Gospel in our personal lives, in our families, at work and in our social life, we will change society, making it more just and more human. Our Lord, from the stable of Bethlehem, urges us to do so. Don't be discouraged because it seems as if what is around us is of little importance. That was how the first Christians transformed the world: with their ordinary daily work, which at first sight was a humble enough thing in many cases.

---

[15] *ibid*, 14
[16] St. J. Escrivá, *Friends of God*, 172
[17] *ibid*, 172-3

THE CHRISTMAS SEASON
– 30 DECEMBER

36. *DO NOT BE AFRAID*

36.1 Jesus Christ is always our safeguard against the difficulties and temptations we may have to undergo. We win every battle with him at our side.

The history of the Incarnation opens with these words: *Do not be afraid, Mary.*[1] And the Angel of the Lord says also to St Joseph: *Do not be afraid, Joseph, son of David.*[2] And again to the shepherds the angel repeats: *Do not be afraid.*[3] This beginning of God's coming into the world marks a style proper to Jesus' presence among men.

Later on, now accompanied by his disciples, Jesus was crossing the little sea of Galilee. *And behold there arose a great tempest on the sea, so that the boat was being swamped by the waves.*[4] St Mark puts this event in its proper context. It was the evening of the day on which Jesus had narrated the parables about the kingdom of heaven.[5] The Gospel explains that Our Lord, tired out after hours of preaching, was asleep in the boat. The storm must have been tremendous, for the disciples, accustomed as they were to the sea, nevertheless saw themselves in danger. And they cried out to Jesus: *Lord save us, for we perish!*

From the start, the apostles understood why Jesus

---

[1] Luke 1:30
[2] Matt 1:20
[3] Luke 2:10
[4] Matt 8:24
[5] Mark 4:35

was asleep. (He must have been very tired not to have been awakened.) They did everything in their power to avert the danger – furling the sails, rowing hard and baling out the water. But gradually the storm began to get the better of them and they were in imminent danger of sinking. Then, overcome with fear, they turned to Our Lord as their one and only recourse. *And they went and woke him, saying, 'Save us Lord; we are perishing'. And he said to them, 'Why are you afraid, O men of little faith?'* [6]

How little too is our faith when we doubt whether the storm will abate! Too often we allow ourselves to be discouraged by circumstances: sickness, work, reverses of fortune, opposition to us in our surroundings. Fear is a phenomenon which covers almost every aspect of life. It is often the result of ignorance or of selfishness stemming from an excessive concern for oneself or anxiety over things that perhaps will never happen. But, above all else, fear often stems from the awareness that the security of our life is based on very weak foundations. Here we are forgetting an essential truth: Jesus Christ is our constant security. This does not mean to say that we are insensitive to events, but that we should have more confidence in using the human means at our disposal. We must never forget that to be close to Jesus, even when he appears to be asleep, is to be safe. When we are confused and going through unpleasant times, Jesus does not forget us. As St Teresa said: *he never fails his friends.* [7]

---

[6] Matt 8:25-26
[7] St Teresa of Avila, *Life*, 2, 4

36.2 The meaning of our divine filiation. Confidence in God. He will never come too late to rescue us.

God never comes to the aid of his sons too late. Even when all seems lost, God will always be there at the right time – although it may be in secret and mysterious ways. Thus, complete confidence in God while at the same time using all the human means available, gives the Christian great fortitude and a special feeling of peace when he is up against the most painful events and circumstances.

If you don't abandon him, he will not abandon you.[8] And we tell him in our prayer that we do not want to leave him. Together with him, every battle is a victory, though at first sight it may seem a defeat. *At the very moment when everything seems to be collapsing before our eyes, we realise that quite the opposite is true, 'because you, Lord, are my strength (Ps 42:2)'. If God is dwelling in our soul, everything else, no matter how important it may seem, is accidental and transitory. Whereas, we, in God, stand permanent and firm.*[9]

This is the medicine to purge from our lives all fears, tensions and anxieties. St Paul comforted the first Christians in Rome, who faced a panorama of great human difficulties, with these words: *If God is for us, who is against us? He who did not spare his own Son but gave him up for us all, will he not also give us all things with him? ... Who shall separate us from the love of Christ? Shall tribulation, or distress, or persecution, or famine, or nakedness, or peril, or sword? ... No, in all these things we are more than conquerors through him who loved us. For I am sure that neither death, nor life, nor angels, nor principalities, nor things present, nor things to come, nor powers, nor height, nor depth, nor*

---

[8] St. J. Escrivá, *The Way*, 730
[9] *ibid, Friends of God*, 92

anything else in all creation, will be able to separate us from the love of God in Christ Jesus Our Lord.[10] By vocation a Christian is a person dedicated to God, and one who has accepted all that may happen to him as being permitted by Him.

On another occasion Our Lord taught the people around him about the love and care God has for every creature. His listeners were simple and honest people who gave praise to the majesty of God, but who lacked that special confidence of children in God their Father.

Probably, just as he was talking to them, a flock of sparrows came around pecking about for what they could pick up. Who bothers about them? Perhaps the housewives of the village would sometimes buy them for a few pennies to flavour their ordinary meals. They were within reach of the most modest purse. They were of little value.

Our Lord would indicate them with a gesture while saying to his audience: *Not one of these sparrows is forgotten before God.* God knows everything. *Not one of these falls to the ground without your Father knowing it.* And Our Lord goes on to give us confidence: *Fear not, you are worth more than a host of sparrows.*[11] We are not creatures of the moment, but his children forever. How could he not take an interest in our plans? *Fear not.* Our God has given us life and he has given it to us forever. And Our Lord says to us: *To you, my friends, I tell you: Do not fear.*[12] St Thomas tells us: *Every man, no matter who he is, is God's friend and should have great confidence in being freed by him from any type of affliction ... And as God helps his servants in a special*

---

[10] Rom 8:33
[11] cf Matt 6:26-27
[12] Luke 8:50

way, he who serves God should live in great peace.[13]
There is only one condition: be friends of God and live as
his children.

36.3 Providence. All things work together unto good for those who love God.

*Take your rest in divine filiation. God is a father full
of tenderness, of infinite love.*[14] In every aspect of our
life, be it human or supernatural, our 'rest', our security,
has no firmer foundation than our divine filiation. *Cast
all your anxieties on him,* St Peter would say to the first
Christians, *for he cares about you.*[15]

Divine filiation cannot be considered as something
merely metaphorical. It does not mean that God simply
treats us as a father and expects us to treat him as sons.
No. Through the indwelling, sanctifying power of God,
the Christian is a real son of God. This is such a profound
reality that it affects man's very being, to such an extent
that St Thomas declares that through it man *is made into
a new being.*[16]

Divine filiation is the foundation for the freedom,
security and happiness of the children of God. In it man
finds the protection he needs and that fatherly warmth
and certainty in the future which enables him to abandon
himself without worrying about the unknown things that
tomorrow may bring. It gives him the conviction that
behind all the hazards of life there always lies a very
good reason: *We know that in everything God works for
good.*[17] Even our mistakes and our wanderings from the

---

[13] St Thomas, *Exp Simb Apost.* 5
[14] St. J. Escrivá, *op cit*, 150
[15] 1 Pet 5:7
[16] St Thomas, *Summa Theologica*, 1-2 q110, a2, ad3
[17] Rom 8:28

right path always end up well, for *God arranges absolutely everything to his own advantage ...*[18]

The realisation that one is a son of God produces in all the circumstances of the Christian's life an essentially loving approach to the world, which shows itself mainly in the virtue of faith. The man who knows himself to be a son of God is always happy and never loses his peace of mind. This awareness frees him from useless stresses and when, out of weakness he goes wrong, if he really feels he is a Son of God, he is able to turn to Him again, confident of being well received.

The thought of divine Providence helps us to approach God, not as a cold, indifferent and distant Being, but as a father who depends on each one of us and who has given us an angel, an angel like those who announced the birth of Our Lord to the shepherds, to watch over us on our road through life.

The peace of mind which this truth brings about in our way of acting and living does not come from turning our back on reality. Rather it consists in viewing it optimistically, because we always trust in God's help. *This is the difference between us and those who do not know God: they, in adversity, complain and grumble; we, on the other hand, are not drawn away from virtue by the things that go against us but are strengthened in it,*[19] for we know that even the hairs of our head are numbered.

Let us always be at peace. If we really seek God, everything will be an occasion for improvement.

As we finish our prayer we resolve to go to Jesus in the Blessed Sacrament whenever the contradictions, the difficulties or the trials of life put us in danger of losing our happiness and peace of mind. Let us go close to

---

[18] St Augustine, *De corresp et gracia*, 30:35
[19] St Cyprian, *De moralitate*, 13

Mary, to her whom we contemplate in the *stable* close to her son. She will be our teacher in these days full of the peace of Christmas and she will show us how to conduct ourselves like children of God, even in the most difficult circumstances.

THE CHRISTMAS SEASON
– 31 DECEMBER

37. MAKING UP FOR LOST TIME

37.1 A day for stock-taking. Our time is short. It is a very important part of the inheritance received from God.

Today is a good day for taking stock of the year now ending and for making resolutions for the year about to begin. It is a good opportunity for asking pardon for our omissions, and the lack of love that caused them, and a good occasion of thanksgiving for all the good things God has given us.

The Church reminds us that we are pilgrims and she herself *being present in the world is, nevertheless, herself a pilgrim.*[1] She stands before her God as *a wayfarer among the persecutions of the world and the consolations from God.*[2]

Our life too is a path full of tribulations and of *God's consolation*. We have a life in time which we are now living, and another life outside time to which we are making our way. The time at our disposal is an important part of the inheritance God has left us. Time represents the separation between the present and that moment when we stand before God with our hands either empty or full. Only now in this life can we obtain merit for the next. In fact, each single day of ours is a *period* given us by God, so that we may fill it with love for him, with love for those around us, with work well done, with

---

[1] Second Vatican Council, *Sacrosanctum concilium*, 2
[2] *ibid, Lumen gentium*, 8

putting the virtues into practice; in a word, a life full of good works pleasing to God's eyes. Now is the time to amass *the treasure that never perishes*. For each one of us it is *the acceptable time. Behold, now is the day of salvation.*[3] Once it is past, there will be no other time.

The time each one of us has at his disposal is short, but long enough to tell God that we love him and to accomplish the work he has given us. For this reason St Paul warns us: *Look carefully then how you walk, not as unwise men but as wise, making the most of the time,*[4] for soon *night comes, when no one can work.*[5] *Short indeed is our life for loving, for giving, for making atonement. It is wrong, therefore, to waste it or irresponsibly throw out of the window such a great treasure. We cannot squander this period of the world's history that God has entrusted to each one of us.*[6]

St Paul, when he considers the brevity of our stay on earth and the insignificance of things in themselves, says: *for the form of this world is passing away.*[7] This life is but a mere shadow of what awaits us in heaven.

The shortness of this life is a continual call to squeeze from it all that we can, to the point of exhaustion, while we keep God before our eyes. Today, in our prayer, we can ask ourselves whether God is pleased with the way we have behaved during the past year. Have we spent our time well or, on the contrary, has it been a year of wasted opportunities in our work, our apostolate or in our family life? Have we often let go of the Cross because of our tendency to complain at the

---

[3] 2 Cor 6:2
[4] Eph 5:15-16
[5] John 9:4
[6] St. J. Escrivá, *Friends of God*, 39
[7] 1 Cor 7:31

first sign of opposition or unwelcome events?

Each year that passes is a call to holiness in our ordinary life and a warning that we are that much nearer to the definitive moment of our meeting with God at death. *And let us not grow weary in our well-doing, for in due season we shall reap, if we do not lose heart. So, then, as we have opportunity, let us do good to all men ...*[8]

37.2 Acts of contrition for our faults and sins committed during the past year. Acts of thanksgiving for the many benefits received.

On examining our conscience we will easily find that during this past year we have at times lacked charity, been too easy-going in our professional work, grown used to a certain spiritual mediocrity, and given little in the way of alms. We have been a prey to selfishness and vanity. We have not done any mortification in our meals. We have ignored the grace offered to us by the Holy Spirit. We have been intemperate, ill-humoured and stubborn in character. We have more or less deliberately allowed ourselves to be distracted in our practices of piety ... So we have countless reasons for ending the year by asking God's forgiveness, by making many acts of contrition and atonement. Let us look at each one of those days. *Every day we must ask forgiveness, for every day we have caused offence.*[9] Not even for one day can we escape from this fact: many have been our sins and faults. Nevertheless, in both the human and supernatural realms, our reasons for thanksgiving are incomparably greater. We cannot count the movements of the Holy Spirit in our soul, the graces we have received in the

---

[8] Gal 6:9-10
[9] St Augustine, *Sermon 256*

sacrament of Penance and in Holy Communion, the times when our Guardian Angel has protected us, the merit gained through the offering of our work and hardships for others, and the times when others have helped us. It doesn't matter if we only perceive a small part of this. Let us give thanks to God for all the benefits we have received during the year.

We must seek new strength with which to serve him and endeavour not to be ungrateful, for that is the condition on which the Lord bestows his jewels. Unless we make good use of his treasures, and of the high estate to which he brings us, he will take these treasures back from us; we shall be poorer than before, and His Majesty will give the jewels to someone else who can display them to advantage and to his own profit and that of others. For how can a man, unaware that he is rich, make good use of his riches and spend them liberally? It is impossible, I think, taking our nature into consideration, that anyone who fails to realise that he is favoured by God should have the courage necessary for doing great things. For we are so miserable and so much attracted by earthly things that only one who realises that he holds some earnest of the joys of the next world will succeed in thoroughly abhorring and completely detaching himself from the things of this earth.[10]

We come to the end of the year asking forgiveness for so many failures to correspond to grace, for all those occasions when Jesus placed himself at our side and we made no effort to see him and so let him pass by. At the same time let us end the year by thanking God for the great mercy he has shown us and for the innumerable and often unseen benefits he has conferred on us.

Together with sorrow and thanksgiving, we resolve

---

[10] *St Teresa of Avila, Life*, 10:3

to love God and struggle to acquire virtues and get rid of our defects, as if next year were to be the last that God was going to give us.

37.3 New Year resolutions.

In these final days of the old year and at the beginning of the new, we like to wish each other a good year. To tradesmen, neighbours, everyone we meet ... we say *Happy New Year!* They wish the same to us and we thank them.

But, what do most people mean by Happy New Year? *Doubtless they mean a year free from illness, pain, trouble or worry; that instead, everyone may smile on you, that you flourish, that you make plenty of money, that the taxman doesn't get you, that you get a rise in salary, that prices fall, and that the news is good every morning. In short, that nothing unpleasant may happen to you.*[11]

It is good to wish these material good things for ourselves and others so long as they do not make us veer away from our final goal. The new year will bring us our share of happiness and our share of trouble, and we don't know how much of each. A good year for a Christian is one in which both joys and sorrows have helped him to love God a little more. It is not a year that comes, supposing it were possible, full of natural happiness that leaves God to one side. A good year is one in which we have served God and our neighbour better, even if, on the human plane, it has been a complete disaster. For example, a good year could be one in which we are attacked by a serious illness that has been latent and unsuspected for many years, provided we know how to use it for our sanctification and that of those close to us.

---

[11] G. Chevrot, *Eight Beatitudes*

Any year can be *the best year* if we make use of the graces that God keeps in store for us and which can turn to good the greatest misfortunes.

For the year just beginning God has prepared all the help we need to make it *a good year*. So let's not waste even a single day. And when we happen to commit sin, or fall into error or discouragement, let us immediately begin again, in many cases through the sacrament of Penance.

May we all have *a good year*, so that when it is over we can come before God with our hands full of hours of work offered to him, apostolate with our friends, innumerable acts of charity with those around us, many little victories over our self-love, and unforgettable meetings with Our Lord in Holy Communion.

Let us resolve to convert our defeats into victories, each time turning to God and starting once again.

And, finally, let us ask Our Lady for the grace to live during this new year with a fighting spirit, as if it were the last that God was going to give us.

OCTAVE OF CHRISTMAS –
SOLEMNITY OF MARY, MOTHER OF GOD
– 1 JANUARY

38. MOTHER OF GOD AND OUR
MOTHER

38.1 Holy Mary, Mother of God.

How often have we contemplated Mary with the Child in her arms! And Christian piety has inspired the countless different works of art which represent the feast we celebrate today – the Motherhood of Mary. This fundamental fact casts a light that shines out in the life of Mary. It is the foundation of all the other privileges with which God has wished to adorn her. Today we give thanks and praise to God the Father because Mary conceived his only Son: *For by the overshadowing of the Holy Spirit she conceived your Only Begotten Son, and without losing the glory of virginity, brought forth into the world the eternal Light, Jesus Christ our Lord.*[1] And from our hearts we sing to her: *Hail Holy Mother, who gave birth to the King,*[2] for truly *the Mother has brought forth the King, whose name is eternal; she who has conceived has at the same time the joy of motherhood and the glory of virginity.*[3]

Mary is Our Lady, full of grace and virtue, conceived without sin, who is the Mother of God and our Mother, and who dwells both body and soul in heaven. Sacred Scripture refers to her as the most exalted of all

---

[1] *Preface of the Maternity of the Virgin Mary*
[2] *Entrance Antiphon of the Mass*
[3] *Divine Office, Lauds, Antiphon 3*

creatures, the *blessed one,* the most praised among women, *full of grace,*[4] *she whom all generations shall call blessed.*[5] The Church teaches us that, after Christ, Mary occupies the place that is highest and closest to God, because of her divine motherhood. *She, after her son, by the grace of God, was exalted over all angels and men.*[6] *Through you, O Virgin Mary, have been fulfilled all the oracles of the prophets who announced Christ: being a virgin you conceived the Son of God and, remaining a virgin, you gave birth to him.*[7]

The Holy Spirit teaches us in the first reading of today's Mass that *when the time had fully come, God sent forth his Son, born of woman, born under the law ...*[8] Jesus did not suddenly appear on earth out of heaven. He became truly man, like us, taking our human nature in the most pure womb of the Virgin Mary. Insofar as he is God, Jesus is generated, not made, by God the Father from all eternity. Insofar as he is man, he was born, *was made,* of Mary. *I am exceedingly astounded,* says St Cyril, *that there could be anyone who has any doubt as to whether the Blessed Virgin should be called the Mother of God. If Our Lord Jesus Christ is God, why should the Blessed Virgin, who gave him birth, not be called the Mother of God? That is the faith that Our Lord's disciples transmitted to us, even though they did not use this exact expression. And that too is what the holy fathers have taught us.*[9] Thus it was defined by the

---

[4] Luke 1:28

[5] Luke 1:48

[6] Second Vatican Council, *Lumen gentium*, 63

[7] *Magnificat*, Antiphon of 27 December

[8] Gal 4:4

[9] St Cyril of Alexandria, *Letter 1*, 27:30

Council of Ephesus.[10]

All the feasts of Our Lady are great events, because they are opportunities the Church gives us to show with deeds that we love Mary. But if I had to choose one from among all her feasts, I would choose today's, the feast of the Divine Motherhood of the Blessed Virgin ...

When the Blessed Virgin said Yes, freely, to the plans revealed to her by the Creator, the divine Word assumed a human nature, with a rational soul and a body, formed in the most pure womb of Mary. The divine nature and the human were united in a single Person: Jesus Christ, true God and, thenceforth, true man: the only-begotten and eternal Son of the Father and, from that moment on, as Man, the true son of Mary. This is why Our Lady is the Mother of the Incarnate Word, the Second Person of the Blessed Trinity, who has united our human nature to himself forever, without any confusion of the two natures. The greatest praise we can give to the Blessed Virgin is to address her loud and clear by the name that expresses her highest dignity: Mother of God.[11]

Our Lady will be well pleased to hear us, on this her feast day, repeating many times the aspiration: *Holy Mary, Mother of God, pray for us.*

38.2 Our mother. The help she gives us.

Our Blessed Mother is the loving and consoling title we often give to Mary. She is truly our Mother in that she continually gives birth to the supernatural life within us.

She conceived, brought forth and nourished Christ, she presented him to the Father in the temple, shared her Son's sufferings as he died on the Cross. Thus in a

---

[10] *Dz-Sch*, 252
[11] St. J. Escrivá, *Friends of God*, 274

wholly singular way she co-operated by her obedience, faith, hope and burning charity in the work of the Saviour in restoring supernatural life to souls. For this reason she is a mother to us in the order of grace.[12]

This motherhood of Mary *will last forever ... until the perpetual consummation of all the elect. For, having been assumed into heaven, she has not left behind this salvific mission but, through her constant intercession, continues to obtain for us the gifts of eternal salvation. With her motherly love she looks after the brothers of her Son, who are still wayfarers and a prey to danger and uncertainty until they at last reach their heavenly home.*[13]

Jesus gave us Mary as our Mother when, after he had been nailed to the cross, he addressed her in these words: *'Woman, behold your son.'* Then he said to the disciple, *'Behold your mother.'*[14]

Thus, in a new way, he bequeathed his own mother to the man: the man to whom he has transmitted the Gospel. He has bequeathed her to all men ... From that day onwards the whole Church has her as Mother. And all men have her as Mother. The words pronounced upon the Cross are understood as being addressed to each one of us.[15]

Jesus looks at us one by one: *Behold your mother,* he says. John took her into his home, received her lovingly and cared for her with the greatest respect. *He brought Mary into his home, into his life. Spiritual writers have seen these words of the Gospel as an invitation to all Christians to bring Mary into their lives. Mary certainly wants us to invoke, to approach her confidently, to appeal*

---

[12] Second Vatican Council, *op cit*, 61
[13] *ibid*, 62
[14] John 19:26-27
[15] John Paul II, *General audience*, 10 January 1979

to her as our mother, asking her to 'show that you are our mother' (Monstra te esse Matrem. Liturgical hymn Ave maris stella).[16]

In giving his mother to be our mother Christ gives proof of his love for his own until the end.[17] And, in accepting the Apostle John as her son, the Blessed Virgin shows her motherly love for all men.

She has had a decisive influence on our lives. Each of us has his own experience. Looking back we see her intervention behind every problem, driving us forward and with the definitive push making us begin anew. *Whenever I get down to thinking about the numerous graces I have received from Mary, I feel like one of those Marian Shrines on the walls of which, covered with 'offerings', there is inscribed only: 'Through grace received from Mary'. In this way, it seems that I am written all over: 'Through grace received from Mary'.*

Every good thought, every good act of will, every movement of my heart: 'Through grace received from Mary.'[18]

We can ask ourselves on this feast of Our Lady if we have known how to resort to her like St John,[19] if we have often said to her, *Monstra te esse matrem. Show that you are our mother,* proving through our deeds that we want to be good sons to her.

38.3 Devotion to Mary is the way to Christ. Beginning the new year with Mary at our side.

Our Lady, close to her Son, fulfils her mission as Mother of all men by interceding continually for them.

---

[16] St. J. Escrivá, *Christ is passing by*, 140
[17] cf John 13:1
[18] Masserano, *Life of St Leonard of Porto Maurizzio*, II, 4
[19] cf John 19:27

The Church gives Mary the titles of *Advocate, Help, Perpetual Succour and Mediatrix.*[20] and with motherly love she takes upon herself the task of obtaining both ordinary and extraordinary graces for us and increasing our union with Christ. What is more, *given that Mary must, in all justice, be considered as the way by which we are led to Christ, the person who encounters Mary cannot but equally encounter Christ.*[21]

Filial devotion to Mary is thus an integral part of the Christian vocation. We are always ready to run instinctively to her who *consoles us in our distress, enlivens our faith, strengthens our hope, gets rid of our fears and invigorates our timidity.*[22]

It is easy to approach God through Mary. The whole people of God, doubtless inspired by the Holy Spirit, have always had this divine certainty. Christians have always seen Mary as a shortcut, *a path which shortens the journey,* to reach God.

O God, who through the fruitful virginity of Blessed Mary bestowed on the human race the grace of eternal salvation, grant, we pray, that we may experience the intercession of her, through whom we were found worthy to receive the author of life.[23]

On this solemnity of Our Lady we begin the New Year. Truly there could not be a better start to the year, and of all the days of our life, than being very close to Mary. With the confidence of sons we go to her, so that she may help us to live in holiness every day of the year; so that she may give us the impulse to begin again each time we fall because we are so weak; so that she may

---

[20] Second Vatican Council, *op cit*, 62
[21] Paul VI, Encyclical, *Mense maio*, 29 April 1965
[22] St Bernard, *Homily on the Nativity of the Blessed Virgin Mary*, 7
[23] *Collect of the Mass*

intercede with her divine Son to lead us to interior renewal, and to strive to grow in the love of God and in the service of our neighbour. We place in Mary's hands our desire to identify ourselves with Christ, to sanctify our professional work and to be faithful apostles.

We repeat her name with ever more fervour whenever difficulties arise. And she, who is forever at the service of her Son, when she hears her name on our lips, will come quickly to our rescue. She will not leave us in error or in disunion.

Today, when we are looking at one of her pictures, we can say to her, at least in our hearts without the use of words: *My Mother,* and feel that she is protecting us and encouraging us to begin this New Year that God has given us with the confidence of one who knows he is well looked after and is being given help from Heaven.

SECOND SUNDAY AFTER CHRISTMAS

39. OUR DIVINE SONSHIP

39.1 What divine sonship means. We are truly children of God. Thanksgiving for this immense gift.

But to all who received him, who believed in his name, he gave power to become children of God; who were born, not of blood nor of the will of the flesh nor of the will of man, but of God.[1] These are St John's words in the Gospel of today's Mass and they are reinforced by St Paul's words to the Ephesians in the second reading: He (God the Father) destined us in love to be his sons through Jesus Christ, according to the purpose of his will.[2]

God has made us his children. We will never completely understand nor value enough this ineffable gift. Child of God! *See what love the Father has given us, that we should be called children of God ... Beloved, we are God's children now; it does not yet appear what we shall be ...*[3]

When we say 'I am a child of God', we are not using a metaphor or a pious phrase. We are children. In the same way as human generation gives rise to 'fatherhood' and 'sonship', those who have been 'begotten by God' are really his children. This incomparable truth is realised in Baptism,[4] in which, thanks to the Passion and Resurrection of Christ, there takes place a new birth into a new life which did not previously exist. *A new*

---

[1] John 1:12-13
[2] *Second reading of the Mass, Eph 1:5*
[3] 1 John 3:1-2
[4] cf Second Vatican Council, *Sacrosanctum concilium*

creature[5] has emerged, by which the newly baptised person is called, and really is, a 'child of God'.

Divine sonship reaches its ultimate perfection in God the Son, *Jesus Christ, the only begotten Son of God, born of the Father before the beginning of time, begotten, not made, consubstantial with the Father.*[6] And to highlight the essential difference between our sonship and the eternal Sonship of the Son, ours is called adoptive. Here below, the word adoption has a specific meaning. The new father has not given life to his son, although he does give him his name, his rights of inheritance and the other privileges his natural children would have enjoyed. This might lead some people to have a somewhat confused idea about the true reality of our divine sonship: it must be understood that we are children of God because God's life is present in our souls in the state of grace.[7]

It will help us in today's prayer to consider that God is more our father than he whom in this life we call 'father' because he has given us our natural life. *To refer to a Christian as child of God is not a mere figure of speech which brings to mind the fatherly protection or watchfulness that God exercises over him. Rather, it must be understood in the strictest sense with the same meaning in which it is said that so and so is the son of such and such ...*

Through the act of conception a new person comes into existence. Just as an animal gives birth to an animal of the same species, a human being gives birth to another human being, similar to the parents. Often enough there is quite a similarity, and people are pleased to see that this or that child takes after his father: in his features, his

---

[5] 2 Cor 5:17
[6] Council of Nicea (325), *Dz-Sch*, 125
[7] cf 2 Chr 8:4

behaviour, his looks, his speech and so on. Well, the Christian, born of God, is his son in the most real sense, so that he must be like his Father in heaven. His condition as a son actually consists in his participation in the same nature as God. Here the words of St Peter find their true meaning: 'participants in the divine nature', which is more than just an analogy, more than a likeness or a relationship. It implies, rather, an elevation and a transformation of human nature into a nature that is proper to a divine being. The Christian enters into a higher (supernatural) world which is above his original nature: the world of God.[8]

In these days of Christmas when that holy night is still so close in the past, and when we can still contemplate the Child Jesus in the crib, we have a great opportunity to thank him for having brought to us the tremendous gift of divine sonship and for teaching us to call the God of heaven our Father: *When you pray, you must say: 'Father ...'*

39.2 The sense of divine sonship defines and guides our relations with God and with our fellow men. Consequences of this.

The Son came sent by the Father, who chose us in him before the foundation of the world and destined us to be adopted sons, for it pleased him to restore all things in himself (cf Eph 1:4-5, 10).[9]

The first fruit of this restoration accomplished by Christ was our divine sonship. Not only did he restore man's fallen nature, but he also gave us a new life, a super-natural life. It is the greatest gift we have received:

---

[8] C. Spicq, *Moral Theology of the New Testament*, Pamplona 1970, vol I, pp 87-88

[9] Second Vatican Council, *Lumen gentium*, 3

*anyone who does not realise that he is a child of God is
unaware of the deepest truth about himself. When he acts
he lacks the dominion and self-mastery we find in those
who love Our Lord above all else.*[10]

The awareness of our divine sonship defines and
channels our way of acting and thus our prayer and
behaviour in every circumstance. It is a way of being and
a way of living. And with this awareness we also learn
how to act in our dealings with our fellow men. *Our Lord
has come to bring peace, good news and life to all men.
Not only to the rich, not only to the poor, not only to the
wise, not only to the simple, but to everyone, to brothers,
for his brothers we are, children of the same Father,
God. So there is only one race, the race of the children of
God. There is only one colour, the colour of the children
of God. And there is only one language, the language
which speaks to the heart and to the mind, without the
noise of words, making us know God and love one
another.*[11]

The knowledge that we are children of God teaches
us how to have peace of mind in the face of all kinds of
events, no matter how painful they may seem. Our life
becomes the active abandonment of children who trust
completely in the goodness of a Father who, moreover,
has control over all the powers of creation. The certainty
that God wants what is best for us leads us to a joyful
abandonment full of peace even in the most difficult
moments of our lives. That is why St Thomas More was
able to write to his daughter from prison: *Keep then your
spirits high, my daughter, and don't worry about me no
matter what happens in this world. Nothing can happen to
me that God doesn't want. And all that he wants, no matter*

---

[10] St. J. Escrivá, *Friends of God*, 26
[11] *ibid*, *Christ is passing by*, 106

how bad it may appear to us, is really for the best.[12]

When we run into a problem or some unpleasantness, the attitude of a child of God is to ask for more help from his Father in heaven, and to renew his determination to live a holy life in all circumstances, even in those that seem to be least favourable.

39.3 Peace and serenity is based on our being children of God.

Divine sonship is the foundation of true freedom, the freedom of the children of God, in the face of every kind of oppression, and especially in the struggle to dominate our evil passions and inclinations.[13]

Divine sonship is also the firm foundation of peace and joy. Being a child of God, the Christian finds the protection that he needs, fatherly affection as well as confidence in the face of an always uncertain future.

No matter what our situation, our awareness of being children of God is the foundation of great peace, even in the midst of privation and difficulty. God always gives us the means to make progress and if we go to him with childlike trust, in many cases he will give us these means in the most unexpected of ways.

We, on our part, should always bear in mind that, in every moment, the essential thing in our life is the search for holiness through these very circumstances.

We will be good children of our Father God insofar as we come close to Jesus. He will always show us the way that leads to the Father and we will often be reminded of this when we go to kiss and adore the Child in the crib. *Pro nobis egenus et foeno cubantem ...,*[14]

---

[12] St Thomas More, *Letter from prison to his daughter Margaret*
[13] cf Rom 6:12-13
[14] Hymn, *Adeste Fideles*

made poor for us he lies amid the straw; we give him warmth and lovingly embrace him. Let us contemplate Jesus at his birth, which in these days is the centre of our attention and devotion. Let us talk to him in our prayer, look at him, listen to him, adore him in silence. *Sic nos amantem, quis non redamaret*[15]: to him who loves us so, who will not return his love? That love which must be practised will be so through putting more love and refinement into our relations with those who are near us.

Divine sonship leads us to hold other people in great respect, since they too are children of God. Our Lady invites us to spend long periods beside the crib looking at her Son. We ask her to re-shape our behaviour in accord with the supreme dignity we have received. We also beg her to help us never to forget, whatever our circumstances, that we are really and truly children of God. *And if children, then heirs, heirs of God and fellow-heirs with God.*[16] We are children for whom a place in heaven awaits, for us prepared by our Father God.

---

[15] *ibid*
[16] Rom 8:17

40. INVOKING OUR SAVIOUR

40.1 Approaching Our Lord in friendship and trust.

In ordinary life, calling a person by his Christian name indicates familiarity. *How decisively it marks a stage, even in casual friendship, when two people begin, without effort and without embarrassment, to call one another by their Christian names! And when we fall in love, and all our experience takes on a sharper edge and little things mean so much to us, there is one Christian name in the world which casts a spell over eye or ear when we see it written on the page of a book, or overhear it mentioned in a conversation; we are thrilled by the mere encounter with it. And it was with this sense of personal romance that people like St Bernard invested the holy name of Jesus.*[1] We too call Our Lord by his first name and for this reason we approach him incomplete confidence.

St Josemaría Escrivá advises us: *Don't be afraid to call Our Lord by his name – Jesus – and to tell him that you love him.*[2]

We call a friend by his first name. Why then don't we call our greatest Friend by his first name too? His name is JESUS; *thus he had been called by the angel before he was conceived in his mother's womb.*[3] God himself gave him his name through the message of the angel, a name that signified his mission, for Jesus means Saviour, he who brings us salvation, security and true

---

[1] R. A. Knox, *Sermon on The Divine Name*, 1956
[2] St. J. Escrivá, *The Way*, 303
[3] cf Luke 1:31

peace: ... *the name which is above every name, so that at the name of Jesus every knee should bend, in heaven and on earth and under the earth.*[4]

How trustfully and with how much veneration we should repeat it! Especially now as we talk to him in prayer: *Jesus, I need ..., Jesus, I would like ....*

Names were of great importance for the Jews, and when a name was given to someone it represented what that person should be in the future. If a person's name is unknown, that person cannot be completely known. Not to acknowledge a name meant to destroy a personality , and to change a person's destiny. His name expressed the reality of his being at its deepest level.

Among all names, the name of God was supremely perfect.[5] *It must be blessed from this time forth and for ever more, from the rising of the sun to its setting,*[6] *for I will sing praise to thy name, O Most High.*[7] And in the Our Father we say: *Hallowed by thy name.*

The Jewish people gave a child its name when it was circumcised. This was the rite instituted by God to single out, by means of an outward sign, those who belonged to the Chosen People. It was the sign of the Covenant that God made with Abraham and his posterity,[8] and it was laid down that it should be carried out on the eighth day after birth. All the uncircumcised were automatically excluded from the pact and, therefore, from the people of God.

In fulfilment of this precept, Jesus *was circumcised on the eighth day,*[9] according to the Law. Mary and

---

[4] Phil 2:9-10
[5] Zech 14:9
[6] Ps 113:2-3
[7] Ps 9:2
[8] cf Gen 17:10-14
[9] Luke 2:21

Joseph fulfilled what had been laid down. *Christ submitted to circumcision at a time when it was still the law,* says St Thomas, *and in doing so gave us an example to imitate, so that we may observe the things laid down by law in our own times,*[10, 11] and not look for exemptions or privileges when there is no reason for doing so.

40.2 The name of Jesus. Invocations.

After the circumcision of Jesus, his parents, Mary and Joseph, would say the name of Jesus for the first time, full of great devotion and love. And this is what we too must often do. To invoke his name is to be saved.[12] To believe in this name is to be counted among the children of God.[13] To pray in the name of Jesus is to be sure of being heard. *Truly, truly, I say to you, if you ask anything of the Father, he will give it to you in my name.*[14] In the name of Jesus we obtain pardon for our sins[15] and our souls are purified and made whole.[16] The preaching of this name constitutes the whole essence of apostolate,[17] for he *is the goal of human history, the focal point of the desires of history and civilisation, the centre of mankind, the joy of all hearts, and the fulfilment of all aspirations.*[18] Mankind finds in Jesus what it most needs and thirsts for: salvation, peace, happiness, the forgiveness of sins, freedom, understanding and friendship.

Let us listen to St Bernard:

---

[10] St Thomas, *Summa Theologica*, 3, q37, a1
[11] cf Acts 15:1
[12] cf Rom 10:9
[13] cf John 1:12
[14] John 16:23
[15] 1 John 2:12
[16] cf 1 Cor 6:11
[17] Acts 8:12
[18] Second Vatican Council, *Gaudium et spes*, 45

O Jesus ..., how consoling you are to those who
invoke you!

How good you are to those who seek you!
What will you not be to those who find you!
Only he who has felt it can know what it is
to languish in love for thee, O Jesus![19]

When we invoke the name of Jesus we see ourselves
at times like those lepers who cried from far off: *Jesus,*
Master, have mercy on us. And Our Lord bids them come
near and cures them, sending them to the priests.[20] Or we
will perhaps use the words of the blind man of Jericho:
Jesus, Son of David, have pity on me, for we too are blind
to so many things. *Don't you too feel the urge to cry out?*
You who are also waiting at the wayside of this highway
of life that is so very short? You who need more light,
you who need more grace to make up your mind to seek
holiness? Don't you feel an urgent need to cry out,
'Jesus, Son of David, have pity on me!' What a beautiful
aspiration for you to repeat again and again![21]

When we invoke the holy name of Jesus many
obstacles will disappear and we will be cured of many
ailments of the soul which so often afflict us.

May thy name, O Jesus, be always deep within my
heart and in reach of my hands, so that all my affections
and all my actions may be directed to thee ... . In thy
name, O Jesus, I have the remedy to rid me of my
wickedness and to turn my defects into perfections; also,
a medicine with which to preserve my affections from
corruption or to heal them if they have already been
corrupted.[22]

---

[19] St Bernard, *Sermons on the Canticles*, 15
[20] cf Luke 17:13
[21] St. J. Escrivá, *Friends of God*, 195
[22] St Bernard, *op cit*

Aspirations will fan the fire of our love for Our Lord, and increase our presence of God throughout the day. At other times, as we gaze at Our Lord, God made Child for love of us, we will trustingly say to him: *Dominus iudex noster, Dominus legifer noster, Dominus rex noster; ipse salvabit nos.*[23] Lord Jesus, in thee we trust, in thee I trust.

40.3 Our relations with the Blessed Virgin and St Joseph.

Along with the name of Jesus the names of Mary and Joseph should also be on our lips. These were the names that Our Lord must have used most frequently. With regard to Mary, the first Christians gave her name many different meanings: *Most lovable, Star of the Sea, Queen, Princess, Light, Beautiful* and so on.

In fact, it was St Jerome who gave her the title *Stella Maris*, Star of the Sea, since it is she who guides us to a safe haven in the midst of all the storms of life.

We must frequently have the saving name of Mary on our lips, especially when we are in need or in difficulty. On our way towards God it is meritable that we will have to endure storms which God permits so as to purify our intentions and to help us grow in the virtues. And it is possible that by paying too much attention to the obstacles on our way, we may yield to discouragement or weariness in our struggle. Then it is time to turn to Mary, invoking her name to help us. *If the winds of temptation rise against you, if you strike against the reefs of temptation, look at the star, call on Mary. If you are tossed by the waves of pride, of ambition, or of envy, look at the star, call on Mary. If anger, greed or*

---

[23] *Divine Office, Antiphon 'ad tertiam' for the Solemnity of Jesus Christ, Universal King*

impurity throw themselves violently against the barque of your soul, look at Mary. If you are troubled by the memory of your sins, confounded at the ugliness of your conscience, fearful at the thought of judgement, and you start sinking in the bottomless pit of sadness or in the abyss of despair, think of Mary. In danger, in affliction, in doubts, think of Mary, call on Mary. Don't let Mary be apart from your tongue, don't withdraw her from your heart; and to obtain her intercession, do not depart from the example of her virtue. You will not go wrong if you follow her, and not lose heart if you pray to her; you will not be lost if you think of her. If she takes you by the hand you will not fall; if she protects you, you will never have cause to fear; you will not grow weary if she guides you; you will reach port safely if she aids you.[24]

Let us invoke her name especially in the *Hail Mary*, and also in all the other prayers and aspirations that Christian devotion inspired over the centuries, and which perhaps our mothers taught us.

And, together with Jesus and Mary, there is St Joseph. *If the whole Church is in debt to the Virgin Mary, since it was through her that she received Christ, in the same way she owes to St Joseph a special gratitude and reverence.*[25]

Jesus, Mary and Joseph, to you I give all my heart and soul. Jesus, Mary and Joseph, help me in my last agony.

Countless millions of Christians have learned at their mothers' knees these and other similar aspirations, which they have later repeated to their dying days. Let us not forget then to have daily recourse, many times, to this *trinity on earth*.

---

[24] St Bernard, *Homily on the Virgin Mother*, 2
[25] St Bernardine of Siena, *Sermon 2*

41. THE PROPHECY OF SIMEON

41.1 The Holy Family in the temple. The meeting with Simeon. Our meetings with Jesus.

When the days of Mary's purification were completed, the Holy Family again went up to Jerusalem to comply with two precepts of Mosaic law: the purification of the mother, and the presentation and ransoming of the first born![1]

Neither of these laws was binding on Mary or on Jesus, by reason of the virgin birth and the fact that Jesus was God. Nevertheless, Mary wished to fulfil the Law. In this she behaved just like any other pious Jewish mother of her times. *Mary*, says St Thomas, *was purified so as to give an example of obedience and humility.*[2]

The Blessed Virgin, accompanied by St Joseph and carrying Jesus in her arms, presented herself at the temple, confused no doubt, just like any other in attendance among the other women there.

Jesus was offered to his Father in the arms of Mary. Never had such an offering been made in that temple before and never again would there be another like it. The next such offering would be made by Jesus himself, outside the city, at Golgotha. And now, thousands of times a day, Jesus is offered in the Holy Mass to the Blessed Trinity, as a sacrifice of infinite value.

Mary and Joseph offered the Child to God and, ransoming him, received him back again. For the ransom his parents paid the price that was usual among the poor.

---

[1] cf Lev 12:2-8; Exod 13:2,12-13
[2] St Thomas, *Summa Theologica*, 1-2, q1, a2

All they could afford was a pair of turtle doves. The Blessed Virgin then went through the rite of purification.

When they arrived at the doors of the temple, an old man named Simeon introduced himself to them. *He was righteous and devout, looking for the consolation of Israel, and the Holy Spirit was upon him.*[3] *He came into the temple inspired by the Holy Spirit.*[4] He took the child in his arms, *and blessed God, and said: 'Lord, now lettest thou thy servant depart in peace, according to thy word; for mine eyes have seen thy salvation which thou hast prepared in the presence of all peoples, a light for revelation to the gentiles, and for glory to thy people Israel'.*[5]

Mary and Joseph marvelled at the things that were said about Jesus. This old man had been counted worthy to recognise the coming of the Messiah, unknown to the rest of the world. His whole existence had been a fervent expectation of the coming of Jesus. At last the purpose of his life has been accomplished. *Lord, now lettest thou thy servant depart in peace ...*

Simeon considers his mission to be accomplished. He has come to know the Messiah, the Saviour of the world. That meeting has been the culmination of his life, the only thing he has lived for. He is not concerned about seeing a baby brought to the temple by some young couple wishing to fulfil the precepts of the Law just like so many other families. He knows that this Child is the Saviour. *My eyes have seen thy salvation.* That is enough. Now he can die in peace. He cannot have lived much longer after this event.

Let us not forget that we, the Christians of today,

---

[3] cf Luke 2:25
[4] Luke 2:27
[5] Luke 2:29-32

have had not just one but many encounters with this Saviour of ours, who is *a light for revelation to the Gentiles*. Perhaps we have received him thousands of times in Holy Communion throughout our lives, encounters more intimate and meaningful than that of Simeon. And now we feel regret for all those communions we have made in a distracted and inattentive way and we resolve that our next meeting with Jesus in the Holy Eucharist will be at least like Simeon's, full of faith, hope and love.

After each Communion, which is unique and un-repeatable, we too can say, *mine eyes have seen the Saviour*.

41.2 Mary, Co-redemptrix with Christ. The meaning of pain.

Old Simeon, having blessed the young couple, turned to Mary and, inspired by the Holy Spirit, opened her eyes to the sufferings her Son would have to undergo and to the sword of sorrow that would pierce her soul. Pointing to Jesus, he said: *Behold, this child is set for the fall and rising of many in Israel, and for a sign that is spoken against (and a sword will pierce through your own soul also), that the thoughts of many hearts may be revealed.*[6]

Commenting on this, St Bernard says: *The time will come when Jesus will not be offered in the temple nor in the arms of Simeon, but outside the city walls on the arms of a cross. The time will come when he will not be ransomed with money but will himself redeem others with his own blood, for God the Father has sent him as a ransom for his people.*[7] The suffering of his Mother, the

---

[6] Luke 2:34-35
[7] St Bernard, *Sermon 3*, On the Child, on Mary and on St Joseph

sword that will pierce her soul, will have as their only cause the agony of her Son, his persecution and death, the uncertainty about when these things will happen, and the resistance to the grace of the Redemption, which will be the ruin of many. Mary's destiny is bound up with that of Jesus, in its operation, and without any other possible reason.

The joy of the Redemption and the pain of the Cross are inseparable in the lives of Jesus and Mary, as if God, through his most beloved creatures in the world, wished to show us that happiness is to be found close to the Cross.

Right from the start then, the lives of Our Lord and of his Mother are stamped with the sign of the Cross. To the joy of the first Christmas is soon added privation and anxiety. From these first moments Mary already knows the pain that awaits her. And when *her hour* comes she will contemplate the Passion and Death of her Son with neither reproach nor complaint. Suffering as no mother could ever suffer, Mary will accept her pain in peace of mind, for she knows its redemptive significance. *Thus the Blessed Virgin advanced in her pilgrimage of faith, and faithfully persevered in her union with her Son unto the Cross, where she stood, in keeping with the divine plan, endured with her only-begotten Son the intensity of his suffering, associated herself with his sacrifice in her mother's heart, and lovingly consented to the immolation of this victim which was born of her.*[8]

Mary's suffering has an especially suitable meaning and is related to the sins of mankind. It is a co-redemptive suffering and that is why the Church gives to the Blessed Virgin the title of *Co-redemptrix.*

We ourselves learn the value and meaning of the sufferings and troubles which are part of every human

---

[8] Second Vatican Council, *Lumen gentium*, 58

life, when we meditate on Mary. With her we learn to sanctify pain, uniting it to that of her Son and offering it to the Father. The Holy Mass is the most suitable moment for offering all that is most painful in our lives. And there we will encounter Our Lady.

41.3 Our Lady teaches us to co-redeem. Offering up pain and contradictions. Atonement. Apostolate with those around us.

Simeon, by the will of God, initiated Mary, from the beginning, into the profound mystery of the Redemption, and made plain to her that God had singled her out to play a special role in the Passion of her Son. Thus, a new element entered into the life of Mary through the prophecy of old Simeon, and it remained with her until she stood at the foot of the Cross of Jesus.

The apostles, despite the teachings and many indications of Our Lord, did not come to understand everything until after the Resurrection, namely that *it was necessary that the Messiah should suffer much at the hands of the scribes and of the chief priests.*[9] Mary had a premonition from the beginning that great suffering was in store for her and that this suffering was in some way bound up with the redemption of the world. She who *kept all these things and pondered on them in her heart,*[10] must have often reflected on these mysterious words of Simeon. Through a process which we cannot fully understand, she identified her heart with that of her Son. Her redeeming pain *is suggested as much in the prophecy of Simeon as in the account of Our Lord's Passion. 'This child,' said the old man, indicating the infant in her arms, 'is set for the fall and rising of many in Israel, and*

---

[9] cf Matt 16:21
[10] Luke 2:19

for a sign that is spoken against, and a sword will pierce through your heart also ...' In fact, when your Jesus, who belongs to all of us but especially to you, gave up his spirit, the cruel lance did not reach his soul. If without sparing him it opened his side, since he was already dead it did not cause him pain. But your soul it did pierce. At that moment his soul was not there but yours was, and could not be totally separated from him.[11]

God has wished to associate us with all Christians in his work of redemption in the world so that we may co-operate with him in the salvation of all. And we will fulfil this mission by carrying out, with a right intention, even the least of our duties, offering them for the salvation of souls. Likewise, we will patiently and with peace of mind put up with pain, sickness and opposition, so as to do an effective apostolate with those around us. Ordinarily, God asks us to begin with the people who, through ties of family, friendship, work, study or locality, are closest to us. That is how Jesus and also his apostles set about this task.

Today, in a special way, we ask our Mother Mary to show us how to sanctify pain and contradiction, that we may know how to unite them to the Cross, that we may make frequent acts of atonement for the sins of the world, and that we may grow each day in the fruits of the Redemption. *O Mother most holy and merciful, who stood by your sweet Son while he was raised on the altar of the Cross for the redemption of all mankind, you who as our co-redeemer joined your suffering to his ... conserve and increase in us the fruits of the Redemption and of your compassion.*[12]

---

[11] St Bernard, *Sermon on the Sunday within the octave of the Assumption*, 14

[12] Pius IX, *Prayer at the close of the Jubilee Year of the Redemption*

42. NATURALNESS AND SIMPLICITY

42.1 Simplicity and naturalness of the Holy Family. Simplicity as an outward sign of humility.

The Messiah came to the temple in his Mother's arms. No one would have paid much attention to the young couple who were taking a little child to present him to the Lord.

The mothers had to wait for the priest at the East gate. Mary went there with the other women and waited for her turn when the priest would take her Son in his arms. Joseph was by her side, ready to pay the ransom. The ceremony of Mary's purification and the ransom of the Child from service to the Temple was no different in appearance from what normally happened on those occasions.

The whole of Mary's life is permeated with a deep simplicity. She always carries out her vocation as Mother of the Redeemer naturally. She appears in her cousin Elizabeth's house to help and look after her during those three months. She prepares the swaddling clothes and everything for her Son. She lives for thirty years with Jesus, never tiring of looking at Him, treating Him with great love, but with complete simplicity. When she obtains his first miracle from her Son in Cana she does it so naturally that not even the bride and groom realise what a wonderful event has taken place. She never makes a show of her special privileges. *Mary, the most holy Mother of God, passes unnoticed as just one more among the women of her town. Learn from her how to live with naturalness.*[1] Our Lady's simplicity and naturalness made her humanly very specially welcoming and

---

[1] St. J. Escrivá, *The Way*, 499

attractive. Jesus, her Son, during the thirty years of His hidden life, is always the model of perfect simplicity. When He begins to preach the Good News He does not carry out a noisy, spectacular activity. Jesus is simplicity itself in his birth, in the presentation in the Temple, or when he manifests his Divinity through the miracles which God alone can work.

Our Saviour shuns all show and vain-glory and false, theatrical gestures. He makes himself accessible to all: to the incurably sick and the most abandoned, who come to him trustingly to beg the remedy for their infirmities; to the Apostles, who ask him the meaning of the parables; to the little children, who embrace him confidently.

Simplicity is a sign of humility. It is radically opposed to anything false, artificial or deceitful. It is also a very necessary virtue for our dealings with God, for spiritual guidance and for our daily life with those around us. *Naturalness. Let your lives as Christian men, as Christian women – your salt and your light – flow spontaneously, without anything odd or absurd; always carry with you our spirit of simplicity.*[2]

42.2 Simplicity and an upright intention. Consequences of spiritual childhood. Being simple in our dealings with God, with others and in spiritual guidance.

If thy eye is clear, the whole of thy body will be lit up.[3] Simplicity demands clarity, transparency and a right intention which preserves us from living a double life, from serving two masters: God and ourselves. Simplicity also requires a strong will which leads us to choose what is good, and controls the disorderly tendencies of a life ex-

---

[2] *ibid*, 379
[3] Matt 6:22

clusively of the senses: and it dominates whatever is disordered and complicated in every person. The simple person judges events, persons and things with a right judgement illumined by faith, not by momentary impressions.[4]

Simplicity is a consequence and characteristic of the spiritual childhood to which Our Lord calls, us especially during these days when we are contemplating his birth and hidden life. *Believe Me, unless you become like little children again – in simplicity and innocence – you shall not enter the Kingdom of Heaven.*[5] We go to Our Lord like children, without pretence or show, because we know that He does not pay attention to external appearances, but *reads the heart*.[6] We feel our Lord's loving glance upon us, which invites us to be authentic, to act with simplicity in his presence, to speak to him in a personal, direct and trusting prayer. This is why we have to avoid any formality in our relationship with God, although *piety has its own good manners*[7] which leads us to be refined, especially in cult, in the liturgy; but respect is not just being conventional, nor is it a purely external attitude – it is rooted in true piety of the heart.

In our ascetical struggle, we have to acknowledge what we are really like and accept our limitations, knowing that God sees them and takes them into account. Far from worrying us, this should lead us to trust in Him more, asking his help to overcome our defects and to achieve the aims which we see are currently necessary in our interior life – those points we are following up more closely in our particular and general examinations of

---

[4] cf I. Celaya, *Simplicity*, in Gran Enciclopedia Rialp, Madrid 1971, vol 21, pp 173-174
[5] Matt 18:2-3
[6] 1 Sam 16:7
[7] cf St. J. Escrivá, *op cit*, 541

conscience.

If we are simple before God we will know how to be simple with those whom we meet every day – our relations, friends and colleagues. The simple person is one who acts and speaks in complete harmony with what he thinks and desires. He is a person who shows himself as he is, without trying to appear to be what he is not, or to have what he does not have. It always gives one great joy to meet a straightforward soul, without nooks and crannies, someone we can trust, like Nathanael who earned Our Lord's praise: *Here comes one who belongs to the true Israel; there is no falsehood in him.*[8] On the other hand, elsewhere Our Lord puts us on guard against *false prophets, men who come to you in sheep's clothing,*[9] against those who think one thing and do another.

In everyday life, any complication places an obstacle between ourselves and others and takes us away from God: *That pose and that self-satisfied manner don't suit you at all: they are easily seen to be affected. Try, at least, to use them neither with God, nor with your Director, nor with your brothers; and between them and you there will be one barrier less.*[10]

In a special way we have to show ourselves with complete simplicity in prayer, spiritual guidance and in Confession, speaking clearly and transparently with the desire that we be known well, avoiding general statements and half-truths and beating about the bush, without hiding anything. Our Lord wants us to show plainly what is happening to us: our joys, worries, the underlying reasons for our conduct.

---

[8] John 1:47
[9] Matt 7:15
[10] St. J. Escrivá, *op cit*, 47

42.3 Things which are opposed to simplicity. Fruits of this virtue. The means to attain it.

Simplicity and naturalness are extremely attractive virtues. To see this we just have to look at Jesus, Mary and Joseph. We need to know that these are difficult virtues, because pride gives us an exaggerated idea of ourselves, making us want to appear before others as more than we are or have. We so often feel humiliated because we want to be the centre of attention or to enjoy the esteem of those around us; because we don't admit that at times we do things badly; because we are not content to act and pass unnoticed; because we seek the compensation of a word of praise or gratitude. We complicate our lives very often because we don't accept our limitations and because we take ourselves too seriously. Pride can lead us to talk too much about ourselves, to think almost exclusively about our personal problems, or to try to attract attention – sometimes in complicated, obscure ways. It can even make us pretend to have non-existent illnesses or joys and sorrows which do not correspond to our state of mind.

Pedantry, affectation, boasting, hypocrisy and lies are all opposed to simplicity, and therefore to friendship. They also make it difficult to live harmoniously with others. They are a real obstacle to a harmonious family life. However, the simplicity Our Lord teaches is not naiveté: *Remember*, he says, *I am sending you out to be like sheep among wolves: you must then be prudent as serpents and yet innocent as doves.*[11] We Christians have to go through the world with these two virtues – simplicity and prudence – which mutually perfect each other.

To be simple we have to be careful to have a right

---

[11] Matt 10:16

intention in our actions, which should be directed to God. Only in this way can we overcome our complicated feelings, our momentary impressions or the confused life of the senses. Together with a right intention we need clear, concise – brutal if necessary – sincerity, to expose our weaknesses without trying to hide or deny them. *Look, the Apostles, for all their evident and undeniable defects, were sincere, simple ... transparent. You too have evident and undeniable defects. May you not lack simplicity.*[12]

To learn how to be simple we contemplate Jesus, Mary and Joseph in all the scenes of the infancy of Our Lord, in the midst of their ordinary life. Let us ask them to make us like children before God, that we may talk to him personally, without anonymity, without fear.

---

[12] St. J. Escrivá, *op cit*, 932

43. THE FAITH OF THE KINGS

43.1 Firmness in faith. Overcoming human respect, comfort, attachment to worldly goods, to seek Our Lord.

Jesus was born at Bethlehem in Judaea, in the days of King Herod. And thereupon certain wise men came out of the East to Jerusalem.[1] They had seen a star and by a certain grace from God they knew that it heralded the birth of the Messiah whom the people of Israel were expecting.

The occupation of these wise men – that of studying the stars – was the circumstance used by God to make them see His will. *God called them by what was most familiar to them and showed them a great, marvellous star, so that it would attract their attention by its very greatness and beauty.*[2] How did they come to know exactly what it meant? We don't know, but they knew and set off. Undoubtedly they received a very extraordinary inspiration from God, who wanted them to be present in Bethlehem, as Isaiah had announced: *Lift up thine eyes and look about thee ..., sons of thine, daughters of thine, come from far away.*[3] They would be the first of those who would come later, throughout all times, from all parts. And they were faithful to this grace.

They left behind their families, their comfort, their goods. It could not have been easy for them to explain the reason for their journey. Probably without talking about it too much, they took the best that they had, to

---

[1] Matt 2:1
[2] St John Chrysostom, *Homilies on St Matthew*, 6:3
[3] Is 60:4

carry with them as an offering, and set off on their way to adore God.

The journey must have been very long and difficult, but they persevered on their way. These men, determined and with none of what we might call worldly respect, teach us what we have to do to reach Jesus – leave aside everything that can lure us from the way or hold us up on our journey. *Sometimes we can be held up – in what refers to following Jesus closely, lovingly – by the fear of what people will say, the fear that our way of acting may be considered extreme in some way or another. You see that these men, who fill our homely feast with joy, give us a lesson in bravery. It is a lesson not to pay attention to human respect, which paralyses many who could already be close to Christ, living with Him.*[4]

We too have seen the star in the depth of our heart, inviting us to be detached from the things that tie us down, and to overcome any human respect which prevents us from reaching Jesus. *Look how gently the Lord invites us. His words have human warmth; they are the words of a person in love: 'I have called you by your name, you are mine' (Is 43:1). God, Who is Greatness and Beauty and Wisdom, declares that we are his, that we have been chosen as the object of his infinite Love. We need a strong life of faith to appreciate the wonder his Providence has entrusted to us. It will be a faith like that of the Magi, a conviction that neither the desert, nor the storms, nor the quiet of the oases will keep us from reaching our destination – the eternal Bethlehem, our definitive life with God.*[5]

Of all those who contemplated the star, only these Wise Men of the East discovered its deep meaning. Only

---

[4] A. M. Dorronsoro *Tiempo para creer*, pp 76-77
[5] St. J. Escrivá, *Christ is passing by*, 32

they understood what for others was only an unusual spectacle in the sky. It is possible that others too received the same special grace from God but did not correspond to it. What a great tragedy for them!

With the Church, let us ask God Our Father: *O God Who enlightened the Wise Men from the East and set them on the way to adore Your Son, enlighten our faith and accept the offering of our prayers.*[6]

43.2 Faith and docility in moments of darkness and disorientation. Letting ourselves be helped.

A life of faith is a life of sacrifice. Our Christian vocation does not take us away from our place in the world, but requires us to cast aside anything that would get in the way of God's will. The light that has just begun to shine is only a beginning. We have to follow it if we want it to shine as a star and then like the sun.[7]

The Wise Men must have travelled along bad roads and slept in uncomfortable places ... but the star was showing them the way and taught them the meaning of their lives. The star made their journey joyful and reminded them all the time that it was worth undergoing any discomfort or danger as long as they came to see Jesus. That is what matters. Sacrifices are borne with elegance and happiness if the goal is worth while.

But when they reach Jerusalem they are left without the light which had been guiding them. The star disappears and they are lost. What do they do then? They ask those who should know. *Where is He that has been born, the King of the Jews? We have seen His star out in the East and we have come to worship Him.*[8] We have to

---

[6] *Divine Office, Vespers of the Epiphany, Preface*
[7] St. J. Escrivá, *op cit*, 33
[8] Matt 2:2

learn from these wise and holy men. Sometimes we too are lost in the dark, because we try to have our lives illumined according to our own whims, which may well lead us along easier paths, instead of seeking the light of God's will. *In our lives we very often make our choices, not according to God's will but according to our own likes and fancies, to our comfort and our cowardice. We are not used to looking up, towards the star, but rather to lighting our way with our own candle, which is a little light, a feeble light, a light which reduces our field of vision to the limits of our own selfishness.*[9]

The Wise Men ask because they want to follow the light which God gives them, even though he shows them rough and difficult roads. They don't want to follow their own light, which will always lead them along apparently easier and more peaceful paths, but along which they will not find Jesus. Now that they no longer have the star, they make use of all the means at hand to reach the stable at Bethlehem. The truly important thing is to reach Jesus.

The whole of our life is a road towards Jesus. It is a road we have to travel by the light of faith. Faith will lead us, whenever necessary, to ask and let ourselves be guided, to be docile. *But we Christians have no need to go to Herod or to the wise men of this world. Christ has given His Church sureness in doctrine and a flow of grace in the Sacraments. He has arranged things so that there will always be people to guide and lead us, to remind us constantly of our way ... Allow me to give you a piece of advice. If ever you lose the way, always turn to the good shepherd ... Go to the priest who looks after you, who knows how to demand of you a strong faith, refinement of soul and true Christian fortitude. The Church allows us the freedom to confess to any priest*

---

[9] A. M. Dorronsoro, *op cit*, p78

provided he has the proper faculties; but a conscientious Christian will go – with complete freedom – to the priest he knows to be a good shepherd, who can help him to look up again and see once more on high the Lord's star.[10] The Wise Men found the star again. It showed them where Our Lord was, because they followed the advice and indications of those who, at that time, had been placed by God's providence to show them the way. Very often our faith is made specific in docility, in this sign of humility, which is letting oneself be helped in spiritual guidance by the person whom we know is the good shepherd for us here and now.

43.3 The only important thing in our life is to reach Our Lord.

The news the Wise Men brought spread throughout Jerusalem from door to door, from house to house. The hope of the Messiah would be rekindled in many good Israelites and they would wonder whether perhaps He had come already. Others, like Herod, in spite of being more educated and having more information, received the news very differently, because their souls were not prepared to receive the new-born King of the Jews.

Jesus, the same Child Who was born in Bethlehem of Judaea, is continually passing close by us. He passes by as he once passed by the Wise Men or as he passed through the life of Herod. There are two positions regarding Our Lord: that of accepting him – then everything of ours is his – and that of denying him by managing our affairs without him, by building our own life as if he did not exist or by fighting against him, as Herod did.

Like the Wise Men we want to reach Jesus even

---

[10] St. J. Escrivá, *op cit*, 34

though we have to leave behind the things others value so highly. We may even have to suffer some setbacks in order to follow the road that leads to Bethlehem.

Every resolution we make to follow Christ is like kindling a little light. What begins as something small and faltering is transformed by time, by constancy in spite of difficulties, beginning over and over again, into a great light – charity towards others who are also seeking Christ. *Whilst the Wise Men were in Persia, they saw only the star, but when they left their homeland, they saw the Sun of Justice Himself.*[11]

Today, on the eve of this great feast of the Epiphany, we could ask ourselves in the depths of our hearts: Why, at times, do I let my life follow the dim light of my whims, my fears, my comforts? Why don't I always go to the light of the Gospel wherein lies my star and my future filled with happiness? Why don't I take a step forward, and abandon what could be a situation of spiritual mediocrity? Isaiah tells us that all men are called to come from afar to meet the Saviour.[12] Our Lord also tells us – and especially those of us who perhaps do not feel as spiritually close to Jesus as we should – that we are invited especially on this day. Let us set out on the way. In this liturgical season[13] let us ask Our Lord to give us such a firm and solid faith on our journey that we may obtain the gifts which he has promised.

As always, we will find Mary very close to Jesus.

---

[11] St John Chrysostom, *op cit*, 6
[12] Is 60:4
[13] cf *Collect, Thursday before the Epiphany*

THE EPIPHANY – 6 JANUARY

44. THE ADORATION OF THE KINGS

44.1 The joy of finding Jesus. Adoration of the Blessed Sacrament.

Behold, the Lord, the Mighty One, has come; and kingship is in his grasp, and power and dominion.[1] Today the Church celebrates Jesus being made known to the whole world. Epiphany means 'manifestation', and in the Kings are represented all peoples of every language and nation who set out, called by God, to adore Jesus. *Gifts shall flow in from the lands of Tharsis and the islanders, tribute from the kings of Arabia and of Saba; all kings must needs bring their homage, all nations serve Him.*[2]

They obeyed the king and went on their journey; and all at once the star which they had seen in the East was there going before them, till at last it stood still over the place where the Child was. They, when they saw the star were glad beyond measure.[3] They were not surprised because they were led to a village, nor because the star stopped over a simple little house. They rejoiced. They rejoiced with an uncontainable joy. How great is the joy of these wise men who have come from so far away to see a King and are led to a little house in a village! How much is there for us to learn here! In the first place we will learn that every rediscovery of the way that leads us to Jesus is filled with joy.

We are perhaps in danger of not realising fully how

---

[1] *Entrance Antiphon of the Mass*
[2] *Responsorial Psalm, Ps 71*
[3] *Matt 2:10*

close Our Lord is to our lives *because God presents himself to us under the insignificant appearance of a piece of bread, because he does not reveal himself in his glory, because he does not impose himself irresistibly, because he slips into our life like a shadow, instead of making his power resound at the summit of all things ... How many souls are troubled by doubt because God does not show himself in the way they expected!*[4]

Many of the people who lived in Bethlehem saw in Jesus a child like any other. The Kings knew how to see Him as the Child, who, from then on, would be adored forever. Their faith gave them a unique privilege: to be the first among the gentiles to adore him when the world did not know him. How immensely happy must these men have been, having come from so far, when they were able to contemplate the Messiah soon after he came into the world! We have to be attentive, because Our lord also shows himself in the normal events of every day. May we know how to recover this interior light, which for us breaks through the monotony of days which are all the same, and find Jesus in our ordinary life!

And going into the dwelling, they found the Child there, with His Mother, Mary, and fell down to worship Him.[5]

We also kneel down before Jesus, God hidden in humanity. We tell him once more that we do not want to turn our backs on his divine call, that we shall never separate ourselves from him, that we shall remove from our path all that may be an obstacle to our fidelity and that we sincerely wish to be docile to his inspirations.[6]

They adored him. They knew that he was the

---

[4] J. Leclerq, *A Year with the Liturgy*
[5] Matt 2:11
[6] St. J. Escrivá, *Christ is passing by*, 35

Messiah, God made Man. The Council of Trent expressly quotes this passage of the adoration of the Kings to teach us the cult which is due to Christ in the Blessed Sacrament. Jesus present in the tabernacle is the same Jesus the wise men found in Mary's arms. Perhaps we should examine ourselves to see how we adore him when he is exposed in the monstrance or hidden in the tabernacle. With what devotion and reverence do we kneel in the moments indicated in the Holy Mass, or each time we pass by those places where the Blessed Sacrament is reserved?

44.2 The gifts of the Kings. Our offerings.

The Kings *opening their store of treasures, offered him gifts of gold and frankincense and myrrh.*[7] The most precious gifts of the East they offer; only the best for God. They offer him gold, a symbol of royalty. We Christians also want to have Jesus in all human activities, to have him exercise his reign of justice, holiness and peace over all souls. We also offer him *the precious gold we receive when in spirit we are detached from money and material goods. Let us not forget that these things are good, for they come from God. But the Lord has laid down that we should use them, without allowing our hearts to become attached to them, by putting them to good use for the benefit of all mankind.*[8]

We offer him incense, the perfume which was burned each evening on the altar as a symbol of the hope placed in the Messiah. Incense is *our desire to live a noble life which gives off the 'aroma of Christ' (2 Cor 2:15). To impregnate our words and actions with his aroma is to sow understanding and friendship. We*

---

[7] Matt 2:11
[8] St. J. Escrivá, *op cit*, 35

should accompany others so that no one is left, or can feel, abandoned ...

The pleasant smell of incense comes from some small, hidden grains of aromatic material placed upon the burning charcoal. Likewise is the sweet fragrance of Christ, noticed among men – not in a sudden burst of flame, but in the constant red-hot embers of virtues such as justice, loyalty, faithfulness, understanding and cheerfulness.[9]

With the Kings we also offer myrrh, because God Incarnate will take upon Himself our weaknesses and be burdened with our sorrows. Myrrh is *the spirit of sacrifice that can never be lacking in a Christian life. Myrrh reminds us of the Passion of Our Lord. On the Cross he is offered wine mingled with myrrh (cf Mark 15:23). And it was with myrrh that his body was anointed for burial (cf John 19:39). But do not think that to meditate on the need for sacrifice and mortification means to add a note of sadness to this joyful feast we celebrate today.*

Mortification is not pessimism or bitterness.[10] Mortification, on the contrary is very closely related to joy, to charity, to making life pleasant for others. *Mortification does not usually consist of great renunciations, for situations requiring great self-denial seldom occur. Mortification is made up of small conquests, such as smiling at those who annoy us, denying the body some superfluous fancy, getting accustomed to listening to others, making full use of the time God allots us ... and so many other details. We find it is the apparently trifling problems, difficulties and worries which arise without our looking*

---

[9] *ibid*, 36
[10] *ibid*, 37

for them in the course of each day.[11]

We make our offering to Our Lord daily, because we can meet him every day in the Holy Mass and Communion. When the priest offers the paten, we can place our offering there too, made up of little things, which Jesus will accept. If we do the little things we offer with a right intention, they acquire a far greater value than gold, frankincense or myrrh, because they are united to the sacrifice of Christ, the Son of God Who offers Himself there.[12]

44.3 Our Lord shown to all mankind. Apostolate.

Afterwards, in obedience to the voice of the Angel, the Kings *returned to their own country by another way,*[13] the Evangelist tells us. What joy those men must have had in their hearts to the end of their days, having seen the Child and His Mother! In these outstanding travellers we see thousands of souls from all over the earth setting out to adore Our Lord. Twenty centuries have gone by since that first adoration, and this long procession of the gentile world continues to make its way to Christ.

Through this feast the Church proclaims the manifestation of Jesus to all mankind of all times, with no distinction of race or nation. He *instituted the New Covenant in His Blood, calling together a people among the Jews and Gentiles who will be drawn into unity ... and will constitute the new People of God.*[14]

The Feast of the Epiphany moves all the faithful to share the concerns and labours of the Church, which

---

[11] *ibid*

[12] cf *Offertory prayer*

[13] Matt 2:12

[14] Second Vatican Council, *Lumen gentium*, 9

prays and works at the same time so that the entire world may be incorporated into the People of God, the Body of the Lord and the Temple of the Holy Spirit.[15]

We can be among those who, being in the world in the midst of temporal activities, have seen the star of a calling from God, carrying within us this interior light, the result of speaking with Jesus each day. Because of this we feel the need to help those who are undecided or ignorant to come closer to Our Lord and purify their lives. The Epiphany is the feast of faith and of the apostolate of faith. *Those who have already reached the faith and those who are on the path to finding it share alike in this feast. They participate, giving thanks for the gift of faith, as did the Kings who, filled with gratitude, knelt before the Child. The Church, more aware each year of the vastness of her mission, participates in the feast. How many people there are still who have to be brought to the faith! How many have to be brought back to the faith they have lost! This at times is more difficult than the first conversion to the faith. The Church, however, aware of the great gift of the Incarnation of God, cannot pause, can never stop. She has to seek continually the way to Bethlehem for all men and for all times. The Epiphany is the feast of God's challenge.*[16]

The Epiphany reminds us that we should use every available means to bring our friends, relatives and colleagues close to Jesus. This may begin by lending someone a book of sound doctrine, by giving to others encouraging words, which help them to start on their way; by speaking to an acquaintance of the need for spiritual formation.

When we finish our prayer today we don't ask these

---

[15] *ibid*, 17
[16] John Paul II, *Homily*, 6 January 1979

holy Kings to give us gold, frankincense or myrrh. It seems more natural to ask them to teach us the way which leads to Christ, so that every day we can take him our own gold, our own incense and our own myrrh. Let us also ask *the Mother of God, who is our Mother, to prepare for us the way that leads to the fullness of love: Cor Mariae dulcissimum, iter para tutum! Most sweet heart of Mary, prepare a safe way!* Her sweet heart knows the surest path on which to find Christ.

The three Kings had their star. We have Mary, Stella Maris, Stella Orientis, Star of the Sea, Star of the East.[17]

---

[17] St. J. Escrivá, *op cit*, 38

45. THE FLIGHT INTO EGYPT. VIRTUES OF ST JOSEPH

45.1 A hard, difficult journey. Obedience and fortitude of Joseph. Trust in God.

The Kings had departed. Our Lady and St Joseph would comment joyfully on the events of that day. Afterwards, in the middle of the night, Mary awoke at Joseph's call. He told her the Angel's message: *Rise up; take with thee the Child and His Mother and flee to Egypt; there remain until I give thee word. For Herod will soon be making search for the Child to destroy Him.*[1] It was a sign of the Cross at the end of a day full of happiness.

Mary and Joseph left Bethlehem hurriedly, leaving behind many necessary items which they could not take with them on a long and difficult journey. They also had the dread of having to escape with the threat of death overshadowing them. It is a profound and amazing mystery that the Son of God made Man cried, slept and sought refuge in the arms of Mary and Joseph.

The journey cannot have been a comfortable one: walking for several days along unfriendly roads, with the fear of being caught in their flight, with tiredness and thirst. The Egyptian frontier, beyond which Herod could no longer pursue them, was approximately a week away at the pace at which they could travel, particularly if they followed, as is most likely, the less frequented roads. It was an exhausting journey through desert regions. God

---

[1] Matt 2:13

the Father did not want to spare those he most loved from this fatigue. Perhaps this is so that we would understand that we can draw great benefit from difficulties. Also, it makes us realise that being close to God does not mean being free from pain or difficulties. God has only promised us the serenity and fortitude to face up to them.

The Holy Family quickly followed the Angel's directions fulfilling the will of God in all circumstances. *Joseph did not become scandalized or say: 'This is an enigma. A short while ago You Yourself let us know that He would save His people and now as He is unable to save Himself, we have to flee, to undertake a journey and suffer a long period away from home: this is contrary to Your promise.' Joseph does not reason in this way because he is a faithful man.*[2]

He obeyed immediately. He showed fortitude, taking charge of the situation, making use of the means at his disposal and trusting entirely that God would not leave him on his own. This is how we have to act in situations which are difficult, even in the extreme, when it costs us a great deal to see the provident hand of God Our Father in our life, or in the lives of those we love. Perhaps we are being asked for something which we think we are incapable of giving. The day after being elected Pope, John Paul I said: *Yesterday morning, I went peacefully to the Sistine Chapel to vote. I could never have imagined what was going to happen. The danger for me had scarcely begun when the two companions at my side whispered words of encouragement. One said: 'Come on, if Our Lord gives a heavy burden, He also gives the help to carry it!'*[3]

---

[2] St John Chrysostom, *Homilies on St Matthew*, 8:3
[3] John Paul I, *Angelus*, 27 August 1978

45.2 In Egypt. Other virtues of the holy Patriarch which we should imitate.

After their long, difficult journey, Mary and Joseph came with the Child to their new country. At that time there were many Israelites living in Egypt, forming small communities. They were mostly tradespeople. Joseph probably joined one of these communities with his Family, prepared to re-make his life again with what little they had been able to bring from Bethlehem. He had brought with him what was most important: Jesus, Mary, and his hard work and effort to look after them, making every sacrifice in the world. Even though those Jews were from his homeland, they were never to know their immense good fortune. The Sovereign of the House of Israel was with them; the true Redeemer who was to free, not only from slavery in Egypt, but also from something immensely worse than any human slavery – sin. All the history of his people came together in him.

St Joseph is for us an example of many virtues: of intelligent and rapid obedience, of faith, of hope, of hard work ... And also of fortitude, both in the midst of difficulties and in the ordinary situations in which a good father of a family finds himself. In Egypt he began as best he could, suffering hardships, at first doing every kind of jobs, finding a home for Mary and Jesus, and supporting them as always by the work of his hands, with his unceasing hard work.

Whenever we suffer contradictions, if Our Lord permits them, we should look at St Joseph, filled with fortitude, and put ourselves in his care, as many saints have done. St Teresa says of his powerful intercession: *I never remember having entrusted anything to him which he has failed to do. I am amazed by the great favours God has given me through this blessed Saint, the dangers from which he has freed me, both of body and soul. It seems that Our Lord gives graces to other Saints to give help in some particular need. I know from experience that this glorious Saint helps in every necessity. And Our Lord wants to make us understand that just as he was subject to him on earth – being his guardian Joseph had the name of father and could command him – so in heaven he does whatever Joseph asks. Other persons have also seen this from experience – persons whom I told to entrust themselves to him and, so, many who have devotion to him have experienced this truth once more.*[4]

45.3 Fortitude in our ordinary life.

After a time, when the danger was over, there was nothing to keep Joseph in that foreign land, but he stayed there for no reason other than that of being faithful to the fulfilment of the Angel's instruction *there remain until I give thee command.*[5] And so he remained patiently in Egypt, without displeasure or protest, doing his work as if he were never going to leave that place.

How important it is to know how to be and to stay where one should be, getting on with one's own work, without giving in to the temptation of changing places continually! Fortitude is needed to do this; a fortitude which *teaches us to appreciate the human and divine value of patience.*[6] *The person with fortitude is one who perseveres in doing what his conscience tells him he ought to. He does not measure the value of a task exclusively by the benefit he derives from it, but rather by the service he renders to others.*[7]

We have to ask St Joseph to teach us to be strong,

---

[4] St Teresa of Avila, *Life*, 6
[5] cf Matt 2:13
[6] St. J. Escrivá, *Friends of God*, 78
[7] *ibid*, 77

not only in difficult circumstances which are out of the ordinary, such as persecution, martyrdom, or a serious and painful illness, but also in the normal events of each day: being constant in our work, smiling when we don't feel like it, or having an affectionate, pleasant word for everyone. We need fortitude in order not to give way when we are tired, or feel lazy, or don't want to be bothered. We need it too, to overcome our fear of fulfilling difficult duties, etc. *By nature man fears danger, discomfort, suffering. Therefore it is necessary to seek brave men not only on the battlefield, but also in hospital wards, or by the sick bed of those in pain,*[8] in the ordinary tasks of every day.

An important part of this virtue of fortitude is the interior firmness to overcome more subtle obstacles such as vanity, impatience, diffidence and human respect. Other manifestations of fortitude are self-forgetfulness, not thinking too much about personal problems so that they get out of proportion, passing unnoticed, and being of service to others without making it obvious.

This virtue has many manifestations in the apostolate – speaking about God without being afraid of what people will say, or what they will think of one; always acting in a Christian way, even though this clashes with a paganised atmosphere; running the risk of taking the initiative to reach more people, and making the effort to put these initiatives into practice.

Mothers frequently have to practise fortitude discreetly and normally in a pleasant, patient way. They will then be the solid rock on which the whole house rests. *The Bible does not praise the weak woman, but the strong one, when it says in the book of Proverbs 'it is kindly instruction she gives' (31:26) – because kindness is*

---

[8] John Paul II, *General Audience: On Fortitude*, 15 November 1978

the summit of fortitude.

The motherly woman has the privilege of this direct and important function – to know how to wait; to know how to be silent; being able, when faced with injustice or weakness, to turn a blind eye; to excuse, to cover shaming things up – which is no less a work of mercy than that of covering the nakedness of the body.[9]

Today we can learn from St Joseph how to care, with fortitude and strength, for all that God entrusts to us in normal life – family, work, apostolate, etc., counting on the fact that it is usual to come across obstacles, which can always be overcome with the help of God's grace.

---

[9] Gertrud von le Fort, *The eternal woman*

46. LIFE IN NAZARETH – WORK

46.1 Our Lord, who worked in Joseph's workshop, is our model in work, to sanctify our daily tasks.

When we meditate on the life of Jesus, we realise that the greater part of his existence was spent in the obscurity of a village which was hardly known even in his own country. We understand how some of the neighbours said: *Go to Judaea, so that thy disciples also may see thy doings. Nobody is content to act in secret, if he wishes to make himself known at large.*[1] The value of Our Lord's actions was always infinite and he gave the same glory to his Father when he was sawing wood as when he was raising a dead man, and when the crowds were following him, praising God.

Many events had taken place in the world during those thirty years which Jesus spent in Nazareth. The peace of Augustus had come to an end and the Roman legions were preparing to resist the onslaught of the barbarians. In Judaea, Archelaus had been sent into exile for his innumerable crimes. In Rome, the Senate had declared Octavian Augustus to be a god ... but the Son of God was then actually in a little village, some ninety miles from Jerusalem. He lived in an ordinary house, probably made of sun-dried bricks like the rest, with his Mother, Mary, because St Joseph must have died by this time. What did God made Man do in that place? He worked, like all the other men in the village. He was no different from them in anything striking, because he was also one of them. He was Perfect God and Perfect Man.

---

[1] John 7:3-4

We cannot forget that the temporal existence of the Son of God consisted of his hidden life as well as his apostolic life.

When Jesus returns later to Nazareth, his fellow countrymen are amazed at his wisdom and the wonders reported of him. They know him because of his job, and because he is the son of Mary. *What is the meaning of this wisdom that has been given him ...? Is not this the carpenter, the son of Mary ...?*[2] St Matthew tells us else-where what they thought of Christ in his village: *Is not this the carpenter's son, whose mother is called Mary ...?*[3] They have seen him work every day, for many years. That is why they emphasise his job.

We also see from Our Lord's preaching that he knows the world of work very well. He knows it as someone who has experienced it at first-hand, and so he uses many examples of people working.

In those years of his hidden life at Nazareth Jesus is teaching us the value of ordinary life as a means of holiness. *The ordinary life of a man among his fellows is not something dull and uninteresting. It is there that the Lord wants the vast majority of his children to achieve sanctity.*[4]

Our days can be sanctified if they are like those of Jesus in those years of his hidden, simple life in Nazareth: if we work conscientiously, and remain in God's presence while working; if we live charity with those around us; if we accept contradictions without complaining; if our professional and social relations are a way of helping others and bringing them close to God.

---

[2] cf Mark 6:2-3
[3] Matt 13:55
[4] St. J. Escrivá, *Christ is passing by*, 110

46.2 What Jesus' work was like. What our work should be like.

If we contemplate the life of Jesus during these years without any external brilliance we will see him working well, with nothing done badly, filling the hours with intense work. We can imagine Our Lord gathering up his tools, leaving everything tidy, with a pleasant greeting for the neighbour who comes in to order something. He will have the same greeting for those who are not very friendly, or whose conversation is not very agreeable. Jesus would be known for doing things in this way because *He has done well in all his doings*, including material things.

All who came near him would feel moved to be better and would receive the help of Christ's silent prayer.

Our Lord's job was not outstanding; it was not light or easy, nor was there in it a great future from a human point of view. But Jesus loved his daily work and taught us to love ours, for, if we do not, it is impossible to sanctify it. *For when one does not love work, it is not possible to find any other kind of satisfaction in it, no matter how one tries to turn to something else.*[5]

Our Lord also felt the weariness and fatigue of daily work, and experienced the monotony of days which were always the same, with nothing of special interest. This consideration is also a great help to us, because *the sweat and toil which work necessarily involves in the present condition of the human race, present the Christian and every one who is called to follow Christ with the possibility of sharing lovingly in the work that Christ came to do. This work of salvation has been accomplished through suffering and death on a Cross. By*

---

[5] F. Suarez, *Joseph of Nazareth*

*enduring the toil of work in union with Christ crucified
for us, man in a way collaborates with the Son of God for
the redemption of humanity. He shows himself a true
disciple of Christ by carrying the cross in his turn every
day in the activity that he is called to perform.*[6]

Jesus, during those thirty years of hidden life, is the
model we should imitate in our life as ordinary people
who work every day. *When we contemplate Our Lord we
have a deeper understanding of the obligation that is
ours to work well. We cannot pretend to sanctify badly
done work. We have to learn to find God in our human
occupations, to help our fellow citizens, and to contribute
towards raising the standards of the whole of society and
of creation.*[7] Someone who is bad at his job – a student
who doesn't study, a shoe-maker whose work is slipshod
... if they don't change and improve, they cannot attain
sanctity in the middle of the world.

46.3 We have to win Heaven with our ordinary work. Mortifications, details of charity, professional competence.

We have to win Heaven with our ordinary work. We
need, then, to try to imitate Jesus *whose labour with his
hands greatly ennobled the dignity of work.*[8]

To sanctify our tasks we have to bear in mind that *a
Christian should do all honest human work, be it
intellectual or manual, with the greatest perfection
possible; with human perfection (professional
competence) and with Christian perfection (for love of
God's will and as a service to mankind). Human work
done in this manner, no matter how humble or*

---

[6] John Paul II, Encyclical, *Laborem exercens*, 27
[7] cf Second Vatican Council, *Lumen gentium*, 41
[8] *ibid, Gaudium et spes*, 67

insignificant it may seem, helps to shape the world in a Christian way. The world's divine dimension is made more visible, and our human labour is thus incorporated into the marvellous work of Creation and Redemption. It is raised to the order of grace. It is sanctified and becomes God's work.[9]

In sanctified work, like that of Jesus, we will find scope for small mortifications which can be made specific by paying attention to what we are doing, in the care and order with which we look after the instruments we use, in being punctual, in the way we treat other people, in offering up our tiredness, in trying to bear contradictions as well as possible, without useless complaints.

In our professional duties we will come across many opportunities for rectifying our intention, so that what we do is really a task offered to God, and not another occasion of self-seeking. By doing this we won't become pessimistic because of our failures, or be separated from God by our successes. This upright intention – working face to face with God – will give us the stability of soul of ones who are continually close to Our Lord.

Today we can ask ourselves in our personal prayer whether we try in our work to imitate the years of Jesus' hidden life. Have I prestige in my profession and am I competent among those I work with? Do I practise the human and supernatural virtues in my daily work? Is my work a way of bringing my friends and colleagues closer to God? Do I speak to them about the doctrine of the Church concerning those truths where there is more ignorance or confusion at the moment? Do I fulfil my professional duties faithfully?

We look at Our Lord's work at the same time as we

examine our own. And we ask him, *Lord, give us your grace. Open the door to the workshop at Nazareth so that we may learn to contemplate you, together with your holy Mother Mary, and the holy Patriarch St Joseph ..., the three of you dedicated to a life of work made holy. Then, Lord, our poor hearts will be enkindled, we shall seek you and find you in our daily work, which you want us to convert into a work of God, a labour of love.*[10]

---

[10] St. J. Escrivá, *Friends of God*, 72

47. FINDING JESUS

47.1 Jesus is lost and found in the Temple. The sorrow and joy of Mary and Joseph. We lose Him through our own fault.

Jesus grew up in an atmosphere of piety and fulfilment of the Law, an important part of which was the making of pilgrimages to the Temple. *Thrice a year keep holiday in My honour ... Thrice in the year all thy menfolk must present themselves before the Lord thy God.*[1] These feasts were the Pasch, Pentecost and the Feast of Tabernacles, and although those who lived far away were not obliged to go, many Jews from the whole of Palestine used to travel to Jerusalem for some of these feasts. The Holy Family used to do this for the Pasch. *Every year His parents used to go up to Jerusalem at the paschal feast.*[2] Although this was obligatory only for males over the age of twelve, Mary, as we see from St Luke's account, used to go with Joseph. Nazareth is just some eighty miles by the most direct road from Jerusalem. When the Pasch came, several families would join together to make the journey, which lasted four or five days.

When the Child was twelve years old, he went up to Jerusalem *as the custom was at the time of the feast.*[3] Once the paschal rites were over, they began the return journey to Nazareth. During these journeys the families divided into two groups, one of men, the other of women.

---

[1] Exod 23:14-17; cf Deut 16:18
[2] Luke 2:41
[3] Luke 2:42

The children could go with either. This explains how
Jesus' absence was not noticed until the end of the first
day, when everyone came together to set up camp.

What did they feel and think then? It seems useless
to try to describe it. They thought they had lost Jesus, or
that he had lost them and was on his own, God knows
where. There were great crowds leaving the city and
along the roads leading to it during those days. It must
have been a terrible night for Mary and Joseph. Very
early in the morning they set off along the way they had
come, back to Jerusalem. They spent three days, tired,
worried, asking everyone if they had seen a boy about
twelve years' old. All in vain.

Mary and Joseph lost him through no fault of their
own. We lose him through sin, through lukewarmness,
through a lack of a spirit of mortification and of sacrifice.
Then our life without Jesus is left in darkness.

When we find ourselves in this darkness we have to
react immediately and look for him. We need to know
who can and should know where Our Lord is. *The
Mother of God who looked for her Son so anxiously when
he was lost through no fault of her own, and experienced
such great joy in finding him, will help us to retrace our
steps and put right whatever may be necessary when,
because of our carelessness or our sins, we have been
unable to recognise Christ. With her help we will know
the happiness of holding him in our arms once more and
telling him we will never lose him again.*

*Mary is also the Mother of knowledge, for it is with
her that we learn the most important lesson of all: that
nothing is worth while if we are not close to Our Lord.
All the wonders of this earth, the fulfilment of our every
ambition, everything is worthless unless the living flame
of love burns within us, unless there is the light of holy
hope giving us a foretaste of the never-ending love in our*

true homeland of Heaven.[4]

47.2 The reality of sin and being far from Christ. Lukewarmness.

Mary and Joseph did not lose Jesus: it was he who went away from them. Our case is different – Jesus never abandons us. It is we who can cast him away from our side through sin, or at least keep him at a distance through lukewarmness. Whenever someone meets Christ, it is always Jesus who takes the initiative. And, on the contrary, whenever there is separation, the initiative is always ours. He never leaves us.

When man commits grave sin, he is lost both to himself and to Christ. He then goes along without meaning or direction in his life, because sin causes an essential disorientation.

Sin is the worst tragedy that could happen to a Christian. In a few moments he is radically separated from God through the loss of sanctifying grace; he loses the merits acquired throughout the whole of his life; he becomes in some way subject to the slavery of the devil and his tendency to virtue is diminished. This separation from God *always breaks the right order that should reign within his being, as well as between himself and other man and all creatures.*[5]

Unfortunately, many hardly give this any importance. It is lukewarmness, a lack of love, which causes us to value the companionship of Jesus very little or not at all. He values being with us. He died on a Cross to rescue us from the devil and from sin, and to be with each of us always in this world and in the world to come.

Mary and Joseph loved Jesus deeply. That is why

[4] St. J. Escrivá, *Friends of God*, 278
[5] Second Vatican Council, *Gaudium et spes*, 13

they searched for him without rest; that is why they suffered in a way we cannot imagine. That is why they were so happy when they found him again. *It would seem that nowadays not many are grievously concerned by his absence from their lives. There are Christians for whom the presence or absence of Christ from their souls means practically nothing. They move carelessly and with equal facility from sin into grace but fail to give the impression of men who have just returned from hell, or of having miraculously passed from death to a new life. One does not see in them the thankfulness, the joy, the peace and serenity of one who has, to his vast relief, rediscovered Jesus.*[6]

Today we have to ask Mary and Joseph to show us how to appreciate Jesus' company and how to be ready to do anything rather than lose him. How dark the world would seem, how dark our world would be, without Jesus! What a great grace it is to realise this! *Jesus, may I never lose you any more ...*[7] We will use all the human and supernatural means not to fall into mortal sin, and not even into deliberate venial sin. If we don't strive to hate venial sin, without the false excuse that it is not 'grave', we will never have a close relationship with Our Lord.

47.3 Using the means not to lose Jesus. Where we can find Him.

In the Temple of Jerusalem there were various areas devoted to cult and the teaching of Sacred Scripture. Mary and Joseph went into one of these. It was probably the portico of the Temple, where people went to listen to the explanations of the doctors of the Law and could ask

---

[6] F. Suarez, *Joseph of Nazareth*
[7] St. J. Escrivá, *Holy Rosary*, Fifth Joyful Mystery

questions and receive a reply. Jesus was there. His
questions by their wisdom and knowledge had attracted
the attention of the doctors.

He was there, one among many listeners, sitting on
the floor, putting questions, as did the others. But his
questioning showed marvellous wisdom. It was in fact, a
way of teaching suited to his age.

Mary and Joseph were amazed when they
contemplated the whole scene. Mary turned to him,
overjoyed at having found him. St Augustine finds in her
words a sign of humility and deference to St Joseph. *For
although she had merited to give birth to the Son of the
Most High, she was most humble and, when naming
herself, does not put herself before her spouse, saying 'I
and your father', but, 'your father and I'. She did not
consider the dignity of her womb, but the hierarchy of
marriage. The humility of Christ was not to be a school
of pride for His Mother.*[8]

The loss of Jesus was not involuntary on his part.
Fully conscious of who he was, and of his mission, he
wished in some way to begin it. Just as he would do later,
he now seeks to fulfil the will of his heavenly Father
without that of his earthly parents presenting an obstacle.
It must have been a painful trial for them, but also a ray
of light revealing the mystery of the life of Jesus to them.
It was an episode in his life they would never forget.

It is very clear to all that Jesus is aware of his
mission and of being the Son of God. In order to
understand his reply better, we would need to have heard
the intonation of Jesus' voice while he was speaking to
his parents. In any case, he makes us see that God's plans
always have priority over human ones and, if at any time
there is a conflict between them, then *God has more right*

---

[8] St Augustine, *Sermon 51, 18*

to be obeyed than man.[9]

If at some time we lose Jesus, let us remember that advice from Our Lord himself, *seek and you shall find.*[10] We always find him in the tabernacle, in those whom God has prepared to show us the way. If we have offended him gravely, he is always waiting for us in the Sacrament of Penance. In this Sacrament we prepare to purify our eyes stained by our frequent lack of love and venial sin.

Perhaps it would be a great help for us today, especially when we are in front of the tabernacle, or when we see the walls of a church, to say in the depths of our heart *Jesus, may I never lose You again.*[11] Mary and Joseph will help us not to lose sight of Jesus throughout the day and throughout the whole of our lives.

---

[9] Acts 5:29
[10] Luke 11:9
[11] St. J. Escrivá, *l.c.*

48. JESUS, OUR TEACHER

48.1 Our Lord is the Teacher for all men. He is our only Teacher.

After three days they found him. He was sitting in the Temple, in the midst of those who taught there, listening to them and asking them questions.[1]

The Rabbis used to comment on Scripture in the Temple. For strangers to Jerusalem, this was their only opportunity to see and hear the most important teachers of Israel. Those who were listening took their seats on mats around the teacher, could ask questions, and also be asked about the text which was being explained. Jesus' questions and answers, although in accordance with one of his age, obviously attracted the attention of everyone. *All those who heard him were in amazement at his quick understanding and at the answers he gave.*

When Jesus began his public life, the Evangelist tells us that the people *were amazed at his teaching, for he sat there teaching them like one who had authority, not like the scribes.*[2] When they were listening to him the crowds forgot their hunger, their cold. He never prevented the people from calling him prophet and master[3] and told his disciples *You hail me as the master and the Lord; and you are right, it is what I am.*[4] Very often Jesus uses the expression 'but I tell you'. He wants to show us that his doctrine carries a special force: it is the Son of God who

---

[1] Luke 2:46-47
[2] Mark 1:22
[3] Matt 21:11
[4] John 13:13

speaks. *From the cloud came a voice which said 'This is my beloved Son; to Him then listen'.*[5] From then on there has been no other to whom to listen.

Moses said to you ... but I tell you. The ancient prophets presented themselves as speaking on God's behalf. 'Thus said the Lord' they would say after their speeches. Jesus speaks in his own name (which no prophet had ever done) and his teaching is divine. He clarifies the meaning and scope of the Commandments of God received by Moses on Sinai and corrects false interpretations. His precepts, continuing the same revelation as in the Old Testament, are, however, absolutely new. No one has shown the sovereignty of God as he has and, at the same time, made it clear that God is a Father, lovingly concerned about the world and, most of all, about mankind, his children. No one has shown the fundamental truth about man as he has: that man is free and has a marvellous dignity.

Jesus' life was one of unceasing teaching. He spoke in the Synagogues,[6] by the lakeside,[7] in the Temple,[8] along the roads,[9] in houses and everywhere. His doctrine has been handed down faithfully and substantially complete through the Gospels. *There is much else besides that Jesus did. If all of it were put in writing, I do not think the world itself would contain the books which would have to be written,*[10] St John tells us at the end of his Gospel. But we know the essentials just as they happened, just as the Master taught. He is our only

---

[5] Mark 9:7
[6] Matt 4:23
[7] Mark 3:9
[8] Matt 21:22-23
[9] John 4:5
[10] John 21:25

Teacher. We feel safe with him. He always tells each one what he needs to hear. When we read the Gospel for a few minutes each day, with a faithful heart, meditating it slowly, we feel urged to say with St Peter: *Lord, thou alone hast the words of eternal life.*[11] Only you, Lord. Let us examine ourselves to see how attentively and in what way we read the Gospel.

48.2 Learning from Him. Meditating on the Gospel.

You have one Teacher, Christ.[12] If afterwards there have been teachers and doctors in his Church,[13] it has been because *he appointed them,*[14] subordinating them to himself; they would repeat and bear witness to what they have heard and seen.[15] The Good News of Christ comes to us through the Church, through the Gospel as it is read in the Church.

Only the one who voluntarily closes his ears will be deprived of hearing his word. Everyone can understand it. The most sublime doctrine becomes accessible to the most simple souls. *Those who are humble, who make themselves like little children, grasp his doctrines effortlessly; whilst those who are 'wise' who let themselves be led by their pride, do not receive the light of the Holy Spirit and remain in darkness, not understanding anything, or deforming the saving truth. Thou hast hidden all this from the wise and prudent, and revealed it to little children.*[16] Jesus is the teacher of all, our Teacher. He knows what is in each person.[17] He is

---

[11] John 6:68
[12] Matt 23:10
[13] cf Acts 13:1, 1 Cor 12:28-29
[14] Eph 4:11
[15] cf Acts 10:39
[16] Matt 11:25
[17] John 2:24

not deceived by our miseries and weaknesses. He knows very well what an abyss of evil there can be in every heart. But he also knows, better than we do, the possibilities of generosity, of sacrifice, of greatness which also exists in every heart, and he can arouse them with his word. The teaching of Christ affects the whole man in the core of his being. *He is a teacher with a knowledge that he alone possesses – the knowledge of unlimited love for God and, in God, for all men. In Christ's teaching we learn that our existence does not belong to us ...*[18] To take Jesus as our Teacher is to take him as our guide, to follow in his footsteps, to seek eagerly his Will for us. It means never being discouraged by our defeats; he will raise us up and turn them into victories time and time again. To take him as our Teacher is to want to become more like him, so that when others see our work, our behaviour at home, with strangers and especially with those most in need, they can recognise Jesus. Just as when we are in close contact with someone we love and admire very much, we end by adopting not only their way of thinking but also their expressions and gestures, so, by making Jesus our inseparable Teacher, speaking to him every day in our prayer and meditating on the Holy Gospel, we will become like him without realising it. *How I wish your bearing and conversation were such that, on seeing or hearing you, people would say: This man reads the life of Jesus Christ.*[19]

48.3 Jesus teaches us in the depths of our heart, through events and the people around us and, above all, through the Magisterium of the Church.

St Paul tells us that the Word of God is something

---

[18] St. J. Escrivá, *Christ is passing by*, 93

[19] *ibid*, *The Way*, 2

alive, full of energy (cf Heb 4:12). The doctrine of Jesus
Christ is always up to date, new for each man. It is a
personal teaching because it is directed to each one of us.
It is not difficult to recognise ourselves in a particular
person in a parable, or to understand in the depths of our
soul that some words of Jesus, twenty centuries ago,
were uttered for us as if we had been the only ones they
were meant for.

In the old days God spoke to our fathers in many
ways and by many means, through the prophets; now at
last in these times He has spoken to us with a Son to
speak for Him (cf Heb 1:1). These times are also ours.
Jesus Christ continues to teach. His words, because they
are living and eternal, are always relevant.

Reading the Gospel with faith means to believe that
everything said in it is in some way taking place now.
The departure and return of the prodigal son is happening
now; the sheep which has wandered and is lost, and the
Shepherd who has gone out to search for it; the need for
leaven to transform the dough; the light which should
illuminate the great darkness, that all too often envelops
the world and mankind. *In the sacred books the Father
who is in Heaven comes lovingly to meet his children and
talks with them. And such is the power and force of the
Word of God that it can serve the Church as her support
and vigour and the children of the Church as strength for
their faith, food for the soul and a pure and lasting fount
of spiritual life.*[20]

But we should learn to hear Christ in our life and in
our soul, in the different ways and circumstances in
which he speaks to us.

One day Our Lord was in the house of a Pharisee
called Simon. *Jesus answered him thus: Simon, I have a*

---

[20] Second Vatican Council, *Dei verbum*, 21

word for thy hearing.[21]

Christ always has something to tell us, each one in particular, personally. In order to hear him, we must have a heart which knows how to listen, a heart which is attentive to the things of God. He is the Teacher of always. He was the Teacher yesterday and will be tomorrow. *What Jesus Christ was yesterday and is today, he remains forever.*[22] And he speaks to every individual, to everyone who is ready to listen to him. Everyone who sincerely seeks a guideline for his life will find it. Our Lord does not deny his grace to anyone who truly seeks it.

When Solomon, who loved Yahweh, was still young, Yahweh appeared to him during the night in a dream and said to him, 'ask me what you want me to give you'. Solomon did not ask for riches, or power or a long life ... but wisdom to govern the people of God. This was very pleasing to the Lord, and He granted him a wise and intelligent heart – a heart quick to learn.[23]

We too should ask above all for a heart capable of listening, and of understanding those interior motions of the Paraclete in our soul, this language of God who speaks to us through the Magisterium of the Church; this doctrine, which comes to us so clearly through the Pope and the Bishops in union with him and which demands a practical response. It would be good to check now, in our meditation, what procedures we follow to get to know the doctrine of the magisterium well. And not only to know it, but to live it personally and to spread it among Catholics and among all men of goodwill. The Teacher, Jesus, speaks to us through this doctrine.

---

[21] Luke 7:40
[22] Heb 13:8
[23] cf 1 Chr 3:4

In yet another order of things, we have to understand the language of God who speaks to us through events and through the people around us and, very especially, in those precise suggestions which come to us through spiritual guidance.

We ask Our Lady that we may acquire an ear attentive to the voice of God, who speaks to us today as he did twenty centuries ago, even though at times he uses intermediaries.

49. THE OBEDIENCE OF JESUS – OUR OBEDIENCE

49.1 Jesus, model of obedience.

After the meeting in the Temple, Jesus returns to Galilee with Mary and Joseph. *He went down with them on their journey to Nazareth and lived there in subjection to them.*[1] The Holy Spirit wanted to leave this fact clearly stated in the Gospel. Its source can only be Mary, who, time and time again, saw the silent obedience of her Son. It is one of the few pieces of information we have from those years of hidden life: that Jesus obeyed them. St Augustine comments *Christ, to whom the universe is subject, was subject to them.*[2] To obey His Father, Jesus subjected himself to those who, in his earthly life, were invested with authority; in the first place, his parents.

Our Lady must have reflected very often about Jesus' obedience, which was extremely refined and, at the same time, very natural. St Luke tells us immediately that *His Mother kept in her heart the memory of all this.*[3]

The whole of Jesus' life was an act of obedience to the will of the Father *What I do is always what pleases Him,*[4] he will tell us later; and on another occasion he said clearly to his disciples: *My meat is to do the will of him who sent me; and to accomplish the task he gave me.*[5]

---

[1] Luke 2:51
[2] St Augustine, *Sermon 51, 19*
[3] Luke 2:51
[4] John 8:29
[5] John 4:34

Food is what gives energy for life. And Jesus tells us that obedience to the will of God – manifested in so many different ways – should be what nourishes and gives meaning to our lives. Without obedience there is no growth in the interior life, nor true development of the human person. Obedience *far from lowering the dignity of the human person, leads it to maturity by extending the freedom of the sons of God.*[6]

God is not indifferent to any situation in our life. He is waiting for a response from us at each moment; the response which coincides with his glory and our personal happiness. We are happy when we obey, because we are doing what Our Lord wants for us, which is what is best, although at times it costs us effort.

God's will is shown to us through his Commandments, through those of his Church, through things that happen and, also, through those persons to whom we owe obedience.

49.2 Fruits of obedience.

Obedience is a virtue which makes us very pleasing to God. Sacred Scripture tells of the disobedience of Saul to a command he had received from God. As a result of this, in spite of his victory over the Amalecites and the sacrifices which the king himself afterwards offered, the Lord repented of having made him king. Through the mouth of Samuel the prophet he said to Saul: *The Lord loves obedience better than any sacrifice.*[7] And St Gregory comments: *Rightly is obedience set before sacrifice, because through obedience we offer up our own will.*[8] Through obedience we show our self-giving to God.

---

[6] Second Vatican Council, *Perfectae caritatis*, 14
[7] 1 Sam 15:22
[8] St Gregory the Great, *Morals*, 14

In the Gospel we see how our mother Mary obeys: she calls herself the handmaid of the Lord[9] showing that she has no other will than that of her God. St Joseph obeys – and always rapidly – whatever is commanded on the Lord's behalf.[10] Promptness in doing what is commanded is one of the qualities of true obedience.

The Apostles, in spite of their limitations, know how to obey. Because they trust in Our Lord they cast the net to the right of the boat[11] where Jesus has told them; and they make a great catch of fish, despite its not being the right time, and despite their earlier experience that day of there apparently not being a single fish in the lake. Obedience, and faith in Our Lord's word, works miracles.

Many graces and fruits accompany obedience. The ten lepers are cured by obeying the words of Our Lord: *Go and show yourselves to the priests and thereupon, as they went, they were made clean.*[12] The same happened to that blind man on whose eyes Jesus put clay. *He said to him, Away with thee and wash in the pool of Siloe (a word which means sent out). So he went and washed there and came back with his sight restored.*[13] *What an example of firm faith the blind man gives us – a living, operative faith! Do you behave like this when God commands? When so often you can't see, when your soul is worried and the light gone? What power could the water possibly contain that when the blind man's eyes were moistened with it they were cured? Surely some mysterious eye salve or precious medicine made up in the*

[9] Luke 1:38
[10] cf Matt 2:13-15
[11] John 2:61
[12] Luke 17:14
[13] John 9:6-7

laboratory of some wise alchemist would have done better? But the man believed. He acted upon the command of God and he returned with his eyes full of light.[14] How often we too are going to find the light in that person placed there by God to guide and cure us, if we are docile in obeying! In the Acts of the Apostles we read *God gives the Holy Spirit to all who obey Him.*[15]

The Gospel gives us many examples of persons who knew how to obey: the servants of Cana in Galilee,[16] the shepherds in Bethlehem,[17] the Kings[18] – all received abundant grace from God.

Obedience makes our actions and our sufferings meritorious, in such a way that the latter, which could seem futile, can become very fruitful. One of the marvels performed by Our Lord is having made what was useless, like suffering, become so advantageous. He has glorified suffering through obedience and love. Obedience is great and heroic when one is ready to face death and ignominy in order to fulfil it.[19]

49.3 Obedience and freedom. Obedience for love.

To carry out the will of the Father, Christ inaugurated the kingdom of Heaven on earth and revealed to us his mystery. By his obedience he brought about our Redemption.[20] St Paul tells us: *He lowered his own dignity, accepted an obedience which brought him to death, death on a Cross.*[21] In Gethsemane, the

---

[14] St. J. Escrivá, *Friends of God*, 193
[15] Acts 5:32
[16] cf John 2:3
[17] cf Luke 2:18
[18] cf Matt 2:1-12
[19] R. Garrigou-Lagrange, *The Three Ages of the Interior Life*, Vol II
[20] Second Vatican Council, *Lumen gentium*, 3
[21] Phil 2:8

obedience of Jesus reaches its culminating point, when
he completely renounces his will to accept the burden of
all the sins of the world and thus redeem us. *Father, he
says ... only as thy will is, not as mine is.*[22] We should not
be surprised if, when we embrace obedience, we find the
Cross. Obedience demands, for love of God, the
renunciation of our self, of our most intimate will.
However, Jesus helps and makes the way easier if we are
humble. St Teresa tells us: *Once the Lord told me that I
was not obeying, unless I was determined to suffer. I
must fix my eyes on all that he had suffered and I should
find everything easy.*[23]

Christ obeys for love. This is the meaning of
Christian obedience: that which we owe God and his
Commandments, that which we owe the Church and our
parents – their commands and those of the Magisterium
of the Church – and that which affects all those very
intimate things of our soul. In every case, more or less
directly, we are obeying God, through the authorities.
And Our Lord does not want unwilling servants, but
children who want to do his will.

Obedience, which always involves subjection and
self-giving, is not a lack of freedom or maturity. There
are bonds which enslave and others which liberate. The
rope which attaches a climber to his companions is not a
bond which impedes, but a safety link which prevents
him falling into the abyss. And the ligaments which join
the parts of the body are not bonds which hamper our
movements, but a guarantee that they can be performed
freely, harmoniously and firmly.

On the contrary, true freedom is threatened by
disordered sensuality, narrow-mindedness originating in

---

[22] Mark 14:36
[23] St Teresa of Avila, *Life*, 26

selfishness, and the desire of doing one's own will. These obstacles are overcome by obedience, which raises and broadens one's personality.

Obedience also brings about a true formation of character and great peace to the soul – the fruits of sacrificing and giving up one's own will for a higher good. We acquire true freedom by serving God through obedience: *Deo servire, regnare est* – to serve God is to reign. *We ask, O Lord, that, glorying in obedience to the commands of Christ, the King of the Universe, we may live with him eternally in his heavenly kingdom..*[24]

If we come very close to Our Lady we will learn easily how to obey promptly, joyfully and effectively. *Following her example of obedience to God, we can learn how to serve with refinement, without being slavish. In Mary we don't find the slightest trace of the attitude of the foolish virgins who obey, but thoughtlessly. Our Lady listens attentively to what God wants, ponders what she doesn't fully understand and asks about what she doesn't know. Then she gives herself completely to doing the divine Will: 'Behold the handmaid of the Lord, be it done unto me according to your word' (Luke 1:38).*[25]

---

[24] *Prayer after Communion*
[25] St. J. Escrivá, *Christ is passing by*, 173

50. JESUS GREW

50.1 The growth of Jesus. His Sacred Humanity.

Jesus grew in wisdom, in age and in grace before God and men.[1]

In this brief verse St Luke sums up the years Jesus spent in Nazareth. He loved the Lord because he was a perfect man whose every passing year was accompanied by a steady growth and manifestation of his wisdom and grace.

In his human nature Jesus grew like any one of us. His maturing in wisdom must be understood as the growth in knowledge that was acquired from the things round about him, from his teachers, from the experience of life that every human being gathers in the course of his growing up. In the little school at Nazareth he learned the Sacred Scriptures, with the classical commentaries which usually accompanied their exposition. We are struck by the sight of Jesus reading the Old Testament and learning what it said about the Messiah: that is to say, about himself. We have to think of how he spoke of the Scriptures with his mother. Joseph, the man of the house, would listen to the conversations of them with incomparable attention and wonder, sometimes intervening in the dialogue himself.

Jesus learned many things from Joseph: among other things, the trade by which he earned his living and by which he maintained the household when the Holy Patriarch left this world. The Blessed Virgin was to make a profound impression on her son: she influenced him in his way of being human, in his gestures, his words and manner of speaking, in the very prayers that every Jew learned

---

[1] Luke 2:52

from his parents' lips.

Besides the empirical human knowledge that grows with age, there were two other kinds of knowledge in Jesus. In the first place the knowledge the Blessed have of the beatific vision of the Divine Essence, was his by reason of his human nature being conjoined with his Divine nature in the one Person of God the Son, the Second Person of the Blessed Trinity. That knowledge, proper to God, could not grow: he possessed it in its fullness.

Jesus also had an infused knowledge which perfected his intelligence and by means of which he knew all things, including those that were hidden; he could read the minds and hearts of men. That knowledge was capable of increase.[2]

At times Jesus asked questions: *What is your name?*[3] *How long have you suffered from this sickness?*[4] *How much bread have you?*[5] At other times he was surprised and wondered.[6] For though he possessed the complete omniscience of divine knowledge, he wanted and chose to live a completely human existence. He was not pretending when he showed surprise and wonder, for these are profound and intimate human reactions, proper to and consistent with his human nature.

We, too, must grow in the knowledge of God and of His plans for salvation. We must not grow weary in our process of formation and our knowledge of doctrine. To know the Lord better is to come to understand Him better, and from this relationship of understanding will arise an ever more fruitful love.

---

[2] *The Navarre Bible*, notes to Luke 2:52
[3] Mark 5:9
[4] Mark 9:20
[5] Mark 6:38
[6] cf Matt 8:10

50.2 Our supernatural growth. The theological and moral virtues.

St Cyril says, when discussing the growth of Jesus, that Divine Wisdom required that the Redeemer should be like us in all things.[7] Our maturity in years must be accompanied by a progressive increase in human virtue and the supernatural life.

The growth the Lord requires of us is unique in that instead of leaving our youth behind us as we do in our natural life, we renew and refresh it. In our natural life as human beings the 'not yet' of our youth reaches a point where it becomes the 'not already!' of our old age. The opposite happens in our supernatural life: the Christian life never grows old: at any time I can turn towards God *Who gives joy to my youth*[8] even in old age. God keeps young those who love Him. Perhaps we have known saintly people who, though old in years, have had great interior youthfulness of spirit born from a faithful relationship to Christ and manifested in all their acts.

Growth comes from grace, obtained especially through the Sacraments and continual practice of the virtues. Grace, deposited in our hearts like a seed,[9] struggles to grow and bring us to its fulness.[10] *The obstacle it contends with is sin – in its essentials a diminution of the human person – which prevents a man reaching his fulness of spirit.*[11]

The spiritual man acts through the impulse of the Holy Spirit[12] by practising the virtues, and reaches his fulness of

---

[7] St Cyril of Alexandria, *One in Christ*
[8] Ps 42:4
[9] John 3:9
[10] Eph 4:13
[11] Second Vatican Council, *Gaudium et spes*, 13
[12] Eph 3:16

being with the help of the gifts of this same Holy Spirit, whose mission it is to perfect the supernatural life by means of the yet imperfect theological virtues. These gifts are found in every soul in a state of grace.

Maturity, both human and supernatural, is not something we achieve instantaneously. It is a task of each day, of many small successes gained by responding to grace in small things. We have to assume the task of repeatedly practising the virtues by concrete acts. By practising the virtues with a care for detail we fashion a true character, a spirit submissive to the action of the Holy Spirit, a will fixed on the things of God, and on the needs of others for God's sake.

50.3 Human maturity which must accompany a true interior life. Human virtues.

Jesus grew. He wanted our supernatural growth also to accompany our human growth to maturity. The natural virtues are the ground and foundation of the supernatural. One cannot conceive of a good Christian who is not at once a good parent, a good citizen, a good friend. In fact, one's true human vocation is to be found somehow subsumed within one's supernatural Christian vocation. *When a soul strives to cultivate the human virtues, the heart is already very close to God. The Christian sees that the theological virtues – faith, hope and charity – and all the other things that bring with them the grace of God, impel him never to be neglectful of the good qualities that he shares with so many other men.*[13]

Grace does not act obliquely on one's nature, but on the interior reality – physical, psychological, moral – it lights upon. Normally interior supernatural life acquires its fulfilment while its possessor is playing a fully human

---

[13] St. J. Escrivá, *Friends of God*, 91

role. The love of God facilitates and strengthens the natural virtues.

Human maturity *shows itself above all in a certain stability of mind, in a capacity for making hard decisions, and in the right way of judging events and people.*[14]

The adult person has a real and objective idea of himself, distinguishes his effective achievements from what is still only a desire or plan, and accepts his limitations. These characteristics give him a feeling of security which enables him to act in a coherent, responsible and free way. He knows how to adapt himself to circumstances without rigid inflexibility or weakness, without yielding or insisting on his rights according to the letter of the law. The immature person frequently deceives himself in his plans and projects because he does not know his own real capabilities; he lives insecurely, avoiding, by way of excuses, accepting his own responsibility, and does not easily recognise and admit his setbacks and mistakes.

High-handed and arrogant behaviour, obstinacy, opinionated vanity, unwillingness to correct one's own errors, a mode of behaviour inappropriately out of correspondence with one's age, frequent flights by daydream and fantasy into an unreal world as a refuge and escape – all these are signs of immaturity.

The Christian has to be serene, as our Lord was, never lacking composure, not liable to be buffeted by fits of ill-humour or carried away by impulsive reactions out of all proportion to their cause, and ready to accept the situation in which he finds himself with a smile or with a modicum of patience.

The balanced person has a prudent confidence in himself without relying on himself totally, because he knows that although he has 'his feet on the ground' he can

---

[14] Second Vatican Council, *Optatum totius*, 11

go astray and make mistakes. When the matter requires it he will know how to ask for suitable advice so that he can then decide for himself and take responsibility for his own actions.

Many weaknesses are related to immaturity and are signs of it: laxity, inability to accept a reverse without seeking the sympathy of others, fear of exertion, frequent complaints against the setbacks and disappointments that are part and parcel of every human life, a search for ease and comfort above all else, and lack of effort in study and work.

Maturity makes one realistic and objective. *The dreamer is seldom one who is prepared to struggle: it is easier and more amusing for him to seek refuge in comfort in an imaginary world of his own creation in which by wishful thinking he is always the leader who grasps reality and understands and controls it or makes it serve his ends. Thus the dreamer becomes a spineless, weak-willed creature*[15] – the very opposite of a man who could be a disciple of Jesus.

Maturity requires the tenacity to continue a work once begun, to its very end, without giving up the struggle in the face of this or that obstacle that stands in the way.

Our Blessed Mother Mary, *the model and living school of all the virtues,*[16] including the human ones, will *help us to reach a perfect maturity according to Christ Jesus.*[17]

---

[15] F. Suarez, *About being a Priest*
[16] St Ambrose, *Treatise on Virginity*, 2
[17] Eph 4:13

SUNDAY AFTER THE EPIPHANY: THE BAPTISM OF THE LORD

51. THE LORD'S BAPTISM – OUR BAPTISM

51.1 Jesus wished to be baptised. The institution of Christian Baptism. Thanksgiving.

And when Jesus was baptised, he went up immediately from the water, and behold, the heavens were opened and he saw the Spirit of God descending like a dove, and alighting on him; and a voice from heaven saying: This is my beloved Son, in whom I am well pleased.[1]

In today's feast we celebrate the baptism of Jesus by John in the waters of the Jordan. Though he himself had no stain to be washed away, he wished to submit himself to this rite as he submitted himself to the other requirements of the Law. As a human being he submitted himself to the laws that ruled and governed the lives of the people of Israel who had been elected by God to prepare the way for the Redeemer. John the Baptist carried out energetically his mission to prophesy and arouse a great movement towards repentance as an immediate preparation for the coming of the Messianic Kingdom.

The Lord desired to be baptised, says St Augustine, *so that he might freely proclaim through his humility what for us was to be a necessity.*[2]

By his baptism Jesus left for us the Sacrament of Christian Baptism, directly instituted by Christ with what

---

[1] Matt 3:16-17
[2] St Augustine, *Sermon 51, 33*

would be a further progressive determination of its elements, and be imposed as a universal law from the day of his Ascension. *All authority in heaven and on earth has been given to me*, the Lord was to say on that day. *Go, therefore, and make disciples of all nations, baptising them in the name of the Father, and of the Son, and of the Holy Spirit.*[3]

In Baptism we receive faith and grace. The day we were baptised was the most important day of our lives. *Just as the parched land does not yield its fruits if it does not get water, so also we who were like dried sticks can produce fruits of life only if we receive freely the gentle and abundant rainfall of grace from on high.*[4] Before we received baptism we were outside the locked gates of Paradise, unable to bring forth the slightest supernatural fruit.

Today our prayer enables us to thank God for this totally undeserved gift, and to rejoice in the countless good things He has so lavishly bestowed on us. *Thanksgiving is the very first emotion that should be born in us in response to our baptism: the second is joy. Never should we think of our baptism without deep feelings of interior gladness.*[5]

We must rejoice in the cleansing of our souls from the stain of original sin, and of any other sin we may have committed before our baptism. All men are members of the same human family which was originally damaged by the sin of our first parents. This *original sin is transmitted as an inextricable part of our fallen human nature, by generation, not by imitation, and is to be found individually in each one of us.*[6] But Jesus gave us Baptism as a specific means of purifying our human nature and freeing it from the terrible affliction of this sin we were born with. *The*

---

[3] Matt 28:13
[4] St Irenaeus, *Treatise against Heretics*, 3,17
[5] Abbott Marmion, *Christ, the Life of the Soul*
[6] Paul VI, *Credo of the People of God*

baptismal water operates in a real way signifying what the use of natural water signifies – the cleansing and purification from every blemish or stain.[7]

Thanks to the Sacrament of Baptism you have been turned into a temple of the Holy Spirit, says St Leo the Great. *Don't ever let it happen,* he exhorts us, *that you drive away so noble a guest by your evil deeds, or ever again submit to the power of the demon: for the price you were bought with is the blood of Christ.*[8]

51.2 The effects of baptism: cleansing from original sin, new life, divine filiation etc. Entry into the Body of the Church.

Almighty ever-living God, who when Christ had been baptised in the River Jordan and as the Holy Spirit descended upon him, solemnly declared him your beloved Son, grant that your children by adoption, reborn of water and the Holy Spirit, may always be well pleasing to you.[9]

Baptism initiates us into the Christian life. It is a true birth into supernatural life. It is the new life preached by the Apostles and spoken of by Jesus to Nicodemus: *Truly I say to you that he who is not born again from on high cannot enter into the Kingdom of Heaven: what is born of the flesh is flesh but what is born of the Spirit is spirit.*[10]

The result of this new life is a true divinisation of man that gives him the power to bring forth supernatural fruit.

Often the dignity of the baptised person is veiled, unfortunately, by the ordinary circumstances of his life so, like the saints, we must strive hard to live in accordance with that dignity at all costs.

---

[7] cf 1 Cor 6:11 and John 3:3-6
[8] St Leo the Great, *Christmas Homily*, 3
[9] *Collect of the Mass*
[10] John 3:3-6

Our highest dignity, that of being children of God, conferred on us by baptism, is the consequence of our rebirth. If human birth gives as its result 'fatherhood' and 'sonship', in a similar way those engendered by God are really his children. *See what Love of God the Father has for us that He has called us children of God! We really are! Beloved, now we are children of God and it is not yet shown what we shall be.*[11]

The miracle of a new birth is achieved at the moment of Baptism by the outpouring of the Holy Spirit. The baptismal water is blessed on Easter night and in the prayers we ask: *Just as the Spirit came upon Mary and produced in her the birth of Christ, so may it descend on the Church and produce in her maternal womb (the baptismal rite) the rebirth of the children of God.*

The profound reality corresponding to this graphic expression is that the newly baptised person is born again to a new life, the life of God and thus is His 'son': *And so we are sons, and heirs too, heirs of God and co-heirs with Christ.*[12]

Let us give thanks to our Father God for bestowing such gifts, gifts beyond all measure, upon us, upon each one of us. What great joy it is to think often about those realities! *'Father', said that big fellow, a good student at the university (I wonder what has become of him), 'I was thinking of what you said to me – that I am a son of God! – and I found myself walking along the street, head up, chin out, and a proud feeling inside ... a son of God!'* With sure conscience I advised him to encourage that 'pride'.[13]

---

[11] cf 1 John 3:1-9
[12] cf Rom 8:14-17
[13] St. J. Escrivá, *The Way*, 274

51.3 Vocation to sanctity and the apostolate. The baptism of children.

In the Church nobody is an isolated Christian. From the time of baptism each person is part of a people, and the Church presents itself to the world as the true family of the children of God. *It was the will of God to sanctify and save mankind, not in isolation, separated from one another or without forming a people that would acknowledge it in truth and serve it in holiness.*[14] *And Baptism is the door through which we enter the Church.*[15]

And in the Church, precisely through Baptism, we are all called to holiness,[16] each one in his own state of life and condition, and to the exercise of the Apostolate. The call to holiness and the consequent need for personal sanctification, is universal. *Everyone – priests and laity – is called to holiness; and we have all received in Baptism the first fruits of a spiritual life which by its very nature will tend to maturity.*[17]

Another truth intimately connected to the condition of being a member of the Church is the sacramental character *a sure and indelible spiritual sign imprinted on the soul.*[18] It is like Christ's seal of possession on the soul of the baptised. Christ took possession of our souls at the moment we were baptised. He rescued us from sin by His Passion and Death.

With these thoughts in mind we appreciate the Church's desire that children should receive early these gifts of God.[19] It has always urged parents to have their

---

[14] Second Vatican Council, *Lumen gentium*, 9

[15] *idem*, 14; *Ad gentes*, 7

[16] *idem*, 11,42

[17] A. del Portillo, *On Priesthood*

[18] *Dz-Sch*, 852

[19] Sacred Congregation for the Doctrine of the Faith, *Instructi*

children baptised as soon as possible. It is a practical demonstration of faith. Neglect to do so is not caring for their freedom, just as if one were to cause them hurt in their natural life, to neglect to feed, clothe, clean or care for them when they were unable to ask for those things for themselves. On the contrary, they have a right to receive this grace. What a wonderful apostolate there is for us to exercise in many cases – among friends, companions, acquaintances ...!

Baptism brings into action something greater than any other good: grace and faith; perhaps, eternal salvation. It can only be by ignorance and a distorted faith that many children are deprived, even by their own Christian parents, of the greatest gift of their lives. Our prayer goes up to God this day asking that He may never allow this to happen.

We have to thank our parents who brought us, perhaps just a few days after we were born, to receive this holy sacrament.

1980; cf *Code of Canon Law*, Canon 867

SUBJECT INDEX